Jonathan's Loves,
David's Laments

Jonathan's Loves, David's Laments

Gay Theology, Musical Desires, and Historical Difference

DIRK VON DER HORST

Foreword by Rosemary Radford Ruether

PICKWICK *Publications* · Eugene, Oregon

JONATHAN'S LOVES, DAVID'S LAMENTS
Gay Theology, Musical Desires, and Historical Difference

Pickwick Publications
An Imprint of Wipf and Stock Publishers
199 W. 8th Ave., Suite 3
Eugene, OR 97401

www.wipfandstock.com

PAPERBACK ISBN: 978-1-62032-702-9
HARDCOVER ISBN: 978-1-4982-8852-1
EBOOK ISBN: 978-1-4982-4485-5

Cataloguing-in-Publication data:

Names: Von der Horst, Dirk, 1971–. | Ruether, Rosemary Radford, foreword.

Title: Jonathan's loves, David's laments : gay theology, musical desires, historical difference / Dirk von her Horst.

Description: Eugene, OR : Pickwick Publications, 2017 | Includes bibliographical references and index.

Identifiers: ISBN 978-1-62032-702-9 (paperback) | ISBN 978-1-4982-8852-1 (hardcover) | ISBN 978-1-4982-4485-5 (ebook)

Subjects: LCSH: Homosexuality—Religious aspects—Christianity. | Homosexuality in the Bible. | Gays—Religious life.

Classification: BR115.H6 V65 2017 (paperback) | BR115.H6 V65 (ebook)

Manufactured in the U.S.A.   03/14/17

To Vicki Garvey

Contents

Foreword

GAY PEOPLE, SHAPED BY their same-sex erotic feelings, are deeply hurt by the traditions of biblical faith and their ecclesiastical supports due to their repudiation of the validity of gay relations and the morality of those who identify themselves as gay. Those who wish to identify with a biblical faith, and also affirm their gay identity, are deeply torn by this contradiction. Dirk von der Horst, a biblical theologian, is one such person. In his book *Jonathan's Loves, David's Laments: Gay Theology, Musical Desires, and Historical Difference*, he writes for those who experience this conflict and for the Christian church, that it may change its ways toward gay people.

Gay folk in the Christian Church, as well as in the Jewish tradition, have looked particularly at the story of Jonathan and David in the books of Samuel in Hebrew Scripture. Here we have the vivid story of two men who loved one another. Jonathan's soul is said to have been bound to the soul of David "and he loved him as his own soul" (1 Sam 18:1). David acknowledges this great love, saying to Jonathan, "greatly beloved were you to me, passing the love of a woman" (2 Sam 1:26). Gay people in the churches and synagogues cling to these texts as proof that two men's love for one another is acknowledged and affirmed in the Bible.

Von der Horst focuses on these texts and their meaning in the Jewish and Christian traditions. But was this an erotic love? Did David and Jonathan have sexual relations with each other and is this also affirmed by these texts? Von der Horst devotes a chapter of his book to biblical scholars' exegesis of these texts in 1 and 2 Samuel, recognizing that these scholars conclude that the texts are ambivalent on this point. There was clearly love between the two men, but whether there was sex is unclear.

Von der Horst also summarizes his studies of gay and feminist theologies that focus on homoerotic love. These theologies draw on the 1 and 2

Samuel texts as part of their development of theologies of love relationships. For such theologies, loving friendship is linked to the nature of God. God is defined as mutuality in loving relationship. Thus, statements of Jonathan about his love for David can be understood as not only affirmed by God, but as an expression of the divine in this love. This is key to the lifting up of homoerotic love as an expression of divine presence, and hence the basis for a gay theology. Homoerotic love can be seen, not as rejected by God, but rather an expression of God.

Von der Horst then moves to examine musical pieces that draw on the texts in 1 and 2 Samuel on the love between Jonathan and David. In seventeenth-century England there were many such musical pieces that lifted up these texts of love and also of lament. Von der Horst listened closely to such musical pieces, particularly from English Church music of this period that focused on the 1 and 2 Samuel texts of the love between Jonathan and David. Not only the words, but the music itself of these pieces allow the listener to experience this homoerotic love through musical beauty. This examination of the musical expression of this love adds an extraordinary dimension of von der Horst's reclamation of these Biblical texts. This is an experience which the reader can not only appreciate intellectually, but reclaim through turning to these musical pieces in their own experience. Von der Horst also draws in the musical work of George Frederick Handel on Saul and the relation of Jonathan and David. Handel, according to historians of music, was himself probably gay and his creative work thus lifts up a love relationship in biblical tradition which he may have reflected in his music.

Von der Horst's new book on gay theology is an extraordinarily creative contribution to the literature on the biblical roots of homoerotic love. With his reclaiming of early modern musical pieces that reflect this biblical tradition, he adds a new dimension to this discussion that has not been there before. This is a book that should become a classic in the literature on gay theology and its relation to both an understanding of God and the need for the Church to play a positive role in welcoming gay people into its communion.

Rosemary Radford Ruether

Introduction

BOY MEETS BOY; EVERLASTING love ensues. This is the kernel of the biblical story of Jonathan and David to which many queer people committed to biblical religions turn for support. Several aspects of this relationship give rise to queer identification with the couple. Jonathan's life force (נפש) instantaneously binds with David's; David and Jonathan make covenants with each other; Jonathan saves David's life; Saul uses sexually charged language to describe their friendship; the final parting of David and Jonathan is erotically suggestive; after the death of Saul and Jonathan, David asserts that Jonathan's love was great, "passing the love of women."[1] In light of biblical traditions that are largely opposed to same-sex eroticism, and which conservative Jews and Christians have routinely and anachronistically mobilized to denounce the mere existence of homoerotic desires, this narrative stands out and even acts as a lifeline for many LGBT people.[2] While several queer or queer-friendly biblical scholars have explored sometimes counter-intuitive ways to access the Bible, the relation between Jonathan and David remains one of the clearer entry points for a gay theological or otherwise queer dialogue with biblical faith.[3] Indeed, the very title of one of

---

1. Examples are from 1 Sam 18:1, 3; 20:1–23, 30, 35–41; 23:18; and 2 Sam 1:26–27.

2. Conservative religious voices are increasingly ceding that homoerotic preferences are innate, and shifting arguments from calls for conversion to heterosexuality to calls for life-long celibacy on the part of those whose erotic desires are exclusively for members of the same sex. For one example of such an argument, see Grenz, *Welcoming, But Not Affirming*.

3. For some of the more adventurous queer work in biblical studies, see Stone, *Queer Commentary and the Hebrew Bible*; Stone, *Practicing Safer Texts*; Guest, *When Deborah Met Jael*; Jennings, *Jacob's Wound*; Boer, *Knockin' on Heaven's Door*; Moore, *God's Beauty Parlor*; and Guest et al., eds., *The Queer Bible Commentary*.

the early treatments of "homosexuality and the Bible" gives Jonathan and David paradigmatic status for the task at hand.[4]

Boy meets boy; what kind of love ensues? Not all interpreters agree that the love between David and Jonathan was of the erotic variety. Each of the elements that queer people have seen as evidence of a homoerotic relationship in the Bible is open to dispute. It is this dispute that puts queer people in a vulnerable position if we wish to argue for full inclusion in communities informed by biblical traditions, either Jewish or Christian. Simply claiming Jonathan and David as a prototype for modern same-sex relations is insufficient for the work of gaining full participation in biblically-identified communities. This does not mean, however, that the resonance queer people have found with the story is not a starting point for theological reflection. What this book seeks to provide is a way to strengthen that resonance.

Boy meets singing boy; the historical tradition credits David with authorship of the psalms and healing Saul with musical gifts. If we are looking for ways to strengthen resonance with the love of Jonathan and David, David's status as the Bible's paradigmatic musician provides an obvious point of entry, thanks to a vibrant body of work in queer musicology that explores the importance of music in the creation of queer identities. Musical interpretations of the story provide another means by which queer people can identify with it. Furthermore, a long tradition of musical settings of David's lament over Saul and Jonathan is a rich source of theological reflection that brings reflection on the relationship into a wider range of possible meanings and connects contemporary modes of identification with a history, or even a tradition.

Boy meets boy; love at first sight quickly shifts to an ethically shady takeover of one monarchic dynasty by another and the subsequent establishment of state centralization. This is a different way of narrating the story; and one which queer people have generally ignored in our appropriation of the Jonathan and David narratives. Jonathan is the son of Saul, the first king of Israel; David is Israel's paradigmatic king. But if David's trickster ethics play well into a queer mode of resistance, his role as the creator of a monarchy that is in tension with ancient Israel's prophetic radicalism does not. The biblical canon holds the divergent perspectives of prophetic radicalism and Davidic monarchism together; the confrontation between David and Nathan brings the clash into open view. At the same time, a variety of

4. Horner, *Jonathan Loved David.*

reading strategies that aim to highlight ideological division within the Bible bring our attention to just how much work it takes to reconcile radical and conservative voices in a reading of the entire Bible. Queer interpretations generally bypass this difficulty. In order not to evade this problem, I turn to seventeenth- and eighteenth-century musical interpretations of Jonathan and David, in which monarchical assumptions still hold.

Boy meets boy; some kind of love ensues and various people try to make sense of it. Talmudic rabbis, sixteenth-century Protestant reformers, composers from antiquity to the present, novelists and dramatists, biblical commentators, theologians, television show producers, and others have all tried their hands at making the story cohere. As motley a crew as these people are, they share a task of bringing an ancient text into a later context. Playing off the shared nature of the task of bringing the past into the present against the diversity of people engaged in the task helps us to see how these people are in relation to each other—relations of love, of enmity, of mere co-existence. These various relations form a dynamic field that relational theologians call "God." The theological affirmation that this whole, shifting field of relations is revelatory of the divine is a decisive starting point for this book.

So, "boy meets boy" ends up having several layers. Let's remove some of them for a moment and focus on how has music enabled people to use the Jonathan and David story to explore queer identities. Between the end of the Second World War and the Stonewall uprising in 1969, at least two American composers—Ned Rorem and Lou Harrison—set the text of David's Lament over Saul and Jonathan from 2 Samuel 1 to music. In both cases, the composers found an opportunity to explore ways in which music could bring gay identity to expression in the words David says or sings of Jonathan, "Your love to me was wonderful, passing the love of women."[5] Rorem, as much an openly gay writer of memoirs as a composer, composed his setting for baritone and string quartet, "Mourning Scene," while a student at Juilliard in 1947.[6] Rorem described how a group of friends he was visiting at Eastman recognized both the homoeroticism of the text and the fact that the faculty at Eastman would be "outraged" by it.[7] The issue was

---

5. 2 Sam 1:26, translations follow the New Revised Standard Version unless otherwise noted.

6. Recorded by William Parker on *The Listeners*.

7. Rorem, *Knowing When to Stop*, 336.

charged because Eastman had recently gone through "homosexual purges" under the leadership of the director Howard Hanson. Nevertheless, the baritone Warren Galjour performed the piece "glowingly." What is clear from the situation Rorem describes is that in the music school setting, where the Bible had cultural value but not religious authority, the potential homoeroticism of a biblical text outweighed the Bible's cultural pedigree insofar as a biblical source could not neutralize the offense raised by an expression of love between men. What the incident also shows is that even before the rise of the Gay Liberation Movement twenty two years later, the homoerotic nature of David's Lament over Jonathan was easily recognized and, in certain contexts, not a matter of dispute. As we shall see, after Gay Liberation, biblical scholars found much to dispute on the matter.

Rorem's contemporary Harrison was also an openly gay composer— in 1942, he candidly let a draft board know he was gay, and in 1971, he responded to a commission for an opera with *Young Caesar*, which focused on the love affair between Caesar and the King of Bithinia. He first composed a version of David's Lament for voice and piano in 1941, and revised it as one of three songs commissioned by the Portland Gay Men's Chorus in 1985. This movement from unpublished solo song to performed choral work offers a neat synecdoche of the "Stonewall narrative" of post-War American gay history: the notion that Stonewall marked a national "coming out" moment that finally allowed homosexuality to be a publicly discussed phenomenon.[8] The contemporaneity of Rorem's version with Harrison's earlier version belies this of narrative of progress. Rorem's version attests to a much more subtle negotiation between the private and public articulations of homoerotic desire in the pre-Stonewall era than does the stark contrast of Harrison's private/solo versus public/communal compositions. The compositional history of two twentieth-century gay musical interpretations of David's Lament over Saul and Jonathan already points to multiple ways in which music, historical change, and queer identification intersect.

Harrison's 1985 setting of the lament musically enacts this interaction of multiple temporalities with queer identity. It follows a seventeenth-century technique of juxtaposing a static bass figure—here, a descending tetrachord, or collection of four notes—with a melody that attempts to assert independence from the stasis of the bass.[9] The technique generates tension

8. Duberman, *Stonewall*. For a critique of this narrative see Bravman, *Queer Fictions of the Past*.

9. Rosand, "The Descending Tetrachord."

because the bass is constantly pulling the melody back into a space from which it tries to escape. This particular tension can be heard as a kind of erotic tension between desire and constraint. The relation between bass and melody also juxtaposes two kinds of temporalities, a cyclic organization of time in the bass, and a linear projection of time in the melody. Harrison also provides surface level rhythmic tension that accentuates a difference between flowing lyricism and mild disruptions of temporal expectations. Rorem's technique, by way of contrast, moves through a series of different textures, with a return to the opening material at the end. The relation of voice to instrumentalist is more variable, with the instrumentalists sometimes anticipating the voice's melody, sometimes embellishing it, but rarely creating such a stark tension between two different ways of relating sound to time on a moment to moment basis. Music's play with time, then, does not simply mean moving from beginning to end, but can evoke many senses of relating past, present, and future over the course of music's unfolding.

In both Rorem's and Harrison's settings of David's lament, musical sound does more than simply illustrate the words; it has a direct sensual impact regardless of the text. A major reason turning to music is helpful for articulating erotic identities is the sheer sensuality of musical meaning, in which what determines meaning is not abstract referentiality, but sonic envelopment. Focusing on music as sonic envelopment over against analyzing its rhetorical strategies or mathematical formulas is the first step in understanding the extent to which music and eroticism can fuse. Queer and feminist musicologists have explored the nature of this connection from a number of angles. However, because eroticism is such a fundamentally subjective matter, it is crucial to note that *whether* music is eroticized, and if so, *what* music is eroticized, is something that can never be determined in advance, just as what counts as erotic, or even sexual, varies among people. This caveat, which Eve Kosofsky Sedgwick posits as axiomatic for queer theory,[10] delimits but does not negate the fact that music and sexuality can mutually constitute each other. Within this multiplicity of responses, the sensuality of music retains its power in creating various sexual identities. For this reason, music's sensual power can secure a gay affirmative and other queer readings of Jonathan and David.

Both Rorem and Harrison explored precisely that overlap in their settings of David's Lament insofar as music was a means through which they expressed their gay identities. But although both composers used the text

10. Sedgwick, *Epistemology of the Closet*, 22–27.

to a similar end—exploring homoerotic desire—the models of desire their compositions produce do not add up to a unified "gay identity." Their larger stylistic choices situate the identities they put forth in relation to very different social contexts. Rorem worked on the East Coast and spent considerable time in Europe, and was particularly inspired by Francis Poulenc, a French composer. Harrison worked on the West Coast and was influenced heavily by ethnomusicology and Asian music. Their pacing of sound, selection of text, and cultural reference points interpret the Lament in ways that make it say very different things, even while they both say "David and Jonathan were gay." In this context, the fundamentalist or foundationalist dream of finding "the right answer"—of moving from textual ambiguity to doctrinal clarity—makes no sense whatsoever. But this does not mean that the quest to glean theological meaning from the text is futile.

The stories of Jonathan and David have been productive of many insights in queer theological reflection over the last half century. Just as Rorem and Harrison took a biblical text and used music to employ it in the creation of a modern gay identity, so have non-musical interpretations of Jonathan and David been helpful for religious attempts to wrest biblical religions away from heterosexist presuppositions. As Jewish and Christian queer people found new ways to dialogue in the contexts of the Sexual Revolution, LGBT liberation movements, and queer theory, we turned to the stories of Jonathan and David as precedent for gay experience within our traditions.[11] With the development of queer theologies, Jonathan and David moved to the forefront of biblical theological reflection on gay and lesbian issues. While queer biblical reflection has in many cases moved past Jonathan and David to less obvious examples, recent publications attest to their enduring power as a source for working through both the productive and destructive tensions of biblical faith and queer identity.[12]

However, the use of Jonathan and David for contemporary gay theological purposes splices experiences of the first millennium BCE and now, skipping over two or three millennia in which various members of the Jewish and Christian traditions have interpreted this text. The erasure of the history of interpretation of this passage reveals contradictory assumptions about the relation of gay identity to history. It allows gay theologians to

11. See discussion in chapter 1.

12. For recent queer biblical writings that deal with, but do not privilege, Jonathan and David, see Stone, "1 & 2 Samuel"; Boer, *Knockin' on Heaven's Door*. Important publications on Jonathan and David and queer identity include Heacock, *Jonathan Loved David* and Harding, *The Love of David and Jonathan*.

speak about the relationship from a "social location," while ignoring the necessary historicity of the social.[13] Thus, identification with Jonathan and David as emblematic for contemporary gay relationships creates a trans-historical identity, in which "we" have been everywhere, always. On the other hand, bypassing the history of interpretation of the biblical passages reinforces a social constructivist narrative in which "we" arrived, most spectacularly at the Stonewall riots, as a product of modernity. Further-more, one's position on the history of homosexuality has a huge bearing on the simple exegetical question, were Jonathan and David friends or lovers?

For these reasons, recent scholarship on Jonathan and David has turned to reception theory to advance more nuanced claims about the love of Jonathan and David. General investigations of the reception of David include the edited volumes *The David Myth in Western Literature* and *David et Jonathan*.[14] The turn to reception and historicity has also informed queer writings on the subject. Devan Hite explores the limits of our ability to read Jonathan and David as "gay," by following the lead of David Hal-perin in teasing out the shifting meanings of same-sex acts before and after the invention of "sexuality." He searches for something that transcends our categorization of same-sex acts because the very act of categorization closes off a number of experiences that may help us understand what the biblical narrative actually addresses.[15] James Harding takes for granted that until the nineteenth century, no one interpreted Jonathan and David's love as erotic. His examination of the intersection of the development of explicitly homoerotic identities and homoerotic interpretations of Jonathan and Da-vid aim to answer the question, "what were the historical conditions that made the question 'were David and Jonathan gay?' even possible?" Anthony Heacock examines the reception of the text in a self-contradictory double argument. On the one hand, he advances the idea that the reception of the biblical text reveals how inescapably ambiguous the stories are—both "gay" and "straight" readings are equally plausible in light of the "openness" of the text. On the other hand, he closes the interpretive openness in the last part of his book by providing "the real meaning" of the text. According to Hea-cock, Jonathan represents gay men and David represents straight men in the text's illumination of gay/straight relations. Heacock never resolves the

13. For social location as central to biblical interpretation, see Segovia and Tolbert, *Reading from This Place: Vols 1 and 2*.

14. Frontain and Wojik, *The David Myth* and Courtray, *David et Jonathan*.

15. Hite, "Pursuing the 'Root of Jesse.'"

contradiction in his understanding of the text as open and his move to close the meaning of the text, but this non-resolution illuminates the tension between the desire to identify with the text and the problematic bases for such identification very well. The arguments of Hite, Harding, and Heacock wrestle with how to balance a desire to identify with Jonathan and David with the slipperiness of textual indeterminacy and historical relativity.

This book likewise grapples with that slippery tension by arguing that a historicist examination of Jonathan and David evaporates the story's ability to provide a simple basis of identification for queer people, but that musical performance can re-embody an ambiguous heritage regarding this text in a grounded and queer-affirmative way in the present. Furthermore, such an understanding of musical performance complements the dialogical and relational solution to the problems of the connections between past and present upon which the theologians I am engaging depend. Following Martin Buber's emphasis on relation and dialogue, the lesbian Episcopal priest and theologian Carter Heyward and the gay theologian Gary David Comstock challenge prescriptive understandings of biblical authority by emphasizing that dialogue with the past is an interaction in which one does not shut down one's own perspective when listening to past voices. As the opening examples of Harrison's and Rorem's settings of David's lament demonstrated, music provides concrete examples of how such interactions work. Opening a score to sing or play the music or listening to a recording are acts that engage the present by retrieving the past. In both cases, imaginative reconstruction and disciplined historical analysis are of necessity intertwined. But disciplined historical analysis can render the oddity of the past inescapable, to the point that some kind of historical relativism makes one aware of the ephemeral quality of all perspectives. Musical interpretations can heighten our awareness of the tension between identification with, and distinction from, past articulations of desire—a tension that often leads relational theologians into confusion. By examining this complex interpretive process, my argument moves from a primarily exegetical to a theological question. In short, Jonathan and David are a focal point through which I will answer the question, "How can music bridge contemporary theologies of erotic mutuality and radical historical differences that give rise to historicist and even relativist philosophies?"

The bridge between theologies of erotic mutuality and historical difference allows me to address two distinct, but interrelated questions. The first question is exegetical. Does the biblical text provide a firm basis for a homoerotic reading of the story of Jonathan and David? The second question is historical. Is homosexuality, or even the more amorphous homoeroticism, a meaningfully trans-historical category with which to read the narrative? The primary link this book will make between the disparate concerns is the history of the interpretation of the text in question. However, rather than answering those interrelated questions with a firm "yes" or "no," I find the evidence to yield decidedly mixed results. I do not find the biblical text to provide a firm basis for a homoerotic reading, though it certainly provides a solid opportunity for one. In this refusal to pin down the meaning of the text, I participate in a growing academic consensus. Heacock's and Harding's books pursue a similar task of asking to what extent and in what way the Jonathan and David might model queer subjectivities when the text itself is open. Similarly, the historical contexts in which we might explore homoeroticism in the early modern era show very different mappings of same-sex desire to conceptualizing experience on a number of levels than modern day queer people might find useful. Stopping to ask questions about the relatively recent past allows us to see how quickly basic assumptions change. This process can provide us with a better sense of just how distant biblical assumptions are from our own.

Another pair of contrasting approaches highlights what is at stake in the tension between the exegetical question and the historical question: the pastoral and the critical. I approach the question of the nature of Jonathan and David's relationship as a pastoral question for queer people wrestling with religious desires to maintain—or reject—a connection with biblical religions. In this sense, and presuming a positive answer to the exegetical question about the sexual nature of their relationship, Jonathan and David function as an anchor for queer identity that connects to uncompromising theological affirmations of cultural self-determination, such as James Cone's articulation of Black Theology or Mary Daly's feminist philosophical vision.[16] However, theological perspectives that seek to pursue uncompromising visions of queer identity in tandem with fidelity to biblical traditions often end up ignoring significant historical differences between ancient Israel and modern times, creating a rigid sense of identity between the two that does not stand up to close scrutiny. The early work of Robert Goss and Robert Williams provide examples of how uncompromising demands for queer self-determination in relation to biblical traditions can

16. See particularly Cone, *Black Theology and Black Power* and Daly, *Beyond God the Father.*

lead to a superficial reading of biblical texts.[17] Since the publication of *Jesus Acted Up*, Goss has deepened his engagement with biblical texts in articles on various New Testament texts in *The Queer Bible Commentary*, which all read the texts strictly as reflective of contemporary queer experience.[18] Rather than trying harder and harder to prove continuity between modern queer identities and the cultural realities of the biblical world, turning to specific mediations of the text over time shows a multiplicity of interpretive strategies and understandings of the sexual politics of same-sex desire. Furthermore, because Goss and Williams engage only contemporary theology and the Bible, their work ends up bypassing both problems and resources of historically contextualized engagement with tradition. On the other hand, Eugene Rogers' engagement with Aquinas and Barth (theologians with whom Daly and Cone engage, respectively) in his revisioning of the Christian tradition as favorable to homoerotic relations lacks the sense of contemporary urgency that fuels Goss's and Williams's pastoral proposals.[19] To engage with musical interpretations of the story in a variety of contexts opens the possibility of keeping radical demands for social justice in the present in balance with the conceptual richness offered by the kind of historical analysis that is often dependent on critical detachment for its success.

To turn to musical renditions of the text allows me to bypass the question of fidelity and apostasy to biblical traditions and open biblical meaning-making to queer people in a wider variety of contexts. Because musical canons have their own dynamics apart from those of religious traditions, shifting attention from exegesis and homiletics to musical interpretation allows for queer people to engage with a biblical construction of homoeroticism regardless of their relation to specific Western religious traditions.[20] In using this method, I aim to strengthen queer solidarity across religious and secular differences, which can at times be extremely divisive within queer communities.

---

17. Goss, *Jesus Acted Up* and Williams, *Just As I Am*. While Williams' text is more popular than scholarly, it is relevant here insofar as he was mentored by Carter Heyward, the theologian whose perspective grounds the larger project.

18. Robert Goss, "Luke," "John," and "Ephesians," in Guest et al., *The Queer Bible Commentary*, 526–47, 548–65, 630–38.

19. Rogers, Jr., *Sexuality and the Christian Body*.

20. See Bergeron and Bohlman, *Disciplining Music* and Kerman, "A Few Canonic Variations," 33–50.

Although I am interested in finding spaces within which religious and secular queer people can find common ground, my argument is also positioned within two basic convictions specifically regarding religious community. The tension here is as follows: The Bible is a source for communal deliberation in religious communities, but all communities have exclusionary dynamics that marginalize various people Liberal religion often turns to "inclusivity" as a term that ameliorates this tension, but queer and other critical perspectives often resist liberal inclusivity as masking different dynamics of exclusion at work in the name of community.[21] I find wisdom in both sides of this debate. Yet, to the extent that any identity has a logic of exclusion built in—we are this, not that—diversity within a religious community will bump against limits that marginalize somebody. This marginalization has been damaging to queer people. My own experience of pain, while being caught in the intersection between a conviction that spirituality is fundamentally communal and the experience of being objectified in the process of communal deliberation in churches, drives much of my argument. Thus, while my book aims to counter the raw violence of homophobic rhetoric and praxis, it participates in a different level of violence, the struggle between heterosexist and counter-heterosexist forces in biblical interpretation and ecclesial reflection. If I have found being in the midst of this pull exhausting on occasion, this book documents and performs that same violence on Jonathan and David.

What I seek to provide in my turn to music is a method by which queer people committed to biblical religions can explore a vantage point of identification with the biblical text that provides a temporary escape from the dynamics of the rabbit hole of arguing over "homosexuality" in religious communities.[22] This escape does not settle the question of fidelity or apostasy, because queer people are left with the choice as to whether or not they can bring the distinct subject positions formed through private engagement with music back into dialogue with religious communities.

Finally, the pastoral arguments I make are based on the fact of my identification as a gay man with various musical representations of the relation between Jonathan and David. Thus, I turn explicitly to a confessional or auto-ethnographic mode of discourse in the latter chapters when I describe the present relevance of music for theological reflection. I do not

21. See Warner, *The Trouble with Normal* and Sycamore, *That's Revolting!*

22. On music as "escape" from heteronormativy, see Cusick, "On a Lesbian Relation with Music."

expect all queer people to have the same patterns of identification, and there may be straight people whose patterns of identification mirror mine more closely than do those of some queer people. The aim is not to prescribe patterns of identification around which queer people can rally in a sense of absolute unity. Rather, the aim is to spur deeper reflection on the processes of self-constitution. In this regard, I pursue a historicist interrogation of the music as a reminder that every step of identification is provisional and open to critique. Music does not provide a final step to guaranteeing that a queer biblical identity is possible. It is simply another angle that can lend support to existing articulations of queer identifications with the Jonathan and David narratives.

In contrast to the factual questions of "did David and Jonathan exist and did they sleep with each other," for which definitive answers should correspond to an objective set of very specific facts, a thoroughly historicist approach to the text highlights the multiplicity of answers to these questions by pointing out various literary layers, from oral sources, to canonization, to subsequent reception, to modern attempts at historical reconstruction.[23] François Langamet's reconstruction of the "Book of Jonathan," provides different possibilities for interpretation than the canonical text does.[24] Indeed, strictly at the level of the canonized text, multiple meanings are possible.[25] In order to stress that the meaning of David and Jonathan shifts in relation to the literary contexts in which readers place them, I have ordered the terms "David and Jonathan" when stressing the canonical context, but reversed them to "Jonathan and David" when stressing the potential for homoerotic appropriation of the narratives. This re-ordering of their names honors the diverse ways in which people actually read the text and the fact that readers make meaning both in alignment with and as resistance to the canonical parameters. This emphasis on the text not as simply the contents of the printed page, but as an ongoing chain of transmission and interpretation means that combating specifically modern heterosexist readings of Jonathan and David can never simply be a matter of replacing one authoritative reading with another. Rather, it is a matter of shifting the

23. For the inescapable literary character of historical writing, see White, *Metahistory* and *Figural Realism*.

24. Langlamet, "De 'David, Fils de Jessé' au 'Livre de Jonathan'" and "'David-Jonathan-Saül' ou le 'Livre de Jonathan.'"

25. See Jobling, *1 Samuel*.

terms of making meaning from the text so that a wider range of people can be empowered by it.

But if the ability of readers to make meaning from the text is the precondition for empowerment, this comes at the price of holding all readings to be indeterminate. How my argument differs from Heacock's and Harding's studies, which also treat the reception of the David and Jonathan story as an opportunity to explore the interplay of gay identity and textual indeterminacy, is in allowing music to take the indeterminacy a step further. While a composer may interpret a biblical passage in a certain way, the amount of control a composer has or wants over a performer or listener varies widely. Performers inevitably interpret compositions in a variety of ways, and listeners approach performances with a variety of listening strategies. This book describes a serial process in which various agents re-open previous interpretations that chose among possible meanings of the Jonathan and David story. To use starker imagery, I describe a number of detonations that keep the text's meaning from becoming fixed—either by radical queer activists, conservative preachers, or any position in between.

For this reason, Jonathan and David as presented in the biblical text are not the primary object of study. Rather, I focus on the interrelations between various interpretations of their relationship as presented in the biblical text. This method follows deconstructive patterns of thought in dispersing the "book" into a "text." As Jacques Derrida notes, "a text always has several epochs and reading must resign itself to this fact."[26] Yet, contrary to Derrida, I do not see this primarily as a matter of "resignation." Rather, I see this sense of multiple interpretations as creative of agency. Like Ernst Troeltsch, who sees the "essence of Christianity" as *an act* springing from an impulse in the Gospel, yet never identical with that Gospel, or Judith Butler, who sees gender as "the repeated stylization of the body," I see interpretive conflict as a sign of agency and creativity more than a reason to mourn a lost foundation.[27]

A line of thought that holds the various pieces of the book together is the debate around the history of sexuality, and more specifically the history of homosexuality.[28] The central tension in this debate is whether "homosexuality" is a category that can be meaningfully applied across cultural and

---

26. Derrida, *Of Grammatology*, 102.

27. Troeltsch, *Writings on Theology and Religion*, 124–81, and Butler, *Gender Trouble*, 33.

28. Greenberg, *The Construction of Homosexuality*.

historical differences. Foucault's multi-volume *History of Sexuality* was an early attempt to historicize sexuality.[29] In contrast to theorists who worked to formulate thoroughly historicized notion of "sexuality," the historian John Boswell offered an "essentialist" argument for homosexuality.[30] One limited example of what is at stake in the conflict between essentialist and historicist understandings of homosexuality can be found in two essays on sodomy in Dante's *Divine Comedy*.[31] In Joseph Pequigney's essentialist reading of Dante, the movement from the treatment of sodomites in the *Inferno* to the *Paradisio* reflects Dante's growing tolerance over the course of his career. In contrast, Bruce Holsinger shows that importing modern notions of both homosexuality and tolerance into the medieval setting distorts what is at stake in Dante's treatment of sodomy, and provides a counter-reading that treats sodomy as conceptually different than homosexuality and does not get as mired in confusions over the difference in Dante's different expressions. In a groundbreaking work of queer theory, *Epistemology of the Closet*, Eve Kosofsky Sedgwick successfully recast the terms of the debate of the essentialist/constructivist controversy.[32] In contrast to Rollan McCleary's recent explorations of gay spirituality, who takes recent developments in biology as warrant to lay the historicist/essentialist controversy to rest in favor of the essentialist side of the controversy, I am arguing for continued engagement with historicist and constructivist notions of sexuality.[33]

Sexual relations take place in many contexts—both sanctioned and unsanctioned. One context that may or may not sanction sexual activity, depending on cultural expectations, is friendship. The biblical narrative characterizes Jonathan and David as friends.[34] Yet friendship takes on many valences and varies in cultural importance in different historical situations. The medieval background of early modern society placed a high value on friendship, as investigated by C. Stephen Jaeger and Brian Patrick McGuire.[35] A major point of historical difference emerges in the understanding of the

---

29. Foucault, *The History of Sexuality*.

30. Boswell, *Christianity, Social Tolerance, and Homosexuality*.

31. Pequigney, "Sodomy in Dante's *Inferno* and *Purgatorio*," and Bruce Holsinger, "Sodomy and Resurrection."

32. Sedgwick, *Epistemology of the Closet*.

33. McCleary, *A Special Illumination*.

34. 1 Samuel 20:41—איש אח־רעהו, "man and his friend," usually translated as "they."

35. Jaeger, *The Envy of Angels* and McGuire, *Friendship and Community*.

relation of friendship to gender hierarchies. For the early modern ideal of friendship, it was an expression between equals; this fact precluded understandings of friendship between men and women. The resulting fact that male friendship could have deleterious effects for women has been explored by Lorna Hutson in *The Usurer's Daughter*.[36] Contemporary feminist theological perspectives often construe friendship between women as part of lesbian resistance to patriarchal mores.[37] Thus, early modern and contemporary understandings of friendship add another historical contrast that makes transhistorical assumptions impossible to sustain.

In close proximity to the question of the historicity of homosexuality is the larger question of the historicity of experience and its significance in liberal theology. Liberal theology since Schleiermacher has treated experience as a foundational category for theology. However, several critiques of the idea that religious experience is historically and linguistically unmediated emerged in the later twentieth century.[38] In chapters 1 and 3, I examine more closely the significance of historical and cultural mediation of experience for religion. One of the ways in which I explore the historical mediation of experience is by examining the contingencies of musical perception.

The theologians I engage in chapter 1 are primarily relational theologians, rather than liberal theologians. While relational theologians draw in part from the liberal theological tradition that emphasizes "religious experience" as the starting point for theological reflection, their primary point of departure is liberation theology, which begins with social analysis instead. Although the Jewish philosopher and pioneer of the significance of relationality, Martin Buber, strictly differentiated between experiential and relational theologies, siding with the latter, the theologians whom I discuss in chapter 1, Gary David Comstock and Carter Heyward, bring experiential and relational views together.

David is an obvious candidate for bridging musical and theological concerns because his covenant with God in the biblical narrative founds the messianic expectation that is an important component of all Abrahamic religions and the biblical narrative characterizes him as a musician and tradition credits him with the composition of the Book of Psalms.

36. Hutson, *The Usurer's Daughter*.

37. Hunt, *Fierce Tenderness* and Stuart, *Just Good Friends*.

38. Most prominently Proudfoot, *Religious Experience*. See also the two essays by Davaney, "The Limits of the Appeal to Women's Experience" and "Problems with Feminist Theory," as well as Sharf, "The Zen of Japanese Nationalism."

This connection remains implicit in this book however; Jonathan's desire is more central to the argument than David's characterization. The Bible reports repeatedly and insistently that Jonathan loved David; we only know of David that he appreciated this love, perhaps out of genuine affection, perhaps out of cynical motives. The text gives us no clear statement that David loved Jonathan.

Musical treatments of David's Lament over Saul and Jonathan may possibly go back to David himself, if he was a historical figure, though textual analysis of 1–2 Samuel shows this to be extremely unlikely.[39] However, there is a large body of musical works that touch on David and Jonathan in one way or another, the earliest of which I have found is a late eleventh-century lesson.[40] The twelfth century is represented by Abelard's "Planctus David." It is this setting that clarifies important conventional parameters of the seventeenth-century anthems discussed in chapter 4 as they are bonded to the medieval genre of the *planctus*.[41] The clearest way in which one can see that early modern musical laments remained bonded to the genre of the *planctus* is in the fact that the most important late-medieval form of the *planctus* were those setting the grief of the Virgin Mary, a lament form that retained importance into the early modern era, seen most clearly in the continued settings of the sequence "Stabat Mater."[42] The *planctus* genre is one which raises questions pertinent to historicity in general because it expresses the fact of temporality through the prior/posterior relationship. This temporal relation is fundamentally one of loss—what was present now is gone. As Juanita Feros Ruys notes, it is the genre of the *planctus* that allowed Abelard to explore biblical figures as expressions of personal grief, as the typological figures in his *planctus* have different functions than in his theological work.[43] Thus, whereas Benjamin prefigures Paul in Abelard's theological writings, in his "Planctus Jacob," he is a child lovingly remembered by an aging father; whereas Samson was an *exemplum* against marriage and a *figura* for Christ in earlier writings, in Abelard's "Planctus Israel," he is "a man who suffered." The *planctus* can express the loss of

39. For the late composition of David's lament, see Tov, "The Composition of 1 Samuel 16–18." For the debate on David's historical reality, see Lemche and Thompson, "Did Biran Kill David?" vs. Halpern, *David's Sacred Demons*.

40. Steiner, "David's Lament for Saul and Jonathan."

41. Stevens, "Planctus," Ruys, "*Planctus magis quam cantici*," and Lammers, "The *Planctus* Repertory in the *Carmina Burana*."

42. Stevens, "Planctus," 890, on the closeness of *planctus* and sequence, 892.

43. Feros Ruys, "*Planctus magis quam cantici*," 37.

what one had either collectively or individually. One of the earliest *planctus* is a lament for Charlemagne's death in 814. Here a personal relation to a political leader bridges intimate aspects of experience and larger political configurations. This precise dynamic *may* have been at work in some of the seventeenth-century settings under consideration, as it is possible that some of them were sung for the death of Henry, Prince of Wales in 1613. This possibility, and problems with this hypothesis, will be discussed in chapter 4. However, a distinct difference between the generic expectations of the *planctus* and the perspective of a central figure of this book, the gay theologian Gary David Comstock, emerges when one notes that the *planctus* expresses grief for the loss of a concrete person; Comstock, however, uses the story of Jonathan and David to grieve for possibilities of forms of love that could not be actualized in the past. This difference between the generic conventions of the *planctus* and a contemporary theological stance points to a recurrent theme in the book: there are multiple ways of relating past to present.

Other versions include sixteenth-century motets by Pierre de la Rue and Josquin des Prez.[44] In the seventeenth century, the Roman composer Giacomo Carissimi, best-known for his extremely influential oratorio on the story of Jephthah composed an oratorio on David and Jonathan. The French seventeenth-century composer Marc-Antoine Charpentier composed a Latin and a French version. In 1993, Susan Hulsman Bingham composed a chancel opera, "Scenes from the Life of David and Jonathan," for the Gay Christians Reading Group at Christ Church Parish in New Haven, Connecticut.[45]

It would be appropriate for a study in historical theology to investigate the entire complex of musical interpretations as a manifestation of an aspect of tradition. However, as a work in constructive theology, this book turns to a small selection of these works in order to ask pointed questions about the historicity of modern gay theology. In this respect, it must be acknowledged that the selection of works from seventeenth- and eighteenth-century England is somewhat arbitrary, given that any version would serve the purpose of highlighting the historical differences between the assumptions of contemporary gay theology and the interpretive contexts composers in the past worked in. The selection of early modern treatments in particular

---

44. See Borgerding, "Sic ego te dilegebam," for an analysis of Josquin's setting in its historical context.

45. www.chancelopera.com/aaCHAN%20OPS/DavidJonathan.html.

is motivated by a number of factors. First, seventeenth-century music has an important place for me personally, as the Venetian opera *Orontea* by Marc'Antonio Cesti articulated parameters of my intellectual and sexual development before I could name what was at stake.[46] This musical/intellectual experience is part of a larger aesthetic response to Early Music. And, an examination of that experience's larger context shows my investment in Early Music not to be simply a personal whim, but a clear example of how the self is interpellated by larger cultural and ideological forces, as Early Music is one of the most vibrant directions in contemporary classical music institutions.

The various ways these seventeenth- and eighteenth-century musical interpretations can both strengthen and relativize contemporary queer interpretations of Jonathan and David is the subject of this book.

---

46. von der Horst, "*Gelone mio.*"

CHAPTER 1

Jonathan and David as Emblematic of Erotic Relational Theology

SINCE THE MID-TWENTIETH CENTURY, readers have connected the love of Jonathan and David depicted in 1 Samuel to queer identities. This connection has strengthened the quest to reconcile biblical faith and gay identity, perspectives that often seem at odds. One way scholars have bridged these perspectives is to cede religious and spiritual questions of ultimacy or holism to a strictly psychoanalytic/cultural understanding of the text.[1] Roland Boer provides a particularly good example of this "secularizing" approach to queering the Bible in his intertextual weaving of biblical motifs, Lacanian psychology, and popular cinema.[2] In contrast, theologians working within various queer perspectives attempt to connect the homoerotic elements of the biblical text with a theological sense of ultimacy.[3] They seek to push a quality of relation—love or mutuality—to the farthest possible reach of the imagination, that symbol which speaks both to cosmic holism and personal spiritual transformation, God.[4] This chapter will elaborate the theological

1. See the literature in Introduction, n. 3.

2. Boer, *Knockin' on Heaven's Door*.

3. The explicit connection between biblical faith and ultimacy as an attribute of divinity should recall readers to Paul Tillich's *Biblical Religion and the Search for Ultimate Reality*. Tillich holds an important and ambivalent place in the theologians who are the focus of this chapter.

4. For the macrocosmic/microcosmic relation underlying this understanding of God, see Eliade, *The Myth of the Eternal Return*. Also helpful is Berger, *The Other Side of*

hermeneutics with which gay and lesbian theologians approach the stories of Jonathan and David and demonstrate that the theological position underlying the hermeneutic can not be separated from historicist presuppositions.[5] Yet, relational theology holds an ambivalent position with regard to historicism. Fault lines between presentist and historicist modes of thought within relational theology require a rethinking of the relation between contemporary relational theology and various aspects of historical existence.

For several gay, lesbian, or queer-friendly theologians, the relation between Jonathan and David is paradigmatic for the concept of mutual relation at the heart of their work. That is, they understand God to consist in concrete relations of mutuality—a quality that goes beyond egalitarianism in its dynamism. The emphasis on concreteness in relational theology means that it finds its primary expression in praxis, "the total complex of action, including all the reflection embedded in that action," rather than in formal logic.[6] The praxis in question is both social and sexual; these theologians see God both in socialist struggles against transnational corporate capitalism and the dynamics of sexual friendships. This emphasis on praxis is the main reason a turn to music will be a logical move later in the argument. Music requires performance, in which thought and action are inherently, if often only implicitly, conjoined. This combination of thought and action is definitive of praxis.

How do relational theologians get from the friendship of Jonathan and David to God? A very simple version of this movement can be found in Elizabeth Stuart's articulation of a gay and lesbian theology, *Just Good Friends*.[7] She moves from a reconsideration of various aspects of the Christian tradition, including a revaluation of Jonathan and David's friendship as a biblical precedent for gay relationships, to a discussion of the "Friend God." In *Engendering Judaism*, Rachel Adler explores ways in which the

---

God. For a particularly clear statement of what is at stake in construing God as a symbol, see Kaufman, *God the Problem*, 82–115.

5. See ch. 2 for exegetical problems surrounding the Jonathan and David narratives.

6. The definition of praxis is from Harrison, *Making the Connections*, 248. See also Heyward, *The Redemption of God*, 12. Both Harrison and Heyward dialogue with liberation theologians, who often foreground praxis over doctrine. See Segundo, *The Liberation of Theology* and Boff, *Theology and Praxis*. Carter Heyward is a central figure of this chapter; her emphasis on praxis to the exclusion of metaphysics is what differentiates her thought from that of process-relation theologians, with whom she shares many commitments. Some representatives of the latter school of thought include Keller, *From a Broken Web*, *Face of the Deep*, Brock, *Journeys by Heart*, and Christ, *She Who Changes*.

7. Stuart, *Just Good Friends*.

feminist theories of object-relations that are widely used by relational theologians can re-envision the method and meaning of *halacha*, the legal aspect of Talmudic literature.[8] She uses the covenant between Jonathan and David in her "Lover's Covenant," an alternative to conventional—or even *halachic*—marriage that is equally applicable to same-sex and different-sex couples. Her proposal here arises from critiques of marriage that make the interconnection between sexism and heterosexism clear.[9] While the gay theological use of Jonathan and David often occurs within an attempt to stake out a specifically queer space within the biblical tradition, Adler offers a transformed version of sexual politics that does not simply assimilate queers into straight spaces, but transforms the common ground between us. In this case, Jonathan and David are representative of an approach to ethics that sees rules within relational commitments, an approach intimately connected with the theological positions of relational theologians.

The gay theologian Gary David Comstock makes the most explicit assertion that this particular story reveals the nature of the divine, and it is his explication of this relationship that will form the primary point of departure for the argument of this book. In arguing that Jonathan and David manifest the love that is God, Comstock goes far beyond simply claiming them as a legacy for gay men. Rather, he invests their relationship with a theological position that has very specific components rooted in late-twentieth century social and religious struggles. A detailed look at the work Jonathan and David have to do in Comstock's theology is necessary to make the real and deep differences between his work and the perspectives of early modern composers discussed later in the book clear. The following chapter will grapple with problems raised by Comstock's approach to Jonathan and David. Comstock forges a "non-apologetic" gay theology that aims to fit the Bible and the Christian tradition into queer experiences. His model of biblical reading is engaging it as a friend. Just as our disagreements with friends do not negate our commitments to our friendship, within Comstock's commitment to biblical faith, he sees an ethical mandate to challenge it on its homophobia.[10] He builds something like a systematic

8. Adler, *Engendering Judaism*. Adler shares this approach to *halacha* with the lesbian-feminist Jewish theologian Judith Plaskow, though Adler emphasizes the Talmudic side of the equation much more than does Plaskow. See Plaskow, *Standing Again at Sinai*, 60–74.

9. Adler, *Engendering Judaism*: The covenant itself appears on pages 214–15. The theoretical underpinning of the covenant is on pages 169–207.

10. Comstock, *Gay Theology Without Apology*, 11. For a very similar position to Comstock's, see Linscheid, "Our Story in God's Story."

theology by moving through arguments that engage specific books of the Bible, though not in canonical order. He treats the Exodus and the life, death, and resurrection of Jesus as norms by which he judges the rest of Scripture. He then proceeds to do exactly that in a direct confrontation with the well-known admonitions against homoerotic practice, in each case setting aside apologetic arguments and stating that the admonitions are wrong.[11]

In addition to confronting biblical heterosexism, Comstock retrieves various passages as points of positive dialogue. In particular, he singles out Queen Vashti from the Book of Esther and David and Jonathan from 1 and 2 Samuel. For Comstock, Vashti, who refuses to obey an order to show herself before the king's guests and then disappears from the narrative altogether, mirrors the marginalization of queer people in heterosexist society. She also models direct rebellion as opposed to the more pragmatic approach of Queen Esther. He highlights Jonathan's role as an "unconventional nurturer," a description which unites resistance to social norms and an ongoing commitment to social relations. He builds a Christology, not on the person of Jesus, but on Jesus' mandate to build a community of friends.[12]

When Comstock pulls the argument together and applies it to the categories of systematic theology, the relationship of Jonathan and David assumes pride of place in explicating the doctrine of God. He describes the covenant they make with each other, noting that they make it without reference to Yahweh and renew it before Yahweh. He draws from this juxtaposition the idea that God is not a party to the covenant but the love between them. He contrasts his understanding of Jonathan's love as Yahweh's action to a more conventional notion of God as directing action. This line of reasoning culminates in the claim that "God is not the facilitator of mutuality but is the mutuality itself: 'Yahweh shall be between me and you forever.'"[13]

In contrast to a popular understanding of David and Jonathan, Comstock does not treat them as role models who give legitimacy to same-sex erotic desires. Comstock is absolutely clear that he does not seek legitimacy from biblical texts, even as he maintains a critical fidelity to the biblical tradition.[14] Instead, Jonathan and David are carriers of a mutuality that is

11. Comstock, *Gay Theology*, 27–48.

12. Ibid., 91–103.

13. Ibid., 128–29.

14. The kind of critical fidelity Comstock practices has been most fully developed by the feminist New Testament scholar Schüssler Fiorenza. See *In Memory of Her*; "The Will

constitutive of the divine; that they do so homoerotically highlights the fact that other homoerotic relations can embody such mutuality. It is not that the Bible grants legitimacy to Jonathan and David that is at stake here. Rather, the biblical story of Jonathan and David is one locus among many across cultures and historical epochs in which homoeroticism expresses itself in a sacred context.[15] Shifting the context to historical struggles to articulate such manifestations means one can discern a sacrality to the biblical text because it transmits this relation, not because it is *a priori* a revealed text.

Comstock notes that relationships create us—"God is the mutuality and reciprocity in our relationships, the compelling and transforming power that brings together, reconciles, and creates us."[16] Indeed, although Jonathan dies a violent death in battle, destroying both Jonathan's life and the possibility of a narrative in which Jonathan and David "live happily ever after," Comstock focuses on the narrative as an opportunity for ongoing relational possibilities. He imagines a different ending, in which Jonathan does not return to Saul's court, but escapes with David. He points to the power of the story as the tension between the social conditions that made this ending impossible and queer desires to see it realized.[17] Comstock here reads the story not as a simple model of gay friendship, but as a mandate to actualize a form of liberation in the present that was impossible in the past. He furthermore points to a tragic ambiguity at the heart of sociality—it is both necessary for human flourishing and structured in a way that prevents that flourishing for many.[18] Yet, Comstock repeatedly refuses to grant total power to seemingly hegemonic structures of oppression, instead looking to ways in which queer people have successfully established agency, even within limits.[19] Finally, the notion that God is the mutuality in relations that constitute healthy lives makes the easy exchange of humane and divine in

---

to Choose or Reject," and *But She Said*. Mosala uses a similar method of "critical fidelity" in *Biblical Hermeneutics and Black Theology in South Africa*.

15. See Conner, *Blossom of Bone* and McCleary, *A Special Illumination*.

16. Comstock, *Gay Theology*, 127.

17. Ibid., 90.

18. On this point see Niebuhr, *Moral Man and Immoral Society*. Feminist and relational theologians, however, take issue with Niebuhr's division between private virtue and public vice, as well as his inability to see grace in sociality. See particularly Plaskow, *Sex, Sin, and Grace* and Vaughan, *Sociality, Ethics, and Social Change*.

19. For a fuller description of agency within seemingly insurmountable limits, see Welch's argument in *A Feminist Ethic of Risk*.

Comstock's text not simply a reduction of the divine to the human, but a clear statement that the human and divine are inextricable.

The theologian Comstock depends on most to aver that Jonathan and David embody a manifestation of God is the lesbian theologian and Episcopalian priest Carter Heyward. Everything in her thought flows to and from the simple, but radical, definition: "God is our power in mutual relation."[20] She derives this definition from a number of sources, most obviously the Jewish philosopher Martin Buber's explication of the I-Thou relation. This understanding of God differentiates itself from pantheist notions of God by making a clear distinction between "right relations" (a synonym for mutual relations in Heyward's terminology) understood to be the locus of God, and "wrong relations," the locus of sin. In Buber's less pedantic formulation, the distinction is between the relation to a Thou, as opposed to a relation to an It.[21] Heyward moves Buber's thought in a different direction, however, when she insists that God is not simply the latent possibility of relating to another as a person rather than an object, a possibility Buber refers to as the Eternal Thou.[22] God, in Heyward's view is "our power," the increase of agency through mutual empowerment. This mutuality can take a number of forms ranging from cooperative labor to sexual friendship; Heyward seeks for a dynamic that accounts for "right relation" across disparate activities and emotions.

In such a relational conception, God is clearly not a "thing" or "object" or even "a person." Rather, as transpersonal spirit, God is movement between persons that generates power. There are a number of concepts and metaphors that clarify and delimit the significance of this assertion. One such concept is "transcendence," which Heyward reclaims and redefines for feminist purposes.[23] Many feminist theologians have abandoned "transcendence" as a useful term, and Heyward begins by acknowledging

20. Heyward, *Touching Our Strength*, 188.

21. Buber, *I and Thou*. See, however, Sands, *Escape from Paradise* for a critique of a simplistic division of relations into "right" and "wrong." This might be the place to point out that an extremely important interpreter of Buber, Emmanuel Levinas, has not received attention from the relational theologians I discuss here. See Levinas, *Totality and Infinity*.

22. Buber, *I and Thou*, 160.

23. Feminist theologians generally assert that masculinist theology over-emphasizes other-worldly dimensions of spirituality and seeks in transcendence an escape from embodiment. The tendency is to search for ways to balance transcendent and immanent understandings of deity. See for example, Ruether, *Sexism and God-talk*, 70–71.

this critique. She notes that "transcendence" often refers to a superior deity, who is in control of the world. In contrast, Heyward notes that the root of transcendence is "crossing over"—an act of going beyond the self and making connections with others. This power to cross beyond the self into connection with others is the relational God, a God whose presence the sexual desire to connect with others intensifies.[24] A good metaphor for God in this understanding would be the synapse, the movement of communication in the space between nerve endings. Along these lines, the feminist relational ethicist Beverly Harrison has described God as an electric circuit.[25] As a transpersonal movement, God is better understood as a verb than a noun. The radical lesbian-feminist philosopher Mary Daly, who pioneered the redefinition of God as verb rather than noun, discusses the metaphoric activities of "sparking" and "spinning" at length in her work *Gyn/Ecology*.[26] Heyward goes as far to suggest that acting in right relations is godding; when we act free of non-mutual dynamics, we god.[27]

Relational theologians can take 1 John 4, which defines God as love, and Jeremiah 22, which equates the knowledge of God and the doing of justice, as biblical precedent for their work.[28] Comstock's primary biblical resources are the Song of Songs and the Greatest Commandment.[29] Drawing on the argument of the feminist biblical scholar Phyllis Trible, Comstock notes that Yahweh emerges as an external administrator only in the breaking of mutuality between Adam and Eve; in the Song of Songs, the characters re-establish this mutuality, at which point God ceases to be an external character again.[30] Comstock also highlights the simultaneity, equality, and unity of the two parts of the Greatest Commandment, to love God and love

24. Heyward, *Our Passion for Justice*, 244–46.

25. Mud Flower Collective, *God's Fierce Whimsy*, 108–13.

26. Daly, *Gyn/Ecology*," 352–424.

27 Heyward, *Touching Our Strength*, 190.

28. 1 John 4:7–8, 11–12: "Beloved, let us love one another; for love is of God, and he who loves is born of God and knows God. He who does not love does not know God; for God is love . . . . Beloved, if God so loved us, we also ought to love one another. No man has ever seen God; if we love one another, God abides in us and his love is perfected in us." Jer 22:15b–16: "Did not your father eat and drink and do justice and righteousness? Then it was well with him. He judged the cause of the poor and needy; then it was well. Is not this to know me? says the LORD."

29. Comstock, *Gay Theology*, 129.

30. Trible, *God and the Rhetoric of Sexuality*.

the neighbor, as indicative of a relational theology.[31] While these biblical assertions of God as relational power do not exhaust the pluriform biblical witness to Israelite understandings of deity, they provide a basis upon which assertions that Jonathan and David manifest such relational power can be made without imposing an external frame of reference on the biblical narrative. They furthermore demonstrate that relational theologians do not need to "invent" a new understanding of God wholesale.

Queer theologians often turn to relational theologies because our desire for relations that do not fit prescribed patterns forces us to reflect on the nature of the relations we do desire. In this context, relational theologians often cite the work of object-relations theorist Carol Gilligan. Gilligan explored how the moral development of girls challenged the frameworks of psychological theory, in the process noting a pattern that girls would often prefer to make decisions that would perpetuate relationship rather than enforce rigid standards of fairness.[32]

Heyward explores precedents for exploring dynamics of relational power outside of set forms. In her reading of the Gospel of Mark, Heyward elaborates on an opposition between the Greek terms *exousia* and *dunamis*, the former being socially-licensed power, while the latter is a spontaneous, unmediated power.[33] *Dunamis* manifests an intimacy that is both the essence of relation (and therefore is a necessary aspect of God), which cannot be held by a single person to lord over others, and stands in opposition to institutionalized forms of power.[34] The emphasis on relationality places socially prescribed gender roles in a secondary position to ethical criteria of mutuality and solidarity.

---

31. Comstock, *Gay Theology*, 129. This position is in tension with Heyward's early interpretation, in which she asserts that the love of the neighbor as self *rather than* the love of God is the only norm of Christian ethics, a position she seems to move away from as she becomes clearer about her definition of God as mutual relation. See Heyward, *The Redemption of God*, 2, 48–49.

32. Gilligan, *In a Different Voice*. For a set of arguments refining and disputing this position, see Held, *Justice and Care*.

33. Heyward, *Redemption of God*, 40–48. One disturbing aspect of Heyward's use of the *exousia/dunamis* opposition is that it echoes Christian law/grace rhetoric that has been a staple of the anti-Semitism Heyward wishes to undermine.

34. Heyward's most rigorous attempt to reflect on the difference between institutional forms of power and relational transcendence of those forms can be found in her exploration of an experience of therapy, *When Boundaries Betray Us*. This book is valuable in highlighting some tragic elements of relational theology that some critics assert it misses. See particularly Sands, "Uses of the Thea(o)logian."

Comstock explicitly notes the way in which Jonathan's behavior fits with such an emphasis of relation over rules. He draws attention to the difference between Jonathan's and Saul's attempts to approach God in preparation for battle. Saul goes through appropriate cultic rituals and consults priests. Jonathan, by contrast, approaches Yahweh directly and acts impulsively in a manner that finds popular approval. Furthermore, it is not military victory, but the immediate relation to Yahweh that establishes Jonathan's authority.[35] Just as Comstock points to Jonathan as a model of the flexible approach to rules and law demanded by relational ethics, David also offers examples of such bending rules to meet the needs of a relation. This use of David is not just restricted to contemporary relational theologians. A saying of Jesus common to all the synoptic gospels uses David's eating of consecrated bread to justify the breaking of the Sabbath.[36] To the extent that a homoerotic interpretation of Jonathan and David's relationship is valid, it would transgress the prohibitions against homoerotic activity elsewhere in the biblical canon, making it a prime example of why queer theologians turn to this text.[37]

These theologians also draw on relational theologies because they see them as suited to the task of reconnecting spirituality with sexuality. Their use of relational theology thus moves into a distinct erotic relational theology. Specifically, they synthesize a general relational sense of the divine with a definition of the erotic forged by the African-American lesbian poet Audre Lorde. In her essay "Uses of the Erotic: The Erotic as Power," Lorde explores an understanding of the erotic as a resource that is rooted in the power of unexpressed or unrecognized feeling, "a measure between the beginnings of our sense of self and the chaos of our strongest feelings," feelings which are distinctly sensual.[38] She seeks to let this power become all-pervasive. Like a packet of yellow dye kneaded into margarine, "when released from its intense and constrained pellet, it flows through and colors

---

35. Comstock, *Gay Theology*, 83. Note, however, that the military context of Jonathan's actions is something toward which relational theologians might respond with ambivalence. See Hunt, "Medals on Our Blouses?" versus Carter Heyward, *God in the Balance*.

36. Matt 12:1–8, Mark 2:23–28, Luke 6:1–5. Note that the dependence of Jesus on David breaks down the opposition between the "Old Covenant" of law and the "New Covenant" of grace, a staple of anti-Semitic rhetoric, by grounding grace within the Hebrew scriptures.

37. See ch. 2 for fuller discussion of the various claims surrounding this statement.

38. Lorde, *Sister Outsider*, 53–54.

my life with a kind of energy that heightens and sensitizes and strengthens all my experience."[39] In a move that puts Lorde at odds with some queer forms of identity, she juxtaposes feeling to sensation, noting that the erotic has often been confused with the pornographic, which, according to Lorde, emphasizes sensation at the expense of emotion.[40] This deep connection to the chaos of feeling and sensuality functions in several ways for Lorde.[41] It provides a power in sharing that is the basis for understanding that which is not shared, lessening the threat of difference. It underlines the capacity for joy at every level of experience, in such disparate activities as dancing, building a bookcase, writing a poem, or examining an idea: she sees "no difference between writing a good poem and moving into sunlight against the body of a woman I love." Finally, the erotic places a demand to live this life within the knowledge that the satisfaction of joy is possible, knowledge she distinguishes from traditional religious loci of such satisfaction: marriage, God, or the afterlife.

Theologies of erotic mutuality go beyond the interpersonal dimension to address larger political realities. Indeed, in Lorde's conception, the erotic is the bridge between the political and the spiritual, in that it brings out the common element of sharing in each.[42] Heyward notes that the largest misconception of her work is that "mutual relation" refers strictly to one-on-one interpersonal relationships.[43] But the fact is that breathing, the most basic act of survival, puts one in relation to all life on earth. We are always in relation to those we do not know. Expanding on his understanding of mutuality, Comstock identifies God as "the accepting, the interacting and loving that go on in the neighborhood and make it an open, diverse, inclusive, productive community."[44] Heyward has emphasized relations in community, as opposed to simple one-on-one relationships, through her work in two theological collectives, one which explored aspects of feminist theological pedagogy and another which immersed itself in the revolutionary

39. Lorde, Sister Outsider, 57.

40. Ibid., 54. Some theorists of queer identity would part ways with Lorde on this point, seeing pornography as an important resource in the shaping of erotic subjectivities. See, for example, Champagne, The Ethics of Marginality and Fung, "Looking for my Penis."

41. Lorde, Sister Outsider, 54.

42. Ibid., 56.

43. Isherwood, "Interview by Lisa Isherwood with Carter Heyward," 109.

44. Comstock, Gay Theology, 129.

society of Nicaragua.[45] Her most probing account of a one-on-one relationship, *When Boundaries Betray Us*, a narrative of her experience with therapy, provides another example of this sense of the centrality of community. It is in a circle of friends that Heyward finds some redemption and healing from the tragic outcome of an intense interpersonal relationship she describes.[46] The importance of community in these theologians' work belies the impression that relational theology is simply about friendships and romances.

In such an erotic relational theology, sexual relations are part of a larger field of relations—it is not the "union of opposites" as one finds in Jungian psychology that guarantees right relation.[47] Rather, sexual pleasure, repression, and violation cannot all be understood apart from the social institutions that give sexuality meaning. Kelly Brown Douglas, who incorporates Heyward's analysis in her critique of heterosexism in the Black Church, powerfully describes the impact of white racism on the practice of African-Americans' sense of sexual freedom.[48] She highlights various roles imposed on African-Americans, such as the Mammy or the Jezebel; Nina Simone gave a devastating musical expression to these stereotypes in her song "Four Women."[49] Writing in a context of a lesbian separatist vision of spiritual quest, Mary Daly addresses the dependence of the rightness of interpersonal relations on just social conditions when she notes that various social experiences, such as the gap between the desire to learn and the sterility of academic protocols or the conflict between a passion for justice and professional demands can throw women into situations of isolation. The result can be a temptation to lean upon friends and lovers to ameliorate such frustrations: "when women bond out of weakness, there is a danger of victimizing each other."[50] In this regard, Heyward is insistent that sexual justice must be a part of all justice-seeking programs.

---

45. Mud Flower Collective, *God's Fierce Whimsy* and Heyward, *Revolutionary Forgiveness*.

46 Heyward, *When Boundaries Betray Us*, 125–38, also 116–17, 123–24, and 155–57.

47. Jung is a frequent target of critique in feminist theology. A succinct statement is Goldenberg's "Archetypal Theory and the Separation of Mind and Body." See also Ruether, *New Woman/New Earth*, 151–58; *Sexism and God-talk*, 190; Daly, *Pure Lust*, 81–82. For a retrieval of Jung for queer purposes, see Hopcke, *Jung, Jungians, and Homosexuality*.

48 Douglas, *Sexuality and the Black Church*.

49. Simone, "Four Women" on *The Best of Nina Simone*.

50. Daly, *Gyn/Ecology*, 368.

A central point of social analysis in erotic relational theologies is the insistence that patriarchy is not only the subjugation of women by men, but also fundamentally the context for homophobia and heterosexism.[51] Comstock locates a crucial part of the problem of the Bible for gay men in the fact that it is a patriarchal document that names a hierarchical form of family with clearly demarcated gender roles.[52]

In contrast to the easy fit between Jonathan and David and a relational trumping of rules, the biblical narrative does not lend itself as well to a model of queer solidarity with feminism. In respect to the understanding of patriarchy as the explanatory category for homophobia, it must be noted that the gay appropriation of Jonathan and David occurs at the expense of Jonathan's sister and David's wife Michal. In 1 Samuel 18, when David's adventures at Saul's court begin, Michal and Jonathan have a roughly parallel relationship to David. They both love him and later they both save his life. But though Michal survives into the reign of David, the narrative does not deal kindly with her.[53] Yet to root for the relationship of David and Jonathan as an erotic pairing is implicitly to wish for Michal's desire to be unrequited. A more transgressively queer reading could move easily toward a polyamorous interpretation that expresses a desire not for Jonathan and David to form a couple, but for Jonathan and Michal to share David's affections.[54] Yet this is not the desire Comstock expresses. Feminist and queer uses of the narratives in 1 Samuel work at cross-purposes here. Curiously, even feminist and lesbian uses of David and Jonathan for queer purposes pass over the erasure of Michal in this strategy.

While patriarchy and homophobia are obvious targets of critique by queer theologians, they also insist on pushing their analysis to help move struggles for racial and class equality forward.[55] In Comstock's case, this

51. Comstock, *Violence Against Lesbians and Gay Men*, 96–101; Harrison, *Making the Connections*, 135–51.

52. Comstock, *Gay Theology*, 33–38.

53. See Clines and Eskenazi, *Telling Queen Michal's Story*; Exum, *Fragmented Women*, 42–60, Hackett, "1 and 2 Samuel," 90–91; and Linafelt, "Taking Women in Samuel."

54. Not only David's polygamy, but the strong parallels between Jonathan and Michal in 1 Sam 18 would reinforce this reading.

55. To clarify what is at stake here, Ruether's typology of liberal, radical, and socialist feminisms is helpful. Liberal views seek formal and legal equality; radical views seek distinctive positions and autonomy; and socialist views press critique into an analysis interlocking forms of oppression. See *Sexism and God-talk*, 216–34. See also Eisenstein, *Capitalist Patriarchy*. For queer perspectives on class and class struggle see Fernbach, *The Spiral Path*, Gluckman and Reed, *Homo Economics*, and Raffo, *Queerly Classed*.

analysis remains largely at a very local, grassroots level. In the case of Heyward, however, it moves toward a full-fledged critique of imperialism and an advocacy of socialist economics.

Comstock sets the tone for his theology by recounting his experience as a volunteer with the Gay Men's Health Crisis working with Estaban, a poor Puerto Rican HIV-positive gay man.[56] Although Estaban's dignity and refusal to apologize for his choices in life form the guiding spirit of Comstock's argument, the solidarity the two men form across racial and class lines is significant in its own right. It grounds in praxis the multicultural vision of queer tradition that he forges when he draws on figures from the Harlem Renaissance as crucial to a sense of gay identity. Comstock here does not simply argue for "equal rights" with straight society, but engages in a thorough and ever-widening vision of inclusive society that takes the experience of oppression and liberation as fundamental, regardless of context.

But again, the presence of other characters makes it difficult to sustain a direct identification of Jonathan and David with the particular vision of gay identity that Comstock envisions. For example, the *locus classicus* of the gay reading of David and Jonathan is David's utterance in the lament over Saul's and Jonathan's death, "Oh my brother Jonathan, great was your love to me, passing the love of women." Yet the narrative embeds this lament not only within a larger context of ethnic strife, but the immediate context of the murder—to use the standards Comstock himself would use to adjudicate the situation—of an anonymous Amalekite messenger, a murder that is part of a divinely sanctioned genocide against one of Israel's neighboring tribes.[57] This kind of erasure of context points toward a kind of abstraction from historical reality—either ethnic strife at the turn of the first millennium BCE or the subsequent experiences that fed the imaginations of those writing the accounts of the David stories—that the overall argument of this book will combat.

Comstock does turn to larger political configurations, as well. In his chapter on Leviticus, he draws parallels between the post-exilic situation of the priestly writers and the United States in the 1980s in order to draw attention to a basic structure of sexual regulation as a form of compensatory

56. Comstock, *Gay Theology*, 1–4. For anthologies of writings by queers of color, see Smith, *Home Girls*, Roscoe, *Living the Spirit*, Ratti, *A Lotus of Another Color*, and Eng and Hom, *Q & A*.

57. For a recent confrontation with violence in the Bible, see Lüdemann, *The Unholy in Holy Scripture*. For the narrative construction of ethnic difference in the Deuteronomistic History, see Mullen, *Narrative History and Ethnic Boundaries*.

micromanagement.[58] He notes the general expansion of protection of sexual freedoms between the mid-nineteen-fifties and mid-nineteen-seventies as emerging in tandem with overall post-War economic growth, and a shift in both political and ecclesial spheres toward greater restrictions in connection with economic decline.[59] Comstock offers a decidedly non-utopian horizon of continued struggle. Indeed, one of his lessons from this chapter is that given that the generosity of the powerful in regard to sexual freedom "dries up" during economic crises, contemporary people can not look to them for permission to get on with the work of creating just and inclusive communities.[60]

Just as Comstock argues for a political struggle for personal freedom in the context of forging solidarity in the face of the consolidation of capital in a corporate class, so Heyward also connects the need to explore sexual liberation as inseparable from struggles for class equality. Heyward's commitment to socialism is most explicit in her dialogue with various liberation theologies.[61] In 1983, she participated in a collective that worked in revolutionary Nicaragua, an experience which deepened her commitment to radical politics, liberation theology, as well as a deep spiritual rejuvenation that gave meaning to the term resurrection.[62] Based on her experiences with churches in Nicaragua, Cuba, and the United States, she articulates the importance of religious communities making a commitment to a socialist solution to poverty and offers an analysis of the relation between ecclesial communities and socialist struggle in different political contexts.[63]

For Jonathan and David to function as models of an erotic egalitarianism, as Comstock and others wish them to, a distortion of the biblical texts is necessary. In this case, one of the characters is a major agent of the

---

58. It is not my purpose at this point to dwell on the accuracy of Comstock's analysis of either Leviticus or the United States under the Reagan administration—there are legitimate points of debate in his treatment of both.

59. Comstock, *Gay Theology*, 68–76.

60. Ibid., 76.

61. Heyward's most explicit acknowledgements of her debt to Latin American liberation theology can be found in *The Redemption of God*, 205–8; and *Our Passion for Justice*, 103–15. For an overview of the North American reception of Latin American liberation theology, see Nessan, *Orthopraxis or Heresy*.

62. Heyward, *Revolutionary Forgiveness*; on the spiritual rejuvenation and reclamation of resurrection, see Heyward, *Staying Power*, 19–21.

63. Heyward, "Doing Theology in a Counterrevolutionary Situation."

increasing centralization of monarchical power in Israelite politics.[64] David is responsible for moving the capital to Jerusalem and making the steps toward political consolidation. Saul, David's predecessor, only commences the monarchy after the prophet Samuel warns the Israelites that rejecting the kingship of God in favor of a human king will lead to various forms of oppression.[65] In the hands of David's successor, such centralization leads to a stark instance of alienated labor, when Solomon institutes forced labor.[66] While there is a major anti-monarchical strand of Israelite political thought, David is not the place to look for it. For Jonathan and David to work as models of erotic *egalitarianism* in the large sense prescribed by queer theologians, one must split their interpersonal relationship from the larger field of political relations in a manner that queer theologians would balk at in modern contexts. To be sure, none of the relational theologians under discussion labor under the illusion that "right relation" can be established universally, or once and for all. But even keeping this caveat in mind, it is noteworthy that Comstock does not pause to ask questions about the connections between the personal relationship of David and Jonathan and the larger political forces that undermine the mutuality Comstock describes in the relationship. Rather, Comstock highlights the very real ways in which their relationship challenges established political configurations in the shake-up of the Saulide dynasty. Both the importance of Comstock's larger political analysis to his understanding of queer resistance to heterosexism and his refusal to idealize the biblical record in general on this front make for a stark contrast with his idealization of Jonathan and David as agents of mutual relation who embody the love of God.

RELATIONAL THEOLOGY IS INHERENTLY HISTORICIST

On a number of fronts, the theology of erotic relations that subtends the gay theological appropriation of Jonathan and David would be completely unrecognizable to the early modern musicians to whom I will turn later. It is not that sexual relations or homoeroticism would have been unrecognizable, nor would sacred contexts for homoeroticism have been *a priori* ruled out. The queer theorist and historian of early modern culture Richard Rambuss has examined early modern English sacred art and literature in

64. See particularly, Pixley, *Biblical Israel*.

65. 1 Sam 8:10–18.

66. 1 Kgs 5:27–30.

detail to discern sacred art as one of the few outlets for homoerotic expressions, even of the "hard core" variety.[67] What pre-modern people would have had trouble recognizing is that such insights could be the basis for non-heretical formal Christian theological doctrines.

Erotic relational theology has a number of entailments that are historically specific to its Cold War context. First, there is a clear analytic preference for seeing homophobia and heterosexism under the umbrella of patriarchy; queer perspectives and feminist perspectives are firmly, if uneasily, linked by a common ambivalent relation to the sexual revolution. Secondly, a strong critique of mind/body dualisms emerges from these feminist perspectives, leading to a widespread agnosticism about the afterlife and continuity with religious traditions focused on establishing justice in the here and now. Third, eroticism is understood as part and parcel of a larger political egalitarianism. Indeed, eroticism often becomes the *sine qua non* of a spontaneity and authenticity of an anarchic strain of political radicalism.[68] Finally, Queer theologians often speak in solidarity with counter-imperialist movements. This solidarity is exemplified in a method closer to liberation theology than liberal theology. None of these entailments will hold true when we turn to early modern renditions of David's Lament over Jonathan later in the argument.

These differences between late twentieth-century theology and early modern theology alone would warrant a historicist interrogation of relational theology. However, there are intrinsic reasons relational theology must turn to history and historicist modes of thought. Most prominently among these reasons is the insistence that relation occurs among embodied persons who are bound to the flow of change, and that it is within history that all efforts to establish "right relation" in the forms of justice and love must take place. Heyward began her investigation of mutual relation in part as a way of finding an answer to the question "to what extent are we responsible for our own redemption in history?"[69]

---

67. Rambuss, *Closet Devotions*. Other scholarly literature along this line of inquiry includes Holsinger, *Music, Body, and Desire in Medieval Culture*, Dinshaw, *Getting Medieval*; Bredbeck, *Sodomy and Interpretation*, 187–231, Borgerding, "Sic ego te dilegebam," Gaunt, "Straight Mind/'Queer' Wishes in Old French Hagiography"; Lavezzo, "Sobs and Sighs Between Women"; and Holsinger, "Sodomy and Resurrection," 243–74. I do not always find the arguments of these theorists of the Queer/Early/Modern nexus convincing. See Freccero, *Queer/Early/Modern* for a summation of some of the key issues.

68. See, for example, Marcuse, *Eros and Civilization*.

69. Heyward, *Redemption of God*, 1.

In the succinct statement of Sheila Greeve Davaney, "human historicity . . . entails both being constituted by our past and being agential contributors to new historical realities."[70] The Presbyterian socialist-feminist ethicist Beverly Harrison, who works with Heyward's relational theological principles, lays out the place of historical inquiry within relational theology and ethics, and a number of reasons to pursue "emancipatory historiography." Most importantly for my argument is her assertion that attention to history relieves thought from the poles of sheer chance or grim determinism by focusing on human decisions and agency as primary causal forces.[71] Such reasons include seeking out root causes of current forms of oppression and learning from the success and especially the failures of previous resistance movements.

There is a different tradition of critical historiography that also explores the interaction between historical change and contemporary agency but focuses more on the reality of suffering itself. In the critical theory of Walter Benjamin, the historical reality of suffering calls into question high-minded metaphysical and aesthetic ideals. The task of history is to maintain solidarity with the victims of the past. In the words of Benjamin, "only that historian will have the gift of fanning the spark of hope in the past who is firmly convinced that *even the dead* will not be safe from the enemy if he wins. And this enemy has not ceased to be victorious."[72] In the argument of Marsha Aileen Hewitt, who works to bring the critical theory of the Frankfurt School in dialogue with feminist theology, such attention to real suffering demands that feminist religious thinkers move away from the comforts of theology with its entailments of authenticity and ontology toward social theory.[73]

Both the need to seek out root causes of today's evils in decisions of the past and the search for ways to honor and foster solidarity with the victims of history are important elements of an emancipatory historiography.

---

70. Davaney, *Pragmatic Historicism*, 1. On the prevalence of an American empiricist ideology that resists acknowledgement of our being constituted by our past, see Hughes, *Myths America Lives By*, 45–65. Note also that Davaney's definition parts from Karl Popper's definition of historicism as discerning a *telos* to historical movement, which he strongly rejects. See his *The Poverty of Historicism*. See also Rand, "Two Meanings of Historicism" for further elucidation of the notion of historicism.

71. Harrison, *Making the Connections*, 249. See her *Our Right to Choose* for an example of how she brings this historicist method to bear on a particular ethical issue.

72. Benjamin, *Illuminations*, 255.

73. Hewitt, *Critical Theory of Religion*.

Especially in the way attention to historical change opens a sense of freedom and increase of agency, such investigations are crucial to contemporary political movements. But despite the fact that I affirm and depend on these understandings of history as opening agency, the converse aspect of historical contingency—its ability to make the world seem strange rather than familiar, to disenchant—provides intellectual challenges to, rather than support for, many aspects of relational theology. For example, in making the case for the intrinsic historicity of relational perspectives, Harrison asserts,

> Liberation theologies are intrinsically historical, physical, time-bound. *There is no "core" of life or reality to be "essentialized."* "Reality" is concrete, a material, interactive cosmic-world-historical process. Our agency or action is set within ongoing temporal-historical processes and webs of interrelations. From this perspective an analysis is theological if, and only if, it unveils or envisions our lives as a concrete part of the interconnected web of all our social relations, including our relations to God.[74]

This complex of assertions pushes human agency toward the dissolution of reality as a coherent foundation.

Taking change as an aspect of history seriously means that the differences between past understandings and present ones are significant intellectual challenges. One such approach to the past that emphasizes such differences is contained in the concept of the *episteme* as elucidated by Michel Foucault in *The Order of Things*.[75] The emphasis here shifts from a sense of dependency on the past (which it does not deny) to the radically different ways in which the most basic modes of cognition work from one era to another. In this case, history, like anthropology, works above all to denaturalize what appears to be common sense. For example, Umberto Eco's essay on the perception of color turns both to ancient Roman color schemes as well as those of the Hanunóo of the Philippines to prove that something as seemingly automatic as registering color only occurs with a great deal of cultural mediation. Both the temporal distance of ancient Roman culture and the physical distance of the rural Philippines function in

---

74. Harrison, *Making the Connections*, 245, emphasis added. Note also Harrison's scare quotes on "reality" in the following sentence.

75. Foucault, *The Order of Things*. See also Kuhn, *The Structure of Scientific Revolutions*, and Margolis, *Historied Thought, Constructed World*.

the same way to destabilize modern Western senses of what is natural.[76] It is this sense of historicity that the relational theologians under discussion here neglect entirely.

For many thinkers, perhaps most radically the nineteenth-century German philosopher Friedrich Nietzsche, such an acknowledgement of historicity must necessarily lead to the dissolution of a universal grounding of ethical norms in any kind of metaphysic—expressed in the famous "death of God." Very early in his career, Nietzsche asserted that a lack of historical sense was the fundamental error of philosophers.[77] He pushed this sense of historical perspectivalism to the point of allowing it dissolve even the sense of a natural world. In *Twilight of the Idols*, he offers an encapsulated history of understandings of the "true world" and its relations to human endeavors. The "true world" becomes increasingly remote from people until they abolish it, along with the apparent world, at which point Zarathustra, the fully alive self-creating person begins his quest.[78] Nietzsche here follows through to a radical conclusion the implications of the connection between the freedom contingency offers and the sense of foundation contingency takes away. But for Nietzsche, historicity requires acceptance of the inherent injustice of perspectivalism, an entailment relational theologians would reject.[79] Another tension between Nietzsche and feminist theologians is that for Nietzsche, mortality as an inherent factor in the changeability of existence implies nihilism, while for feminist theologians mortality is simply a limit of existence within which one exercises what agency one has.

The ramifications of such historicist arguments go so far as to render the most quotidian of categories unstable, ushering postmodern ethics around the destabilized category of "woman" and to vehement disputes as to whether "homosexuality" can in any way be construed as a trans-historical given.[80] In this respect, all historicist theologies carry an internal

---

76. Eco, "How Culture Conditions the Colors We See." See, however, the naturalistic account of why humans are dependent on such contingent cultural symbols in Geertz, *The Interpretation of Cultures*.

77. Nietzsche, *Menschliches, Allzumenschliches*, 25.

78. Nietzsche, *Götzen-Dämmerung*, 80–81.

79. Nietzsche, *Menschliches, Allzumenschliches*, 20.

80. The clearest historicist dismantling of "woman" as a coherent category is Riley's *"Am I That Name?"* For a related, though less explicitly historicist, argument, see Butler, *Gender Trouble*. In theology, Davaney made these issues a subject of debate in two essays, "The Limits of the Appeal to Women's Experience" and "Problems with Feminist Theory." One argument that developed from this line of thought, Armour's *Deconstruction,*

tension between seeking a foundation in God and pursuing an awareness of change which, if followed through rigorously, could lead to a point of radical relativism. The German liberal theologian Ernst Troeltsch modeled a particularly rigorous example of thinking in that particular tension.[81]

As Eco's investigation of color perception suggests, aesthetics are a powerful tool with which to investigate historicity because, aside from the question of artistic merit, they make the mediation of perception by social and linguistic parameters clear. Because relational theologians assert that all relation happens within such social and linguistic parameters, they can not afford to neglect the questions raised by aesthetics. Music is particularly tricky in this regard because people often understand its effects as completely unmediated. For example, the musicologist Philip Brett notes how a basic instrument of modern music pedagogy, analysis of Bach's chorale harmonizations, treat Bach's procedures as "standard" harmonic practice, without noting how he often strains to reconcile a fairly new harmonic practice with older modal procedures.[82] Thus, the rudimentary exercises by which many learn the basics of harmony trains ears to accept as "normal" what a historicist argument reveals to be contorted.

The relational theology with which gay theologians interpret Jonathan and David is explicitly a break with classical theism. While Comstock does not make this break a focal point of his theology, Heyward began her theological career with a strong interest in the "Death of God" school of thought of the 1960s, which dramatically heralded a strong sense of discontinuity with traditional and historical understandings of Christian faith. The mere fact of this break demands a historicist analysis of it. For Heyward it is explicit that what she means by "God" is not what John Calvin meant by "God," what Augustine meant by "God," or what the Elohist meant by "God." She vehemently makes a clear distinction on feminist grounds between the God she seeks and the "God" she rejects. She expresses anger at an other-worldly, misogynistic "God" set above human experience and material needs, and notes that if this is Christianity's "God" she is willing

---

Feminist Theology, while admirably elucidating the ethical nature of deconstruction, strikes me as overly concerned with establishing distance from the theologians it critiques, to the point of drastically distorting the record of feminist theologians' connections with class and racial struggles.

81. For an explication of some of the issues, see Wyman, Jr. "Revelation and the Doctrine of Faith."

82. Brett, "Music, Essentialism, and the Closet," 14.

to reject this "God" and the tradition in which "He" is proclaimed.[83] In describing her rejection of a patriarchal "God," Heyward narrates a movement of a transcendent, personal God moving violently over the course of millennia. The nature of the "God" she criticizes and the narration are both significant. Heyward narrates a lasting historical effect of this "God," who does the same sort of things in a line of development that can be traced from ancient Israel to modern Rome. The image of God she criticizes is both male and transcendent, the apex of a static hierarchical structure. Like the radical lesbian religious philosopher Mary Daly before her, she believes that feminism calls for a radical rethinking of the nature of God, and is largely sympathetic with Daly's strategy of moving from using nouns to using verbs to describe God.[84] The point of contention between Heyward, Daly, and other feminist and queer religious thinkers is in how they relate this rethinking to the past.

Unlike Daly, who finds the entire biblical and Christian heritage worse than useless, Heyward believes there is much within the Christian tradition that can be retrieved to good purpose. Heyward especially shares with the extremely influential nineteenth-century theologian Adolf von Harnack a sense that Hellenism was a corrosive force on the early Christian message.[85] This understanding of the relation of Christianity to Hellenism is significant in three respects. First, for Heyward, it bespeaks a betrayal within the Christian tradition of a "Hebrew" voluntary sense of covenant rooted in history that is superseded by a "Greek" emphasis on metaphysics. Second, the very fact of this change again points to a historicist understanding of what religion is. Third, she shares with a wide number of liberal Christian thinkers the opinion that this shift had deleterious effects on Christianity's ability to celebrate sexuality.[86]

Heyward shares with various liberation theologians an insistence that all theological pronouncements are ideologically weighted and historically

---

83. Heyward, *Redemption of God*, 10–11.

84. Daly, *Beyond God the Father*, 33–34.

85. Heyward, *Redemption of God*, 2–5. See Harnack, *What is Christianity?*

86. Most prominently, Nelson, *Embodiment*, 45–52. See also Ruether, *Liberation Theology*, 51–64, and 115–26, *New Woman/New Earth*, 15–18; see, however, her qualifications of her critique in "Asceticism and Feminism." For recent restatements of this perspective, see Jantzen, "Good Sex" and Jennings, *Plato or Paul?*. The Jewish assyriologist and biblical scholar Tikva Frymer-Kensky makes a similar historical case in *In the Wake of the Goddesses*. This line of argumentation should be treated with some caution in light of Hengel, *Judaism and Hellenism*.

specific.[87] She specifically denies that it is the task of the theologian to strive for statements that are universally true. She notes that it is impossible to determine the shared assumptions with which a religious community defines itself prior to the ongoing shared reflection on living together which is praxis. It is this praxis that matters for theology, not the determination of what assumptions have held invariably over the course of Christian history.[88]

This emphasis on praxis places Heyward significantly closer to liberation theologies than classical liberal theologies. For liberal theology since Schleiermacher, the problem to be addressed is the relation between cultural symbols, the element of projection therein, their historical situatedness and the transcendent reality to which those symbols refer.[89] Liberal theologians pursue these questions primarily in dialogue with those for whom modernity renders religious belief untenable. In contrast, liberation theologians pursue accountability to the oppressed, seeing answering the skeptic as a distraction from more important tasks of survival.

But in relation to both liberal and liberationist perspectives, Heyward's insistence on praxis as both central to the theological task and of necessity tied to historical change is not an aberration. The centrality of historical change to conceiving the theological task has been a central aspect of liberal Protestant thought, from the German idealist philosopher Georg Hegel, through later nineteenth-century German liberals such Adolf von Harnack and Ernst Troeltsch,[90] to representatives of the Chicago School of theology such as Shailer Mathews.[91]

In contrast to those who see historicism as pushing to a radical relativism, relational theologians resist this implication. Although the dialogical views of Buber and Heyward are intrinsically open to a variety of perspectives, both writers posit a relational ontology that finally excludes non-relational perspectives. Buber's *I and Thou*, written before advances in religious pluralism, makes firm distinctions between a relational ontology and a number of religious worldviews.[92] Indeed, Buber categorically rejects Schleiermacher's doctrine of absolute dependence, the monism of Advaita

---

87. See particularly Segundo, *The Liberation of Theology*.

88. Heyward, *Redemption of God*, 12.

89. In the context of feminist theology, the most thorough examination of the dynamics of this tension is Schneider's *Re-Imagining the Divine*.

90. Troeltsch, in *Writings on Theology and Religion*, 124–79.

91. Mathews, *The Growth of the Idea of God*.

92 Buber, *I and Thou*, 136.

Vedanta, and even, despite the deeply relational doctrine of dependent co-arising, Buddhist teachings of detachment.[93] In each case, Buber's rejection of the issue in question revolves around their failure to take a relational or dialogic position as the basis for what is ultimately true and practical in this world.

Like Buber, Heyward insists that the relational aspect of living must be pursued to the furthest implications, to the point that any kind of grounding in a non-relational understanding of God or the ultimate must be refused. She opens her argument in *The Redemption of God* with a bald assertion that "God and humanity need to be understood as relational and co-operative, rather than as monistic (synonymous) or dualistic (antithetical)."[94] She implies throughout her work that monistic and dualistic visions of God are false projections of power, whereas relational understandings of God are true, seen for example in her distinction between "God" and God in *The Redemption of God*.[95]

But these assertions of the ultimacy of relation go beyond the questions of praxis that Heyward insists is the proper locus of theological endeavor. Instead, they directly make metaphysical claims on ethical grounds, often by noting that the models other theologies offer have deleterious effects. The question remains to what extent historicity is compatible with either metaphysics or ontology. One relatively successful attempt to integrate historicist insights into a generally ontological framework, *Truth and Method* by the twentieth-century German philosopher Hans-Georg Gadamer actually highlights the fact that an ontological grounding can brake the radical ethical possibilities of historicity, as Gadamer's text has been widely criticized for overly conservative tendencies.[96]

Heyward spells out how she reconciles the demands of ontology and her historicist perspective. When she explicates the centrality of love in

93. For a Buddhist engagement with Buber, see Heisig, "Non-I and Thou."

94. Heyward, *Redeption of God*, 1. An interesting line of inquiry here would be an examination of Karl Barth's use of Buber in light of feminist critiques of Barth as excessively dualistic in his approach.

95. The strongest argument in feminist theology that delineates between projection and truth in theology is Schneider's *Re-Imagining the Divine*. Schneider, however, comes to a monistic position in contrast to Heyward's relational position.

96. Gadamer, *Truth and Method*; for criticisms, see Habermas, "A Review of Gadamer's *Truth and Method*," Ricoeur, "Hermeneutics and the Critique of Ideology," Ingram, "The Possibility of a Communication Ethic Reconsidered," and "The Historical Genesis of the Gadamer/Habermas Controversy," and Frow, *Marxism and Literary Theory*, 224–27.

theology, she notes that it is only possible to realize love of God and neighbor in time and history. She affirms "eternal and transcendent dimensions of reality," but that these dimensions are rooted in temporal experience. This rootedness means that one must begin with a historicist examination of what the words "eternal" and "transcendence" mean to begin to make sense of any claims about them.[97] Unlike radical relativists, Heyward does not completely cede such terms as "God," or "transcendence." Rather, she notes that one can only speak of such matters from within the flow of historical change and contingency.

In the cases of both theologians, the distinction between history and tradition reveals further tensions between presentist and historicist assumptions. There is a tension between Comstock and Heyward on the uses of the past. Comstock is more interested in retrieving or creating a tradition. Heyward is more committed to a historicization that mandates a commitment to radical social change. In both thinkers, however, very strong presentist commitments sit within their attempts to forge dialogues with the past. These presentist assumptions undermine the historicist ethic that locates a mandate for social struggle in the inevitability of change.

Comstock accepts both the standard definition of tradition as "that which is handed over" and its importance for salvation. He sees three theologically standard elements—scripture, tradition, and experience—as buttressing "salvific events." He defines a salvific event as one which "rescues us from pain and suffering and makes us a new people."[98] He builds on the narratives of the Exodus and the ministry, crucifixion, and resurrection of Jesus to advance an understanding of salvation as the transformation of pain. He uses this principle as a Scriptural norm with which to critique Scripture itself. As an aspect of the salvific role of religion, tradition must contribute to the transformation of pain.

In Comstock's vision, tradition is primarily a source of solace, succor, and rest.[99] Above all, it is a further instance of the thoroughly relational vision he advances, for above all, what he seeks in his understanding of tradition is company, a sense of being a part of others' lives, even though they are deceased. He cites an essay by Alice Walker, making a genealogical connection between his notion of tradition and African ancestor venera-

---

97. Heyward, *Redemption of God*, 19. Davaney cites Sidney Hook's 1927 *Metaphysics of Pragmatism* as making a similar point; see *Pragmatic Historicism*, 52, 198.

98. Comstock, *Gay Theology*, 106. See also Soelle, *Suffering*.

99. Comstock, *Gay Theology*, 110–11.

tion closer than Euro-Christian notions of tradition as the handing over of doctrine.[100] Secondary to that fundamental relational sense of connection with the dead are a kind of detached appreciation and observation of past figures simply as past figures or as role models for the present.[101]

Where Comstock differs from "traditional" notions of tradition is in his insistence that as outsiders to a heterosexist social contract, queer people must search out and create a tradition for themselves. The violence done to gay and lesbian people through the mechanisms of the Christian tradition demands the articulation of a counter-tradition. He describes the lack of gay role models in his youth, a fact which demonstrates a sense of being isolated and cut off from a common gay culture.

Comstock establishes a parallel between an "outlandish" aunt with whom he identified as a child and Queen Vashti in the book of Esther, who refuses to obey the commands of the king and whom the narrative drops quickly, to explicate the dynamics of creating a counter-tradition. Comstock's family generally disapproved of the aunt, and as such she became a model of the "ousiderness I kept privatized."[102] Similarly, he finds in Queen Vashti, who makes a defiant gesture at the outset of the Book of Esther and is then dropped from the narrative, both a model of rebellion and resistance and a mirror of marginalized status. What Comstock sees as the "good news" of the story is the active attempt to "turn the story around" from one which marginalizes Vashti both socially and in terms of the narrative.[103] We have already seen this sense of "turning narratives around" in Comstock's naming of the desire to see the story of Jonathan and David end differently than it does. But this insistence that queer people must *create* their own traditions is deeply ambivalent in a historicist sense. For on the one hand, the notion that queer people must *create* a counter-tradition shows a strong sense of how people construct the past in the pursuit of present needs. On the other hand, his search for *tradition* and not *history* demands that he find people who fundamentally, if imperfectly, fit with a common, stable, gay identity. While the creation of a particular coherence of the past through research rather than acceptance of normative sources

100. Walker, "A Name is Sometimes an Ancestor Saying Hi, I'm with You." On retrieving African forms of ancestor veneration for Christian theology, see Hood, *Must God Remain Greek?*, 217–43.

101. Comstock, *Gay Theology*, 111.

102. Ibid., 50

103. For a similar approach see, Pardes, *Countertraditions in the Bible*; Bal, *Death and Dissymmetry*; also Fetterley, *The Resisting Reader*.

fits well with a historicist sense that history is a matter of contingency, the search for a trans-historical anchor of like-minded company is a search for something more solid than the flux of change.

It is striking that the figures Comstock refers to as forebears in his reconstructed tradition are all nineteenth- and early twentieth-century figures from Europe and America. He highlights the turn-of-the-twentieth-century English socialist and sexual theorist Edward Carpenter as a paradigmatic figure of what he means by tradition.[104] In keeping with this tradition rooted in nineteenth-century homoeroticism, Comstock's interpretation of Jonathan and David themselves depends largely on Walt Whitman's poetry and its literary and social context.[105] In short, he turns to a highly modernist version of gay identity with which to dialogue. His list is certainly multicultural, but the geographic and temporal scope of the tradition he defines is shockingly narrow in comparison to understandings of tradition that provide an anchor for identity across hundreds, or even thousands, of years. The very term he is redefining, "tradition," makes glaringly clear that even in his attempt to create an interface between the past and present, he is locked into fundamentally presentist commitments.

This modernist understanding of homosexuality drives his reading of David and Jonathan. One way in which Comstock bypasses the debate over whether David and Jonathan expressed their friendship sexually is to displace the primary locus of homoerotic elements of the text from the relationship proper to a hypothetical redactor or groups of redactors.[106] He notes that it is more important to him that a writer or group of writers "may have used an available framework to tell a story that would be read or heard differently by gay men than by nongay people."[107] It is this knowing wink across generations that Comstock is looking for as the common ground,

---

104. Comstock, *Gay Theology*, 110.

105. See also Katz, *Love Stories*.

106. Comstock, *Gay Theology*, 87–89.

107. Ibid., 89. For varying examinations of authorship in ancient Israel one could use to test the notion that "gay" writers in ancient Israel would have slipped homoeroticism into the narrative, see Friedman, *Who Wrote the Bible?*; Niditch, *Oral World and Written Word*; Thompson, *The Mythic Past* (see also Zwelling's helpful exegesis and contextualization of *The Mythic Past* in "The Fictions of Biblical History"); Schniedewind, *How the Bible Became a Book*; and van der Toorn, *Scribal Culture and the Making of the Hebrew Bible*. A good starting place for considering the issues in relation to David and Jonathan more specifically is Tov, "The Composition of 1 Samuel 16–18."

not necessarily with the historical Jonathan and David, but with crafty biblical authors willing to plant subversive messages in the biblical text.

With this strategy, Comstock shows awareness of historicist arguments about homosexuality, and at the same time, a strong reluctance to give them their due. His primary basis of comparison here is nineteenth-century American literature, *not* ancient Mesopotamian, Egyptian, West Semitic, or even Greek literature. He elucidates ways in which writers coded homoerotic subtexts in literature to communicate to knowing readers while escaping detection from those with the authority to pursue sanctions against people engaged in homoerotic activities. "If the situation in biblical times was similar, such appropriate terms might have been conventional to covenant making. The altering and coding of terms would have been heard by other gay men with a recognizing ear."[108] He does not stop to consider the implications of the text if the situation in biblical times was *not* similar.

What Comstock does successfully achieve with this strategy is divorcing "gay identity" from modernist notions of "authenticity" with which essentialist arguments operate. By acknowledging a complex process of literary composition, the text is no longer a direct expression of an undivided subjectivity.[109] The tension between this perspective and his continued insistence on "gay people" in the ancient Israelite context is real, however.

Furthermore, as noted repeatedly in the first section of this chapter, such presentist commitments radically distort the source on which Comstock bases his doctrine of God as mutual relation. In order to cite Jonathan and David as examples of a mutual relation that not only affirms sexual body pleasure, but inclusive community, Comstock has had to write Samuel's warning of monarchical oppression and its fulfillment in David's son Solomon, Michal's desire for David, and the genocide against the Amalekites out of the narrative. To be sure, Comstock offers the desire to have the story end differently as a potent force from the reception side of the text to grant a kind of flexibility to the reading. But it becomes clear by the sheer magnitude of textual erasure Comstock performs that he needs a text he does not have.

Heyward's emphasis on redemption in history leads her toward an uncompromising presentism. "In history, we begin. It can be *kairos*. There is no

---

108. Comstock, *Gay Theology*, 88. For a scholarly perspective from biblical studies supporting the view of a homoerotically coded covenant between David and Jonathan, see Olyan, "'Surpassing the Love of Women.'"

109. For a particularly forceful account of the importance for divided subjectivity and complex literary processes for gay identity, see Jackson. *Strategies of Deviance*.

time that is not *our* time, *the* time, the *only* time that matters for humanity: *now*."[110] She critiques the patristic theologian Ireneaus for an understanding of God that postpones the fullness of relation to the end of history.[111] Her insistence on radical immanentism puts her work in tension not only with classical theologians, but also with liberal secular messianism. Where Heyward shows an active distaste for understandings of salvation that postpone it to the future, Comstock simply bypasses a concern with the future altogether, focusing on the ministerial tasks that lie before him.[112]

But Heyward's own development shows that an immanent presentism this uncompromising is impossible to sustain. While in *The Redemption of God*, Heyward refuses to waver in the slightest from an affirmation of the here and now, she later turns to a tension between the yet/not yet in regard to coming out. Her main point here is about the tension between revelation and concealment; she plumbs the spiritual implications of the decision whether to state one's sexual preference openly. Her basic point that God is present in our communal actions for justice stands. "We don't realize what is good until we are ready to help generate conditions for it."[113]

Drawing on insights from Rudolf Bultmann, Heyward begins her explanation of the importance of Jesus for theology by noting that Jesus will never be "for us" who he was for Mary Magdalene or the other disciples.[114] This means that we can not simply lift Jesus pure out of the first century and "follow his teachings" or his example. Rather, we must re-image the picture of Jesus in such a way that speaks to contemporary needs. But the fact remains that her re-imagining is of a past figure; the fact that Jesus will mean something different to us than he did to the earliest disciples does not negate the meaning he had for them. Heyward's approach here is consistent with Jesus' admonition to "let the dead bury the dead," and to experience the risen Christ as life-giving in the present. It is, however, inconsistent

---

110. Heyward, *Redemption of God*, 152.

111. Ibid., 108–16.

112. In this regard, Comstock might profitably be read alongside Edelman, *No Future* and Puar, *Terrorist Assemblages*, which theorize non-procreative aspects of queer sexuality as having potential ethical significance and actual cultural significance.

113. Heyward, *Touching Our Strength*, 30. Note, however, the position of Sharon Welch, who similarly idenitifies the divine with relational power in movements for social justice, but is much less sanguine about the possibility of discerning the good. See *A Feminist Ethic of Risk*.

114. Heyward, *Redemption of God*, 27–29. See also Young, *History and Existential Theology*.

with the mandate to seek solidarity with the dead found in other historicist perspectives from Walter Benjamin to Elisabeth Schüssler Fiorenza.

She takes a similar stand in relation to an era she did live through, the 1960s, during which time she learned valuable lessons about the spirituality of social protest—"I really did believe that God is best known in the movements for a better world."[115]

> The meanings of the 60s do not lie behind us but rather are ours to create, for the value of a historical moment is not inherent, self-evident, or static. We are creating the meaning of the 60s *in the relation* between then and now, them and us, ourselves and our forebears and our children ... In the movement of God, the 60s are not over and done, and they never will be.[116]

Again, as with Comstock's elucidation of a gay counter-tradition, both the general principle and the specifics of Heyward's approach are significant. As with the Bible, Heyward does not see past activity simply as a perfect model which can be simplistically appropriated to achieve the same effects, nor as a singular revelation that must be preserved pristine. Rather, Heyward is absolutely clear about our active role in constituting a past that is useful for our efforts to create a future.

But like Comstock, she sees two historically disparate events—the activity of the biblical prophets from Amos through Jesus and the turmoil of the 1960s—as especially revelatory of possibilities for mutual power. Again, like Comstock, despite acknowledgement of historical changes, the end result is to impose a modernist sensibility on the biblical text. In Heyward's case, this modernizing hermeneutic consists of the unapologetic re-imaging of several passages from the Gospel of Mark to make them speak to our contemporary situation.[117] On the one hand, this approach positively acknowledges that an experience can not be confused with a written account of it, showing textual fidelity to be a kind of idolatry in the face of an experience that can only be grasped relationally in a variety of perspectives. On the other hand, the technique refuses the strangeness of the past, and it refuses the opportunity to relate to the dead in terms that give them autonomy.

Heyward devotes more attention to the intervening millennia between biblical times and the present than does Comstock. However, whereas

---

115. Moroney, "A Conversation with Carter Heyward."

116. Heyward, *Staying Power*, 13.

117. Heyward, *Redemption of God*, 36–59.

Comstock flattens the past through simple neglect, Heyward paints an often one-dimensional picture of an unrelievedly oppressive past that becomes a mandate for a total revolution in the present. For example, in her statetment, "the christian [sic] church has been the chief architect of an attitude toward sexuality during the last 1,700 years of European and Euroamerican history—an obsessive, proscriptive attitude, in contrast to how large numbers of people, christians [sic] and others, have actually lived our lives as sexual persons,"[118] she makes a sweeping claim about a nearly two-thousand-year period that would make any good historian cringe. Her description of Christian history flattens the diversity of Christian experience into a monolithic picture of "the church." However, attention to the details of history, which she neglects, makes such a monochromatic picture impossible to paint. To illustrate what is missing, take two examples of medieval Christianity, often understood as the epitome of benighted oppressive tendencies in the popular imagination. The macho asceticism of Thomas of Kempis and the polymorphous exuberance of the Goliards do not line up neatly to form a coherent model for "medieval Christian masculinity." Nor can Heyward's description of Christian history account for the importance of profane lyrics as the basis for liturgical music in the later medieval era.[119] Furthermore, she goes on to gloss only half of the equation—that of Christian teaching, to the exclusion of "how large numbers of people" have practiced sexual pleasure. In this sense, her perspective is much closer to Mary Daly's separatist vision than the accounts of struggle spelled out by Elisabeth Schüssler Fiorenza and Rosemary Radford Ruether with whom she shares a commitment to a Christian feminist vision. In her work, *Gyn/Ecology*, Daly examines in detail the global victimization of women, and charts a radical feminist alternative.[120] But for Daly, this break must be total. In contrast, Ruether and Schüssler Fiorenza are more concerned to retrieve the struggles of women throughout history, and to look at the past as a record of ambiguity.[121]

I want to stress that Comstock's and Heyward's theological and political proposals are strong enough on their own merits that they do not need

118. Heyward, *Touching Our Strength*, 42. She uses a lowercase "c" for "Christian" as a gesture toward undoing notions of Christian superiority to other religions.

119. Falck and Picker, "Contrafactum."

120. Daly, *Gyn/Ecology*.

121. Ruether, *Women-Church* and *Women and Redemption*, Fiorenza, *In Memory of Her*, and *Discipleship of Equals*.

to misconstrue, distort, or even simplify the past. The point here is not to refute their theological insights, but to develop them. To point to a history of oppression, resistance, and survival would give a richer sense of agency, and clearer visions of what is actually possible, than a monochromatic story of a church hierarchy stifling human creativity for a two-thousand-year period.

Relational theologies pose a largely, but not entirely, satisfactory answer to the dilemma posed by the desire to articulate a coherent historicist worldview. Historicism shows all coherent metaphysics or worldviews to be provisional articulations that can change drastically with paradigm shifts. That is, historicism can take away the ground on which relational theologies articulate the divine and ethical norms. Relational theologians insist that the fluctuating interface of the present and the past is part and parcel of the worldview they articulate, which mitigates the sense that historicism will have as radical an effect as "the Death of God." The performance of music from times past provides one concrete example of how a ground can be re-established in a new way after a deep look at historical differences establish a disconcerting relativity.

Before we turn to the question of how music can help bridge the tensions inherent in relational theology's approach to history, the question remains as to how well David and Jonathan actually model an erotic relation. That is the question for chapter 2.

CHAPTER 2

The Conflict of Interpretations Surrounding David and Jonathan in Biblical Studies

THE PREVIOUS CHAPTER DEMONSTRATED that Comstock offers a clear interpretation of Jonathan and David—either in historical reality or in the imagination of biblical editors—as manifesting an erotic and egalitarian relationship. This relationship, read through Comstock's hermeneutic, proved to be emblematic of relational theology, especially as developed by the lesbian theologian Carter Heyward. The chapter also showed that several elements of the biblical narrative—especially in its treatment of gender, social stratification, and ethnic conflict—counter various entailments that Comstock sees in his understanding of Jonathan and David's relationship. This chapter further complicates Comstock's reading by examining exegeses that resist the understanding of Jonathan and David as an erotic couple and pointing out how the text is ambiguous enough to allow for eroticized and non-eroticized readings. The biblical text is similarly ambiguous regarding the political egalitarianism that relational theologians seek in connection with a broader agenda of sexual liberation. These ambiguities both offer agency to readers, who inevitably and often unconsciously shape the narratives into a more specific form, and generate communal divisions over interpretive conflict.[1] Thus, the undecidability of the texts in question has

---

1. This chapter depends on various insights from reader-response criticism,

both the virtue of encouraging responsible reading practices, and the more problematic possibility of creating deadlock in interpretive communities in which biblical authority plays a formative role.[2] It is this deadlock that mitigates the power of interpretations of Jonathan and David such as Comstock's to establish queer legitimacy in religious communities, and establishes a demand for queer religious people to search for additional ways of relating to the text.

Comstock's interpretation of Jonathan and David is part of a larger theological argument that moves through various biblical narratives to explore a revision of Christianity in queer terms. While he is a careful reader of the biblical text, his approach is not primarily exegetical. His main agenda is not to explicate the biblical text, but to use the text theologically. On its own terms, this procedure is perfectly legitimate. However, Comstock's theological vision is vulnerable to conservative attack because the use of the canonical Bible has its own dynamics in various faith communities; some communities would preclude Comstock's critical approach to the Bible from the outset. For this reason, I will now turn to exegetical disputes to show how the conflict of interpretation emerges among biblical scholars, who have the task of simply explicating the text. The disputes at the exegetical level highlight the improbability of reaching consensus in the even more charged context of ecclesial hermeneutics, especially within mainstream Protestant denominations.[3] While the praxis of biblical reflec-

---

reception theory, and deconstruction, as well as attention to the use of the Bible in religious communities. On reader-response, see Fish, *Is There a Text in This Class?*, Suleiman and Crosman, *The Reader in the Text*, Tompkins, *Reader-Response Criticism*; Flynn and Schweickart, *Gender and Reading*. A general introduction in relation to biblical studies is McKnight, *The Bible and the Reader*.

2. Undecidability is, of course, a central point of deconstruction as laid out by Jacques Derrida. However, many biblical readings that adopt the rhetoric of deconstruction to explore ambiguities are fairly shallow, appropriating the terms, but not the philosophical grounding, of deconstruction. While I am in many ways indebted to Derrida for a comfort with thinking into undecideable issues, I do not want to belabor the connections here. For some examples of readings of biblical texts that would have been better served simply attending to contradictions on literary terms without dragging in deconstructive terminology, see Clines, *What Does Eve Do to Help?*, 106–23 and Brueggeman, *Old Testament Theology*, 235–51. More successful, in my view, is Fewell, "Deconstructive Criticism."

3. See for example, Rogers, "Biblical Interpretation regarding Homosexuality." Mainstream Protestant denominations often have to balance liberal and Evangelical approaches to biblical authority, a tension that maps exactly onto a degree of comfort with historicity. This divide does not, however, map neatly onto the queer affirmative/

tion in other religious bodies is more amenable to multiple interpretations than mainstream Protestant ones, queer people are vulnerable to biblically-based heterosexism in any context where the Bible has authority. Unless otherwise noted, all of the scholars discussed in this chapter are biblical scholars working with an array of modern methods.

To engage with modern biblical scholarship is *a priori* to advance an argument on historicist grounds. Nineteenth-century biblical scholarship both responded to and advanced historicist developments in philosophy.[4] The development of the documentary hypothesis was at root a shift from seeing the Bible as immune to dependence on historical contingencies to situating it squarely within those contingencies. While much contemporary biblical scholarship has either rejected historical analysis in favor of literary or anthropological analysis, these latter perspectives do not return the Bible to the static, pre-critical, fideistic perspective envisioned by modern fundamentalism.[5] Rather, they are voices within a larger discussion made possible by historicist developments. Thus, this chapter's engagement with modern biblical scholarship implicitly continues the line of argument advanced earlier that relational theologies and historicist methods are intrinsically linked. A fault line among these historicist readings by scholars of the biblical text, however, is apparent in disputes over the historicity of love and desire.

Comstock's reading of the text favors an erotic understanding of the phrase "Jonathan loved David." While homoerotic readings of Jonathan and David predate the gay liberation and radical feminist movements of the 1970s, the readings in question have assumed special importance in light of these struggles in both the civil and religious spheres.[6] This context de-

---

heterosexist tension. For example, Scanzoni and Mollenkott's *Is the Homosexual My Neighbor?* offers a defense of GLBT equality using an Evangelical hermeneutic, whereas Gagnon's *The Bible and Homosexual Practice* uses historical critical methods in its assault on the dignity of queer people.

4. Craig, "Biblical Theology and the Rise of Historicism," Rogerson, *Old Testament Criticism in the Nineteenth Century* and Howard, *Religion and the Rise of Historicism*.

5. An early theological criticism of the historical-critical method in favor of a more literary approach is Frei, *The Eclipse of Biblical Narrative*. For an anthropological approach that sees the Bible in the context of an ostensibly historically static Near East, see Patai, *Sex and Family in the Bible and Middle East*. An anthropological approach more sensitive to historical dynamics is Eilberg-Schwartz, *The Savage in Judaism*.

6. Horner cites Schmitt's novel, *David the King* and Patai's *Sex and Family in the Bible* as two pre-Stonewall examples that recognized an erotic dimension to the Jonathan-David relationship. See Horner, *Jonathan Loved David*, 37, 39.

mands attention to at least two factors—the reading strategies queer people and their opponents use in approaching texts in general and the question of to what extent one can analogize between an ancient sex/gender system and a modern one. For some readers, a strong correspondence between ancient and modern understandings of sexuality renders the interpretation of Jonathan and David highly charged in terms of its application to modern sexual ethics. This approach can be found in both pro- and anti-queer interpretations.[7] Other scholars see such a radical change on many fronts between ancient and modern understandings of sexuality, including the conceptualization of "sexuality," that Jonathan and David do not pertain to the debate about homoeroticism in contemporary biblically-oriented religions.[8] Finally, for others, this change in conceptions of sexuality indicates the complete irrelevance of the Bible for contemporary sexual ethics.[9]

J. P. Fokkelman, writing from a desire to explicate the text, expresses impatience with pulling the love of Jonathan and David into contemporary political disputes:

> That ardor merits a better fate than falling prey to exegetic factional strife. The love of Jonathan does not have to be nailed to the mast of a late capitalistic liberation front whose members, after centuries of sinister suppression of homosexuals, wish to designate homosexual love the highest form of humanity. It would be even less sound for celibates, who have devoted their best powers to

---

7. A very qualified example of the "pro" side here would be Helminiak, *What the Bible Really Says about Homosexuality* for Jonathan and David (and Saul and David), 123–27. See also Greenberg, *Wrestling with God and Men*, 99–105 for a less equivocal account. Comprehensive accounts that posit unequivocal biblical condemnation of homosexuality in a manner that applies to modern sexual ethics are Wold, *Out of Order* and Gagnon, *The Bible and Homosexual Practice*.

8. See especially Bird, "The Bible in Christian Ethical Deliberation Concerning Homosexuality." For Bird, the absence of interest in affections, as opposed to acts, makes the Hebrew Bible a problematic guide for contemporary sexual ethics, a problem she situates not in a rejection of biblical wisdom, but in the biblical metaphor of wandering before the Promised Land; see 146–47, n. 6, and 169–70. See also Nissinen, *Homoeroticism in the Biblical World*; Römer and Bonjour, *Homosexualité dans le Proche-Orient et la Bible*; and Himbaza, Schenker, and Edart, *Clarifications sur l'homosexualité dans la Bible*.

9. This seems to me to be the position of Halperin. See *One Hundred Years of Homosexuality*, 75–87 and *How to Do the History of Homosexuality*, 48–80. In the latter, Halperin responds at length to Brooten's *Love Between Women*, focusing solely on her treatment of Greco-Roman constructions of sexuality, ignoring her extensive discussion of Paul altogether.

suppressing their own sexuality, to assure us in suspiciously strong tones that Jonathan and David were most definitely not gay.[10]

Fokkelman's position is helpful in elucidating the distinction between a critical perspective that respects historical differences and the political uses of the text that obliterate a sense of critical distance between the reader and the text. Furthermore, Fokkelman's summary nicely lays out how a political engagement with the text forces readers into taking sides in a dispute, whereas critical distance respectful of historical distance dissipates political partiality into a kind of agnostic detachment.

However, contra Fokkelman, confronting the undecidability as to whether or not Jonathan and David had a sexual relationship is a crucial task on practical, political, and ecclesiastical grounds. While queer people will always be free on a personal level to experience resonances between their experience and the story in 1–2 Samuel, the exegetical problems associated with a queer reading mean that heterosexist forces in church and state will be able to refuse to accept a queer reading as normative for polity and policy. Many churches are presently mired in a stalemate over the affirmation of queer people.[11] For some queer people, the personal costs of living in the context of an ecclesial argument over queer issues are so high that they warrant the renunciation of biblical religions altogether.[12] While for some queer people, such a rejection of biblical religions is a feasible option, for others, biblical traditions maintain a genuine power and authority that warrant continued struggle within them. This context precludes a simple stance of critical distance from the text in the name of objective accuracy. Fokkelman is right, however, to highlight the fact that the question is fundamentally a modern concern which will inevitably, regardless of the position one takes, distort the dynamics of the biblical text, which works with radically different assumptions.

10. Fokkelman, *Narrative Art and Poetry in the Books of Samuel*, 196–97.

11. See Siker, *Homosexuality in the Church*; Hartman, *Congregations in Conflict*; Moon, *God, Sex, and Politics*; Alison, "The Gay Thing," Udis-Kessler, *Queer Inclusion in the United Methodist Church*; Helfand, "Gay Issues May Splinter Churches."

12. For some descriptions of these costs, see Fortunato, "The Last Committee on Sexuality (Ever)"; and Rudy, "Subjectivity and Belief." The question of fidelity to tradition had already been raised as a theological issue by feminist theologians—for gay male perspectives on post-biblical spirituality, see Thompson, *Gay Spirit* and Conner, *Blossom of Bone*. Recent court cases and legislation in favor of same-sex marriage indicate that U.S. churches are probably in their last gasp as far as having influence in the civil debate on ethics of homoeroticism.

Another reason to turn to the interpretive conflict here is that discomfort with ambiguity seems to be a fundamental issue of which homophobia is an expression. Homoeroticism and transgender identities introduce gray areas into an ostensibly clearly demarcated sex/gender system where gender dimorphism and complementarity create clear social boundaries. But gender dimorphism has more to do with a desire for clear categories than with the facts that underlie the designation of a person as female or male.[13] The need for clear sexual categories finds a mirror in reading practices that aim to settle on a single meaning with which to wield authority. A dualistic conception of male and female sexes finds resonance with a dualistic conception of right and wrong.[14] Often feminist and queer readings are caught up in precisely the same dynamic of attempting to seize control of a "right" interpretation of the biblical text in order to wield authority.[15] While this approach is tactically necessary in contexts where biblical authority determines communal reflection, and while it can be effective, it does not unsettle the basic assumption that biblical authority equals prescriptive norms, as opposed to, for example, a focal point for communal deliberation or the anchoring of identity in a specific history. While Comstock provides a way of reading the Bible "otherwise," recognition of the ambiguity of meaning requires that his proposal be read alongside other approaches so as not to fall into a new authoritarian single account. On the other hand, a celebration of ambiguity can also lead to a kind of political atrophy. Indeed, a great aporia postmodern ethics wrestles with is how to sustain ethical norms and political objectives after the dissolution of clear foundations.[16] When caught between two readings, one of which claims certainty and the other of which celebrates ambiguity, queer readers may find that their ability to counteract ecclesial heterosexism is severely hampered.

13. See Fausto-Sterling, *Myths of Gender*, Butler, *Gender Trouble*; Epstein and Straub, *Body Guards*.

14. Fuchs has used this correspondence as a heuristic device to interpret various biblical narratives in "Who is Hiding the Truth?" and "'For I Have the Way of Women.'" However, she pushes the dualistic associations into a harder match than is warranted by the narratives themselves.

15. Koch critiques this approach as a "pissing match" in "Cruising as Methodology," 170–72. See a similar critique by Bal in *Lethal Love*, 1.

16. One might look to the experience of collective bargaining as one model that has been successful in praxis, a model that neither holds to some sure foundation, but also firmly asserts the need for effective political struggle. See also Marshall, *Christians in the Public Square*, 35–72, for further discussion of the tensions between ambiguity and political effectiveness.

For the purposes of this book, it is the precisely the interpretative stalemate that arises in relation to the Jonathan and David narratives which is the primary issue that must be addressed.[17] As recently as 2007, a major academic Christian publisher could release a commentary on 1 Samuel that simply presumes heterosexual norms in its interpretation of Jonathan and David without so much as acknowledging that there has been a lengthy debate on the matter.[18] This intransigence demonstrates that continued efforts by queer and queer-friendly biblical exegetes to advance the discussion of biblical ethics in light of queer liberation movements have not effectively disrupted heterosexist norms of scholarship, which bodes ill for future discussion in ecclesial contexts.

To demonstrate the nature of the interpretive stalemate, I will turn to a series of academic articles that lay out the positions particularly concisely, starting with one homoerotic interpretation, followed by a rebuttal. The Swiss biblical scholars Silvia Schroer and Thomas Staubli made a strong exegetical defense of a homoerotic reading in a 1996 German article, which was translated and included in the *Feminist Companion to the Bible, Second Series*.[19] Schroer and Staubli's argument has three main components. First, they delimit the context of biblical prohibitions against homoerotic behavior to clear away the primary argument against a homoerotic reading of Jonathan and David—namely that because the biblical witness is consistent in its condemnation of homoerotic behaviors, it is unlikely or even impos-

---

17. For my purposes here, I bracket the question of historical facticity. In the 1990s, questions of the extent to which the Bible records history, if at all, were disputed with a great deal more heat than light in the "minimalist-maximalist" debate. For an overview, see Grabbe, *Did Moses Speak Attic?* Some scholars who accept the historicity of David have raised the question of the historical facticity of David and Jonathan's friendship. See Halpern, *David's Secret Demons*, 341–43; on the story of David and Jonathan as "inferred or invented," 283. See also Edelman, "The Authenticity of 2 Sam 1, 26 in the Lament over Saul and Jonathan," for an argument that David's association with Jonathan was introduced to the narratives at a relatively late date. Arguing with a painstaking source-critical method for the historical fact of David's friendship with Jonathan is Kaiser, "David und Jonathan." Kaiser's reconstruction strikes me as unlikely in light of Tov's textual study, "The Composition of 1 Samuel 16–18," which shows the Jonathan and David narratives to be part of a late source.

Another vector which deserves detailed analysis is that of naturalizing vs. denaturalizing readings. Many postmodern critics highlight the artificiality of the text, see especially Miscall, *1 Samuel*. For an insistence that denaturalizing conventions must be part of any queer discourse, see Jackson, Jr. *Strategies of Deviance*.

18. Tsumura, *The First Book of Samuel*, 472.

19. Schroer and Staubli, "Saul, David, und Jonatan."

sible that the biblical editors would have allowed for a homoerotic depiction of a major protagonist. They note that the prohibitions against images do not reflect the reality of ancient Israelite religion, which did include images. The situation to which the prohibition against homoerotic behaviors in Leviticus speaks was most likely analogous, in their view.[20] They go further in positing that the Levitical prohibitions postdate the narratives in Samuel.[21] Second, they provide a reading of the David and Jonathan narratives as depicting homoerotic desire. Finally, they turn to ancient near eastern parallels to anchor their interpretation as being consistent with the actuality of recognized same-sex pairings in the ancient world.

Schroer and Staubli approach the Jonathan and David narratives by looking for parallels in the Song of Songs, the most explicitly erotic text of the Bible, to anchor erotic meanings of various phrases within stories about Jonathan and David. They begin by noting that the wide spectrum of meanings of the term "love" has allowed previous commentators and translators to downplay erotic possibilities of the text by focusing on non-erotic aspects of the word. For Schroer and Staubli, this fact prompts a search for

---

20 Ibid., 15. For some assertions along the line that Schroer and Staubli reject here, see, Zehnder, "Exegetische Beobachtungen," 174–75 and McKenzie, *King David*, 85. Stoebe, in his magisterial commentary on the text, dismisses without explanation reflections on 2 Samuel 1:26 as praise of a homoerotic love as "overburdening" the verse. *Das zweite Buch Samuelis*, 96, presumably with a similar argumentation underlying the dismissal.

21. Schroer and Staubli, "Saul, David, und Jonathan," 20; Wilson, *Our Tribe*, 150; Olyan, "'Surpassing the Love of Women,'" 14–15. This strategy raises thorny questions of the dating of each of the texts.

Furthermore, no scholars writing about David and Jonathan address the ideological, ethical, and theological tensions between the Priestly and Deuteronomic sources in relation to the Deuteronomic redaction of 1 and 2 Samuel. The absolute prohibitions in Lev 18 and 20 are not echoed in Deuteronomy, which only includes a possible prohibition of male cult prostitution (but not a general prohibition of homoeroticism) in 23:17–18. For the Deuteronomic editing of 1–2 Samuel, see especially Veijola, *Die ewige Dynastie*. More general studies of the Deuteronomistic History include Noth, *The Deuteronomistic History*; Cross, *Canaanite Myth and Hebrew Epic*, 273–89; Römer, *The So-Called Deuteronomistic History*. For studies of tensions between Priestly and Deuteronomic approaches, see Knauf, "Die Priesterschrift und die Geschichten der Deuteronomisten;" Brueggemann, *A Social Reading of the Old Testament*, 13–42; Lohfink, *Theology of the Pentateuch*; Ellens, *Women in the Sex Texts of Leviticus and Deuteronomy*. In the prophetic context, the trajectory continues into the different views of Jeremiah in the Deuteronomic trajectory and Ezekiel in the Priestly strand, see Leuchter, *The Polemics of Exile in Jeremiah* 26–45. Bird touches briefly on the significance of the tension between Leviticus and Deuteronomy for thinking through issues of the ethics of homoeroticism in "The Bible in Christian Ethical Deliberation," 162–63, but does not relate it explicitly to 1–2 Samuel.

other terms with which to read the story in homoerotic terms. The first terms they explore widen the narrative's presentation of homoerotic desire to include the relation of Saul and David. In 1 Samuel 16:21–22, the text describes Saul as loving David, and David as "finding favor in Saul's eyes." Schroer and Staubli note that "finding favor in one's eyes," like love, has a range of associated meanings, some of which are clearly erotic. They point to Deuteronomy 24:1 and Esther 5:2 for parallels in which the erotic component is clear.

Markus Zehnder rebutted Schroer and Stabuli's case for a homoerotic reading. Zehnder's argument proceeds on the basis of three broad areas of discussion.[22] He begins with a semantic discussion, challenging key terms that Schroer and Staubli see as designating erotic desire or activity, moves to a discussion of the relationship's narrative context, and finally looks to the canonical framework. The most important point Zehnder makes in terms of vocabulary is that neither of the biblical terms that directly and unambiguously designate sexual activity, שכב (shachav, lie (with))and ידע (yada, know), appear anywhere in the narrative's description of Jonathan and David's interactions.[23] His argument on this point is strengthened by the fact that other words commonly designating sexual activity, such as לקח (lakach,take) or בוא (bo,go (into)) also do not appear.[24] Absent such explicit terms, the case for a homoerotic reading of the narratives rests largely on inference.

Zehnder never pushes his conclusion to an absolute refutation of a homoerotic reading, though it is clear that he does not accept one on exegetical grounds.[25] Rather, his task is simply to show that the reading is extremely improbable. Zehnder approaches all of the textual evidence—semantic, narrative, and canonical—with an unstated hermeneutic assumption that the areas of sexuality, politics, and piety are strictly delimited without interaction. Repeatedly, he draws attention to a political or a theological meaning in order to diminish or even rule out the likelihood of an erotic meaning.[26] Where Zehnder succeeds is in conclusively showing that

22. Zehnder, "Exegetische Beobachtungen."

23. Ibid., 167.

24. *Saul*, however, does "take" David in 1 Sam 18:2.

25. For Zehnder's concession that a homoerotic reading of "love" in the Jonathan and David narratives is a possible one, see "Exegetische Beobachtungen," 156.

26. Alter is similar in this regard: "Repeated, unconvincing attempts have been made to read a homoerotic implication into these words [2 Samuel 1:26]. The reported details of the David story suggest that his various attachments to women are motivated by

a homoerotic reading of Jonathan and David is not a necessary reading: the text admits other possibilities. Furthermore, he demonstrates that some readers will not be convinced by erotic readings of the David and Jonathan stories. All of the terms Schroer and Staubli use to anchor a homoerotic interpretation are open to multiple interpretations and one must align several independent factors to secure a homoerotic reading.

Zehnder's argument aims simply to falsify Schroer and Staubli's understanding of Jonathan and David as homoerotically involved with one another. He does not push his argument into an explicit positive statement about "homosexuality in the Bible," although he hews as closely as he can to the position that ancient Israelite religion was consistently opposed to homoerotic behaviors over the course of its history. Nevertheless, Robert Gagnon has taken Zehnder's arguments as "the definitive refutation of a homophile reading,"[27] and connected the refutation of an erotic reading of David and Jonathan to both an exhaustive treatment of homoeroticism in the Bible and policy implications in the present. He connects a disavowal of the homoerotic interpretation of David and Jonathan to a reading of the entire biblical canon in terms that insist on the absoluteness of the sinfulness of homoerotic activity, *per se*. Gagnon is also loathe to recognize any kind of ambiguity in the biblical record. The rhetoric of certainty he wields is perhaps the most violent thing about his writing.

Gagnon furthermore shares with many exegetes a historicist understanding of "homosexuality." However, for Gagnon, the historical and social malleability of sexuality does not lead to ethical reflection on the power of contingency to open agency and foster diversity. Rather, he sees the historical contingency of sexual identity as "giving hope" for queer people to strive to meet a straight norm. In pursuit of articulating this straight norm, Gagnon takes the biblical prohibition to the limit, designating even thoughts of same-sex eroticism as sinful.

Gagnon's exchanges with two other biblical scholars, Dan O. Via and Walter Wink, demonstrate forcefully the way in which discussion on the topic of homosexuality within church bodies leads to a stalemate.[28] In both instances, the positions between Gagnon and his opponents harden

---

pragmatic rather than emotional concerns—and in one instance, by lust. This disposition, however, tells us little about David's sexual orientation. The bond between men in this warrior culture could easily be stronger than the bond between men and women." *The David Story*, 200–201.

27. Gagnon, *The Bible and Homosexual Practice*, 146.

28. Wink, "To Hell with Gays," Gagnon, "Gays and the Bible," 40–43.

and the discussion devolves into talking past one another, rather than constructive dialogue. In the case of the exchange with Wink, conducted in the *The Christian Century*, the discussion quickly derailed into personal attacks and ad hominem accusations. Wink and Gagnon's perspectives, though both rooted in a Christian commitment to biblical faith, strain so violently against one another that it becomes difficult to see how they share a religion, even broadly defined, insofar as a common commitment to the biblical witness fails to "bind together" the disputants.

Gagnon's dialogue with Via is more temperate, conducted in a jointly published book, *Homosexuality and the Bible: Two Views.*[29] In this case, both writers agree that the Bible is the highest authority for Christians and that the Bible uniformly condemns homosexuality. Where they part ways is in their hermeneutical presuppositions about how to place that condemnation in the overall biblical witness. For Gagnon, the combination of the Bible's authority and the scriptural condemnation of homoerotic behaviors settles the matter. However, Via notes that the presence of larger thematic perspectives that counteract the proscriptions shows that Gagnon is not simply reading out of Scripture but brings his own interpretive presuppositions to the text. Regardless of the specific arguments each author makes, the fact remains that by the end of the discussion, the gap between the perspectives has not narrowed.

These interpretive disputes have a direct bearing on the ability of queer people to participate in biblical religions. It is significant that the debates are among men who identify as straight. Openly queer perspectives are missing from the debates with Gagnon in particular; some queer perspectives, religious as well as secular, would balk at having the terms of the debate defined as the opening of sanctioned, blessed monogamous relations to same-sex couples.[30] Other same-sex couples who seek precisely the blessing of their monogamous relations are then placed in the position of either foregoing solidarity with other queer people who explore other options, or weakening the position from which they claim biblical sanction on the terms debated by Via and Gagnon. For many queer people, biblical religion is no longer tenable in light of the constant questioning

29. Via and Gagnon, *Homosexuality and the Bible.*

30. Heyward explores the nature of sexual friendships as a manifestation of mutual relation in *Touching Our Strength*, 119–55, and explores the meaning of "fidelity" as a virtue outside of monogamous relations in *Our Passion for Justice*, 184–99. See also Rudy, *Sex and the Church*, 67–84.

of the validity of one's identity, leading to trends where secular queers and religious conservatives face off against one another.[31]

In contrast to Gagnon, who is unremittingly hostile to queer people, the queer theorist David Halperin uses a non-erotic reading of David and Jonathan to provide a counter-narrative to universalizing understandings of "homosexuality." He provides a very clear example of how Jonathan and David appear when read through a lens that stresses the historical malleability of sexuality.[32] Halperin uses the Jonathan and David story, in tandem with the Epic of Gilgamesh, to draw attention to a historical break within ancient Greek constructions of sexuality. By connecting the relationship of Achilles and Patroclus with those of Gilgamesh and Enkidu and Jonathan and David, Halperin disconnects the *Iliad* from contemporary narratives of "Greek Love" as an originary source for homosexual identity.[33] Rather, according to Halperin, the *Iliad* presents Achilles and Patroclus in terms consistent with "Near Eastern" portrayals of male friendship in which heroes have "pals," with whom they do not engage in erotic behaviors. This interpretation unsettles an understanding of ancient Greece as an undifferentiated source of homoerotic identity, highlighting that pederasty is read retrogressively into the *Iliad*.[34] At the same time, Halperin reinforces a different historical metanarrative, namely that biblical religions and homoeroticism are fundamentally at odds with one another.[35]

A third line of interpretation is simply to assert that the text is ambiguous, or undecidable. It is this position that strikes me as the most defensible; the interpretive stalemate between homoerotic and heterosexist interpretations itself is evidence of this ambiguity. Authors who pursue this approach include Martti Nissinen and Susan Ackerman. Nissinen makes the most thoroughgoing assertion of the indeterminable nature of the question of Jonathan and David's love for each other.[36] Nissinen is adamant that

31. Bull and Gallagher, *Perfect Enemies*.

32. Halperin, *One Hundred Years of Homosexuality*, 75–87.

33. See also Bravman, *Queer Fictions of the Past*, 47–67, for an analysis and critique of the role of ancient Greece in originary narratives of queer identity.

34. Ironically, Halperin thus narrows an originary narrative to pederasty, rather than unsettling the very idea of an originary source for identity. For a critique of "origins," see Said, *Beginnings*.

35. For a large-scale historical exposition of homosexuality in terms of its fundamental incompatibility with Abrahamic religions, see Crompton, *Homosexuality and Civilization*.

36. Nissinen, "Die Liebe von David und Jonathan also Frage der modernen Exegese" and *Homoeroticism in the Biblical World*.

the question of Jonathan and David's sexuality is anachronistic, informed by contemporary assumptions about the nature of homosexuality, and thus not a question which exegetical approaches can answer. Unlike Fokkelman, and in direct response to Zehnder, however, Nissinen affirms the hermeneutical strategies of contemporary queer readers as they approach the text on modern terms.

A different approach to the ambiguity of *eros* can be found in Susan Ackerman's monograph, *When Heroes Love*, a study of homoeroticism in the Gilgamesh epic and in the friendship of Jonathan and David.[37] Ackerman notes that the question of homoeroticism in both the Gilgamesh epic and the stories of Jonathan and David has led scholars to opposite conclusions. She takes this lack of scholarly consensus as a sign that the stories themselves are ambiguous on the question of homoeroticism. Rather than trying to force the evidence into a clear-cut answer, she probes the ambiguities of eros as meaningful in their own right. She finds in the anthropological concept of "liminality," a state of being in between established conceptual spaces, an explanation for why homoeroticism—an example of the ambiguity of eros in a system that presumes heterosexuality—is tolerated in a context that otherwise offers strong cultural sanctions against it. Exceptions to rules are regularly permitted in such liminal spaces, which in turn are circumscribed so that norms can be upheld in more general contexts.

Ackerman notes that the story of "Saul's Fall and David's Rise" describes a liminal situation in that David both is and is not a king of Israel. As the anointed king by Samuel, he is a king in God's eyes. However, as far as the concrete political rule of the Israelite people is concerned, David is still subject to Saul. Thus, the entire narrative seeks to resolve a liminal situation. The friendship of Jonathan and David occurs entirely within this liminal situation. Thus, ambiguous expressions of eroticism highlight the ambiguous state of affairs, both in terms of narrative movement and political reality. It is significant, then, that the narrative resolution of liminality includes the death of Jonathan. Once the ambiguity as to whether Saul is king or David is king is resolved, the subtly eroticized friendship of Jonathan and David ceases, returning David to an unambiguous heterosexual identity.

---

37. Ackerman, *When Heroes Love* and Nardelli, *Homosexuality and Liminality in the* Gilgameš *and* Samuel.

Why is this text able to spawn such contradictory interpretations? Part of the reason is largely hermeneutical—exegetes do not agree on the basic object they are interrogating when they approach the text with the intent of determining the nature of Jonathan and David's friendship. Schroer and Staubli open their argument with a bald statement of fact: "David and Jonathan shared a homoerotic and, more than likely, a homosexual relationship."[38] Although their interpretation does not dwell on the meaning of the distinction between "homoerotic and homosexual," the distinction is one that gets lost in much of the subsequent discussion. Most usages of the distinction consider homoeroticism to be any kind of same-sex desire or activity, whereas homosexuality refers to a form of desire that is constitutive of an identity, the latter being dependent for explication on modern psychological theories. Indeed, one of the major points on which discussion of the nature of Jonathan and David's relationship founders is on the degree to which readers are able to recognize this distinction.[39] In almost all cases, more liberal interpretations are willing to see a range of possibilities—akin to Adrienne Rich's notion of a "lesbian continuum."[40] In contrast, conservative interpreters regularly resort to a binary understanding of gender and sexual orientation, often going as far as to assert that David's marriages to women are themselves proof of the non-erotic nature of Jonathan and David's relationship, as if bisexuality simply does not exist.

Various specific verses in the narrative allow for a closer examination of the work the "ambiguity of eros" does. The disputed points among interpretations of the nature of Jonathan and David's relationship are the following. Most famously, at the beginning of 2 Samuel, David asserts after Jonathan's death, "Wonderful was your love to me, passing the love of women." It is this statement that in some cases may serve as the catalyst to go back through the narratives in 1 Samuel to seek out confirmation for a homoerotic interpretation. The basic question David's praise of Jonathan's love raises is "was Jonathan a better lover than David's wives, or does David consider friendship superior to romance?" Going back to the narratives in 1 Samuel, a number of other issues create interpretive dilemmas. Jonathan immediately loves David, and his life force or whole self knits with David's

38. Schroer and Staubli, "Saul, David, and Jonathan," 22; "Saul, David und Jonatan," 15.

39. See Heacock, "Wrongly Framed?" for a reading that focuses on the historicity of sexuality.

40. Rich, *Blood, Bread and Poetry*, 23–75.

on their first meeting. Jonathan and David's wife Michal are presented in parallel fashion in chapters 18 and 19. Jonathan's father Saul accuses Jonathan of a "shameful" relation with David. The farewell between David and Jonathan in 1 Samuel 20 has possible erotic overtones. David maintains Jonathan's son Mephibosheth after eliminating the rest of the House of Saul as a sign of his love for Jonathan. To these commonly discussed passages, I would add an exchange between David and the priest Ahimelech in 1 Samuel 21. The topics on which the narrative is particularly ambiguous are the meaning of the term "love," Saul's outburst against Jonathan, the farewell of David and Jonathan, and David's interaction with Ahimelech.

The biblical text is doggedly insistent that Jonathan loved David. This assertion guides the narrative presentation of their relationship from the outset, when Jonathan instantly loves David as himself, to the end, when David declares that Jonathan's love was greater than the "love of women." A fundamental issue of undecidability in the interpretation of Jonathan and David's relationship centers on whether the love that Jonathan expresses for David is a manifestation of political loyalty, erotic attachment, recognition of David's divine election, or some combination of those options. It is clear that the word "love," in ancient Hebrew as well as modern English, has such a range of meanings as to make a "plain reading" of the phrase "Jonathan loved David" impossible. Furthermore, while "love" expresses a range of phenomena in both ancient Hebrew and modern English, the respective ranges designated by the term in Hebrew or English are considerably different.

In a literary study of gender and power in Genesis through Kings, Danna Nolan Fewell and David Gunn draw attention to issues of translation in the standard commentary on 1 Samuel by P. Kyle McCarter.[41] They have to deliberately draw attention to this because of the way McCarter breaks up the text, with much textual and exegetical commentary intervening between his treatment of Jonathan's love for David and Michal's love for David.[42] While the Hebrew simply says that both Jonathan and Michal "loved" David, McCarter makes a distinction between Jonathan "loving" David and Michal "falling in love" with David. McCarter's translation is unquestionably ideological insofar as a presumed and strict distinction between heterosexuality and homosociality takes precedence over an accurate rendering of the original Hebrew. McCarter's translation is a clear instance

41. Fewell and Gunn, *Gender, Power, and Promise*, 149.
42. McCarter, *1 Samuel*, 300–23.

of "gap-filling," a practice every reader engages in, but here overdetermined by compulsory heterosexuality. Fewell and Gunn's critique of McCarter's translation practice deliberately tries to unsettle heterosexist assumptions in the standard biblical commentaries.

In a brief, but influential article, the biblical scholar J. A. Thompson provided one examination of the term "love" in the David and Jonathan stories, which hones in on political understandings of the term in the ancient near east.[43]

Even understandings of love that pertain strictly to interpersonal relations, and do not play into macro-political dynamics, are not constant across history and culture. Ellen van Wolde offers a comparison of the cultural construction of the sentiments of love and anger in Hebrew, English, and Japanese.[44] Whereas Thompson showed political associations of the word love, van Wolde hones on those aspects of the meaning of "love" in ancient Hebrew that relate more strictly to personal relations. She brackets the usage in the Song of Songs, examining the use of the word in narrative texts.[45] Her findings in this delimited field show that the concept "love" in ancient Hebrew narrative is quite different than in modern English. Most prominently, in the narratives, "love" is overwhelmingly unidirectional from a man to a woman. This unidirectional nature of "love" indicates a hierarchical understanding that establishes the loved object as subordinate to the loving subject. Furthermore, in the Genesis narratives, "love" is generally a consequence of sexual activity, not a precondition of it. The Jonathan narratives do not fit easily with van Wolde's explication of inter-personal love—demanding a re-reading of the Jonathan stories and/or an expansion of her analysis.

In the Jonathan story, the juxtaposition that Jonathan loves David followed by his giving his armor to David does not sit easily with the notion of love unilaterally establishing the lover as superior to the beloved. Jonathan's love, however, would, in this case, express well a story in which David rises from a subordinate position to a superordinate position. That is, if read as consistent with van Wolde's analysis of "love," the Jonathan-David

---

43. Thompson, "The Significance of the Verb *Love* in the David-Jonathan Narratives in 1 Samuel," 334–38.

44. Van Wolde, "Sentiments as Culturally Constructed Emotions."

45 Ibid., 19. The decision to exclude the Song of Songs seems more determined by the scope of the argument than a conviction that the usage in narrative and poetic texts have little overlap.

narratives would be a story of Jonathan's unsuccessful attempt to establish himself as superior to David.

Narratives in Genesis reveal a strong tendency for love in the narratives of the Hebrew Bible to trigger behavior that is not in one's self-interest.[46] Jonathan would fall into this understanding of love, as he renounces royal succession out of love for David.

In this discussion of the semantic value of "love," one can see a contrast between understandings of the term that assert a fundamental continuity across vast historical differences, and those that see various understandings of love as a marker precisely of historical difference. The elucidations that posit a fundamental continuity often betray unreflective assumptions, rather than a critical principle at work. Thus, McCarter's distinction between Jonathan "loving" and Michal "falling in love with" reflects a twentieth-century common-sense perspective within a world where heterosexuality has already been invented, which McCarter then treats as a constant across millennia.[47] On the other hand, Thompson and van Wolde point out usages of the word love that challenge precisely modern common-sense understandings of what it means to say, "X loved Y." Schneider's examinations of love as destructive of self-interest highlights an aspect of the semantic range that has not been completely obliterated in modern understandings, but which has moved to a more marginal position in the way the word signifies.[48] On the basis of this distinction between essentialist and historicist understandings of "love," one could distinguish between "gay" and "queer" readings of Jonathan and David. The former reading would treat the two men as a romantic couple, with clear desires for a sexual relationship. The latter reading, espoused especially by Ken Stone, would highlight the queerness of the text more in the historical plurality of understandings of love than in same-sex desires, *per se*.[49]

---

46. Schneider, *Mothers of Promise*, 100. For the interconnections between Genesis and Samuel narratives, see Rosenberg, *King and Kin* and Clements, *Abraham and David*; Ho, "The Stories of the Family Troubles of Judah and David," 514–31.

47. See Katz, *The Invention of Heterosexuality* and Sedgwick, *Epistemology of the Closet*.

48. The title of the movie about the dysfunctional relationship of Ike and Tina Turner, "What's Love Got to Do with It?" brings out the ambiguity of contemporary attitudes to love as destructive to self interest by both showing contemporary understandings of love as detrimental to self-interest while literally questioning the validity of the particular notion of love.

49. Stone, "1 and 2 Samuel," 206.

One line of interpretation uses Saul's outburst in 1 Samuel 20:30, in which he describes Jonathan's relationship to David as shameful both to him and "his mother's nakedness," to show that the text draws attention to the homoerotic nature of Jonathan and David's relationship.[50] At the very least, we have one biblical verse that describes the relationship between David and Jonathan as shameful, and uses explicit references to genitalia to do so, drawing the description of the relationship of David and Jonathan into a field of signifiers that are explicitly sexual. Jean-Fabrice Nardelli, furthermore connects this outburst to Saul's rumination that David is gone because he is unclean. According to Nardelli, David's uncleanness could easily have been construed by Saul as the result of sexual activity; Saul suspects David of having slept with Jonathan and hurls an insult at Jonathan as a result. A point against Nardelli's argument, however, would be that Saul does not see Jonathan as likewise unclean.

But Saul—as portrayed by the biblical text—is a notoriously unreliable witness who is consistently—from his meeting of the women at the well, to his inability to discern God's will in his conflicts with Samuel, to his desperation in contacting a medium—out of touch with reality.[51] With attention to Saul's characterization overall, this outburst could perhaps be read as the definitive textual proof that Jonathan and David were *not* lovers; rather the outburst could underscore Saul's unreliability as a witness. In any case, the distinction between the narrator and the character of Saul opens room for multiple ways of relating the outburst to the overall story. What the biblical text offers in the case of Saul, however, is indisputable evidence that at least one person in the biblical world—historical or imaginary—interpreted Jonathan and David's relationship as potentially sexual.

A possible explicit reference to sexual activity may be present in the story relating the farewell between Jonathan and David. Chapter 20 describes a rendezvous between Jonathan and David in a field, where they have arranged to discuss whether or not David is safe at Saul's court. As part of the strategy, Jonathan arranges for a boy to come along and collect some arrows which Jonathan shoots in a coded manner to communicate whether

---

50 Horner, *Jonathan Loved David*, 31; Schroer and Staubli, "Saul, David und Jonatan," 19.

51. Studies on the tragic character of Saul include Gunn, *The Fate of King Saul* and Exum, *Tragedy and Biblical Narrative: Arrows of the Almighty*, 16–44. For an analysis of Saul's meeting of the women at the well as an "aborted betrothal type scene" that encapsulates Saul's ineptness in a narrative episode, see Alter, *The Art of Biblical Narrative*, 60–61.

David is safe to return to Saul's court. Susan Ackerman beautifully connects the phallic symbolism of arrows in the ancient Near East to the references to bows and arrows over the course of the narrative.

> Jonathan's offering of his bow in 1 Sam 18:4, his shooting of arrows in 1 Sam 20:36, and David's subsequent lauding of Jonathan's prowess as an archer in 2 Sam 1:22 might therefore all be read in terms of homoerotic innuendo: a sexual proposition, followed by coitus, and then a fulfilled lover's words of gratitude.[52]

The message Jonathan provides is that it is not safe for David to return, and what follows is an extended farewell, in which Jonathan and David kiss and weep together. The precise description of what happens when Jonathan and David weep and kiss contains a phrase that has posed translators some difficulty (1 Sam 20:41b).

The King James Version gives: "and they kissed one another, and wept one with another, until David exceeded."

The New Revised Standard Version reads: "and they kissed one another, and wept with one another, until David recovered himself."

The Jewish Publication Society translates the verse as: "They kissed each other and wept together; David wept the longer."

P. Kyle McCarter's translation in the Anchor Bible series expresses absolute bafflement: "Then they kissed each other and wept over each other [. . . ? . . .] [sic]"[53] His textual note, like several other commentaries, registers confusion:

> At the end of the verse MT has 'd dwd hgdyl, "until David magnified (?)" The translation of LXX (heōs synteleias megalēs, probably reflecting 'd hgrl hgdl, thus with two attempts to represent hgdl) suggests that dwd should be deleted (cf. Wellhausen). But no easy translation of what remains emerges. Perhaps the sense is 'd hglyl lbkwt, "unto weeping greatly," elliptically expressed.[54]

Confronted with such an array of translations as "exceeded," "recovered himself," "wept the longer," and "[. . . ? . . .]," one might ask what is so obscure about the verse. The last phrase of 20:41 reads.

צד־דוד הגדיל
'd dwd higdil

---

52. Ackerman, *When Heroes Love*, 184.

53. McCarter, *1 Samuel*, 334.

54. Ibid., 341.

until David caused to become large.[55]

The verb הגדיל (*higdil*) is the causative form of גדל (*gdl*), "to become large" or "to become great." The least complicated meaning of a man "causing to become large" in the context of kissing someone would indicate that he formed an erection.[56] This understanding of the passage would eliminate the need for textual acrobatics McCarter performs on the verse. The verb does not take an object, which may indicate a reticence to speak of sexual matters too directly, as with the still common euphemism of "sleeping with someone" to indicate sexual activity. The sexual activity would be understood, but not described in detail. Because of the causative form and the fact that the verb lacks an object, it is unclear as to whether the phrase indicates that David, Jonathan, or both men got erections, if the object is in fact male genitalia. The King James version's more literal reading than most modern translations, "exceeded," could also suggest ejaculation. In light of David's "becoming large" or "exceeding," Jonathan's closing statement in the chapter, "Yahweh be between your seed and my seed, forever," could then not only have a metonymic meaning—seed as offspring, but a literal meaning—a shared orgasm. The image here suggests a non-penetrative act, in which both partners' seed is in the same place at the end.

The possibility that the scene may describe a non-penetrative erotic act radically changes the interpretive strategies because non-penetrative sex may not have counted as "sex" in ancient Israel.[57] In this case, Jonathan and David would have shared an erotic encounter as an expression of friendship and love, but not necessarily of a latent "gay identity." It would also relieve the interpreter of the conundrum of reconciling an erotic expression of love between men with prohibitions against sex between men in Leviticus—and it would defuse the argument of homophobic interpreters that the "biblical prohibition against homosexuality" would allow for Israel's greatest king to be depicted as a lover of men.

It should be noted, however, that to interpret the passage in such explicitly sexual, even genital, terms is a reading strategy dependent on early twenty-first century liberal mores informed by a post-Sexual Revolution ethos. James Harding, who examines how nineteenth-century discourses

---

55. I would like to thank Dr. Tammi Schneider for help with translating this passage.

56. Nardelli also makes this claim in *Homosexuality and Liminality in the* Gilgameš *and* Samuel, 26–27, n. 36.

57. This is one possible implication of Olyan's argument on Leviticus in "'And With a Male You Shall Not Lie the Lying Down of a Woman.'"

of homosexuality made the question "were David and Jonathan gay?" possible, argues vehemently against it.[58] Theodore Jennings, Jr. provides a consistent example of a reading strategy that aims to make sexual references as explicit as possible, as seen, for example, in his treatment of Elijah's and Elisha's healing of boys in 1 and 2 Kings. What anthropologists of religion might look to as ritualized healing, Jennings interprets as sexual healing.[59] But Jennings does not problematize the relation between a modern "gay-affirmative" social location and an ancient Israelite understanding of sexual honor. The historical determinacy of a sexualized reading does not automatically mean that it is therefore an "incorrect" reading. What is open for dispute is whether the standards of propriety that seem to underlie McCarter's confusion about the passage or the ethos of sexual liberation that underlie a more genital reading come closer to the ethos of the ancient Israelite author of this verse.[60] The fact that the verb does not take an object means this tension is an irresolvable ambiguity.

The verse also insists that it is "the man and his friend," who kiss and weep together. The nature of the action between Jonathan and David depends on whether ancient Israelites at any point conceptualized non-penetrative erotic gestures of friendship as distinct from penetrative sexual activity connected with procreation, possession, or violence. Given the paucity of descriptions of friendships in the Hebrew Bible, which dwells more extensively on kinship, it is impossible to say whether or not non-penetrative sexual behaviors would have been understood as normal expressions of friendship in ancient Israel. In some cultures, this is the case. For example, in contemporary Lesotho, same-sex female erotic practices that Western cultures construe as lesbian are seen as chaste expressions of friendship.[61] This non-Western sexual discourse reveals the possibility of distinguishing various behaviors that modern Western sexual discourses aggregate under the umbrella "sexuality." The ambiguity of eros in the Gilgamesh epic can be reasonably read in light of this distinction. Further-

---

58. Harding, *The Love of David and Jonathan.*

59. Jennings, Jr., *Jacob's Wound*, 99–106. For a non-sexualized commentary, see Sweeney, *I & II Kings*, 214–16.

60. The English novelist A. S. Byatt illustrates the collision of an older, more "decent" sense of academic protocols with a newer libidinous one in her novel *Possession.*

61. Kendall, "Women in Lesotho and the (Western) Construction of Homophobia." In contemporary America, adolescents often do not consider oral sex to be sex. See Lewin, "Are These Parties for Real?" I would like to thank Sarah Gregory for drawing my attention to the "rainbow parties" the article discusses.

more, it is also possible that Jonathan and David are deliberately modeled on Gilgamesh and Enkidu.[62] If one reads the passage with an eye to the distinction between penetrative sex and non-penetrative eroticism, there is likely nothing subversive about the passage; it is simply a manifestation of tenderness and pleasure between friends. If this distinction was not operative in ancient Israel, the implications are far more troubling to both ancient and modern readers. In either case, however, reflecting on the verse carefully reveals the need to approach the text with an eye to historical and cultural differences in the conceptualization of sexual behaviors.

It is telling that the verse insists that *David* "causes to become large." Regardless of what (or whom) he makes large, the verse underscores David's agency. One could even see the movement in the designation of the grammatical subject of the sentence from "the man and his friend" to "David" as a synecdoche for the larger dynamic of 1 and 2 Samuel, in which David emerges out of obscurity, establishes a relation with the House of Saul, and goes on to become the main agent of the narrative, independent of the House of Saul. In this regard, it is noteworthy that many relations David has with the House of Saul have either inescapable sexual ramifications or possible sexual undercurrents. Not only have several readers seen an erotic dimension to David's relation to Saul, but David marries Saul's daughter Michal, and possibly Saul's wife Ahinoam, depending on whether one understands the brief notice of David marrying Ahinoam of Jezreel to be referring to Saul's wife Ahinoam.[63] This pattern would simply make an eroticized reading of Jonathan consistent with the way in which David relentlessly uses sex to take over the House of Saul.

While for many commentators, the awkward phrase "until David made large" is cause for considering the possibility of scribal error or some other form of textual corruption, David Tsumura notes that brachyology, the omission of key words in idiomatic expressions, accounts for the unusual form here. He supplies the missing object in light of a non-sexualized reading: in contrast to a genital focus, Tsumura supplies "voice" as the missing object, thus rendering the phrase, "until David cried louder."[64] Tsumura, then, provides a plausible counter-reading that restores ambiguity to what

---

62. Damrosch notes connections between the Gilgamesh epic and the Ark narrative of 1 Samuel in *The Narrative Covenant*, 186–88. He notes similar paralells between Gilgamesh the David and Jonathan stories, 203.

63. 1 Sam 25:43 and 14:50.

64 Tsumura, *First Book of Samuel*, 64–65 (on brachyology), 523–24 (on 1 Sam 20:41).

might look like the definitive statement that Jonathan and David engaged in sexual relations.

A non-sexual reading of the verse, furthermore, becomes eminently defensible if one does not take the reference to kissing in an erotic sense. Like "love," "kiss" can express a range of affective qualities, from formal greeting to erotic passion. That ancient Israelite writers did conceive of kissing in an erotic sense is clear from its use in the Song of Songs. However, in none of the other references in 1 and 2 Samuel do kisses between men seem to carry the erotic connotations that the kisses in the Song of Songs do.[65] However, Fokkelmann points out that the kiss here is the only mutual kiss in 1 and 2 Samuel, a point that indicates that this kiss has a very different valence than the other kisses in the biblical narrative.[66] Further complicating the issue is the fact the repeated prostrations David performs before Jonathan make it more likely that the kiss should be understood as a formal greeting than a passionate exchange. However, while the prostrations David performs push the reading toward a non-eroticized interpretation, they are more consistent with David's self-description as Jonathan's *servant* than the narrator's description of Jonathan and David as *friends*. While the opposition between "servant" and "friend" may be starker in modern society than it was in ancient society, the tension between the two terms should be seen as indicative of the ambiguity with which interpreters wrestle. In any case, the possibility that the kiss in 1 Sam 20:41 is more a formal gesture than a passionate one returns what might look to modern queer readers as a clear indicator of sexual activity to the ambiguity that leads to interpretive discord.

As stressed earlier, the sexualized/genitalized reading of עד־דוד הגדיל (until David made large) depends a great deal on late-twentieth/early-twenty-first century discursive norms. Regardless of whether a sexualized or non-sexualized reading of the passage corresponds more closely to the ancient Israelite conception of the phrase, a sexualized reading breaks with the dominant interpretation in both Jewish and Christian history. Thus, both the medieval Jewish commentator Rashi and Martin Luther interpreted David's "magnifying," as weeping more than Jonathan, not as becoming sexually aroused.[67] This mode of translating or glossing the verse,

---

65. Zehnder, "Exegetische Beobachtungen," 162–64.

66. Fokkelman, *Narrative Art and Poetry*, 350.

67. I would like to thank Emily Leah Silverman for help with identifying Rashi's position. See commentary on 1 Samuel 20:41 in מקראות גדולות עם ל״ב גדולות פירושים. For Luther, see his translation in *Die gantze Heilige Schrifft Deudsch*.

extending back at least to circa 1000, when Rashi was active, gives weight to Tsumura's contemporary construal of the missing object in the final phrase of 20:41 as "voice." However, by the rabbinic period, one can already see a sexual reconstrual of biblical narratives, in some cases "taming" narratives, in others introducing sexual elements.[68] A heightened anxiety about sexual matters seems to underlie the contradictory impulses to play down and to introduce them in inter-testamental revisions of biblical narratives. Thus, by the time of Rashi and earlier rabbinic commentators, a cultural shift concerning sexual discourse may have already changed the frame of reference enough to distort the sense of the text. However, the dominance of this way of translating the text shows at the very least that 1 Samuel 20:41 was not understood by commentators as referring to explicit sexual activity for a large part of the interpretive tradition, a fact that points to a standard theological refusal to see Jonathan and David as erotically involved partners.

One detail that commentators have overlooked in considering the odds that Jonathan and David had an erotic relation is an exchange between David and the priest Ahimelech immediately following Jonathan and David's farewell in 1 Samuel 20. When David asks the priest for bread, the priest stipulates that the men with whom David is going to share the bread "not have touched a woman." David replies, "Of a truth women have been kept from us as always when I go on an expedition; the vessels of the young men are holy, even when it is a common journey; how much more today will their vessels be holy?" One could read this answer as a kind of strategy on David's part, playing with the specificity of "touching women" to avoid discussion of having just "touched a man" in a manner inconsistent with purity laws.[69] An even more adventurous reading might posit David

---

68. Compare, for example, the telling of Joseph and Potiphar's wife in Genesis and in "Joseph and Aseneth," in Sparks, ed., *The Apocryphal Old Testament*, 465–503. In the inter-testamental retelling, the text emphasizes Joseph's virginity, an emphasis on male sexual purity absent from the biblical text. For discussions of this development, see Prusak, "Woman: Seductive Siren and Source of Sin?" and Biale, *Eros and the Jews*, 37–43. It should be emphasized, however, that early Christian hermeneutics took this asceticizing trend much further than did rabbinic ones; the combination of textual interpretation and asceticism in early Christianity reaches its apogee in Jerome. See Cox-Miller, "'Pleasure of the Text, Text of Pleasure,'" Pagels, *Adam, Eve, and the Serpent*, and Clark, *Reading Renunciation*. For rabbinic culture in relation to early Christian exegesis, see Boyarin, *Carnal Israel*. For the interpretive history of Joseph in particular, including the trajectory discussed here, see Kugel, *In Potiphar's House*.

69. Hearkening back to an earlier discussion of the tension between Leviticus and

as not simply evading the priest's question, but implicitly criticizing the priest's concerns without letting him in on the fact that David does not share the priest's ethics. David's characterization as sly reinforces this understanding. If one reads the scene between Jonathan and David in chapter 20 as an erotic scene, this exchange links the tropes of sexuality and flight in both scenes.

On the other hand, David Clines reads David's statement to Ahimlech straightforwardly as direct evidence of a straight masculinity that David ideally embodies.[70] For Clines, such "separation from women," expresses an emphatic division between homosociality and heterosexuality that activates the distinction between men and women on which masculinity depends. Clines furthermore construes the friendship of David and Jonathan within a model of friendship that is not eroticized.

Given that 1 and 2 Samuel is a representation of events, purported or actual, of three millennia ago, it is clear that even the most rigorous of scholars must do a great deal of piecing fragments together to forge a coherent account of either an eroticized or non-eroticized relationship. The dead have surely taken innumerable subtleties of reference with them to their graves. The ambiguities in the text may, *per* various queer critics, bespeak the quest of homoerotically inclined voices to hide the evidence "in plain sight." Or, they may simply register moods which are so foreign to modern sensibilities as to inevitably be distorted by the reading strategies we bring to them. What is clear, however, is that simply turning to the text and reading it carefully will not deliver us from our own agendas, including the scholarly agenda of shedding agendas in the pursuit of understanding. For a way out of the conflict that makes Jonathan's love a lightning rod for disputing parties, another way must be found. Before exploring an alternate path, however, one more area of tension must be elucidated.

CONTESTED EGALITARIANISM

As noted in chapter one, the theology of mutual relation that Comstock imbues into the David and Jonathan stories does not only legitimate non-normative sexual desires, such as homoeroticism. It also relates to larger political struggles for solidarity across class and racial lines. While

---

Deuteronomy, it strikes me that this exchange is one of the few places in the text of 1–2 Samuel where an engagement with Leviticus would be a useful enterprise.

70. Clines, *Interested Parties*, 225.

mutuality is a more dynamic term than egalitarianism, egalitarian political ideals often intersect with theologies of mutual relation, seen particularly in their dependence on liberation theologies. Analysis of oppression forms a common starting point for liberation theologies and theologies of mutual relation. The question in the context of the exegetical investigations of the David and Jonathan stories this chapter address is, then, to what extent do the stories model an understanding of political liberation and egalitarianism that theologies of mutual relation attempt to reinforce?

In contrast to the question of whether Jonathan and David were sexually attracted to or involved with each other, which is a question opened by moments of textual under-determination in the text (multiple meanings of the word "love" or the omission of a key word that could refer to "voice" or "genitals"), the question of egalitarianism is ambiguous because both Israelite social and political structures generally and the relationship of David and Jonathan specifically explicitly attest to both hierarchical and egalitarian visions. Furthermore, the stories of David and Jonathan take place within a larger story in which the House of Saul falls and the House of David rises. David and Jonathan exchange places within a newly established hierarchical system of monarchy.

The biblical canon attests to both egalitarian and hierarchical tendencies in ancient Israelite and early Christian ideologies. Walter Brueggemann provides a binary heuristic for understanding the bulk of the Hebrew Bible along the lines of the tension between egalitarian and hierarchical tendencies.[71] Beginning with a widely recognized distinction between the Mosaic and Davidic covenants, Bruggemann traces the difference between these two covenants to a trajectory of peasant revolt and imperial power. He notes that both of these covenantal paradigms, and their sociological and ideological backgrounds, are simultaneously manifest at every stage of Israelite history. For Christians, the ministry of Jesus often offers a particularly stark example of an egalitarian ethos.[72] In early Christian history, one can see the reinscription of more hierarchical patterns especially clearly in the Pseudo-Pauline Epistles.[73]

---

71. Bruggemann, *A Social Reading of the Old Testament*, 13–53. Compare also the theological application of a fundamentally similar approach in Ruether, "Religion and Society."

72. For example, Schüssler Fiorenza, *In Memory of Her*, 99–154; Crossan, *Jesus*.

73. McDonald, *The Legend and the Apostle*; Schüssler Fiorenza, *In Memory of Her*, 245–315.

Keeping in mind that these tensions persist through various stages of Israel's history—at least as related by the biblical account—it is also crucial to note how the tension between hierarchical and egalitarian ethical priorities inform the shaping of the narratives. There is general scholarly consensus that the books Joshua through 2 Kings went through some sort of Deuteronomic redaction, seen most unambiguously in the farewell speech of Samuel in 1 Samuel 12, which very precisely restates Deuteronomic ideology.[74] This redaction means that the final form of the text comes filtered through the agenda and ideology of a Deuteronomist. The question then arises, is this Deuteronomic ideology egalitarian or not? On this point, scholars are divided, with some seeing Deuteronomy as forging egalitarian social concepts,[75] others seeing it as creating a legal framework for the subjugation of vulnerable populations.[76] Regardless of the extent to which one can credit Deuteronomy with an egalitarian ethic, however, many scholars see the Deuteronomic framework as at least more egalitarian than the Priestly framework. Comstock, for example, highlights an intensification of hierarchical language in Leviticus over against Exodus as part of his critique of the Levitical proscriptions against homoerotic behavior.[77] Although Exodus is not Deuteronomic, read through Bruggemann's trajectories, Deuteronomy maintains a Mosaic sense of covenant, keeping the two texts in the same overall trajectory. Because the final form of 1–2 Samuel comes with Deuteronomic framing devices that guide the reader, the internal tensions of Deuteronomy are *a priori* an aspect of the overall narrative. The fact that the text as it stands is often in tension with Deuteronomic assumptions simply adds a layer of complexity to the question of how to relate Deuteronomic concerns to 1–2 Samuel, but does not justify a complete abandonment of seeking interrelations.

Martin Buber, on whom relational theologians depend, has provided one extended analysis of hierarchy and equality in the stories leading up to the monarchy.[78] Using the structuralist theory of Levi-Strauss, David Jobling explores in depth how the narrative in 1 Samuel works to resolve contradictions in the underlying assumptions of the ideology of the text.

74. See n 21.

75. Berman, *Created Equal.*

76. Bennett, *Injustice Made Legal.* See also Nakanose, *Josiah's Passover.*

77. Comstock, *Gay Theology Without Apology,* 63–7.

78. Buber, *Kingship of God.*

Because covenant is a basic structure governing both political and religious conceptions in ancient Israel, as well as being a basis upon which Jonathan and David define their relationship, an analysis of covenant is necessary. There are both hierarchical and revolutionary readings of covenant. Moshe Weinfeld argues that a common understanding of covenant as "agreement between parties" is radically mistaken.[79] In contrast, he emphasizes that God and kings *impose* covenants on subordinates, and demand unconditional obedience. In this view, all covenant ideologies depend on a set of assumptions in which stark hierarchies are simply a given.

On the other hand, a line of Marxist-inflected scholarship has related Israel's commitment to covenantal root metaphors as at the heart of a revolutionary impulse that the emergence of the monarchy brakes.[80]

David and Jonathan represent different relations to growing state centralization. Jonathan maintains a charismatic authority typical of the book of Judges. David is the inaugurator of state centralization in ancient Israel. Within these different approaches to larger political configurations, how do they relate to each other?

A striking aspect of Jonathan and David's relationship is that they do not separate personal and political concerns.[81] They understand their friendship to have larger ramifications, as they not only make covenants between each other, but also between their houses. Similarly, Saul understands this connection as well, when he tells Jonathan, in the context of descrying their friendship, that as long as David lives, "neither you nor your kingdom shall be established."[82]

Jerzy Woźniak points to the ambiguity of hierarchical versus egalitarian implications of the covenants between David and Jonathan in his comparison of their three covenants with similar treaty covenants in ancient Near Eastern literature.[83] The shifting nature of the hierarchies within the covenants between David and Jonathan has given rise to a number of general images of the relation between David and Jonathan.

---

79. Weinfeld, "ברית."

80. Mendenhall, *Law and Covenant in Israel and the Ancient Near East*; Brueggemann, *A Social Reading of the Old Testament*, 13–69.

81. George, "Assuming the Body of the Heir Apparent." For a larger context, see Stone, *Sex, Honor, and Power in the Deuteronomistic History*.

82. 1 Sam 20:31.

83. Woźniak, "Drei verschiedene literarische Beschreibungen des Bundes zwischen Jonathan und David."

For example, David Halperin, who interprets the story in light of other ancient narratives such as the Gilgamesh epic and the *Iliad*, presents Jonathan simply as a sidekick of David's. In this instance, David is the hero of the story, and Jonathan a subordinate. The actual social hierarchies of royal son versus shepherd disappear in Halperin's reading in light of larger narrative patterns across the ancient Near East. Another reading by Kurt Noll sees Jonathan as naïvely trusting David's intentions, not seeing the way in which David will usurp Jonathan's role as heir apparent.[84]

Fewell and Gunn, who were among the defenders of an erotic reading of Jonathan and David postulate an extremely non-mutual understanding of the dynamics of their relationship. Situating the narrative with the "Bible's First Story," an epic that extends from Genesis to Kings, that, in their view, consistently presents a hierarchical view of gender relations, they see Jonathan as akin to David's wives. In keeping with their understanding of gender hierarchy, however, this parallel means that Jonathan is severely subordinated to David. They note an asymmetry in the affective terms the narrator uses to describe their relationship. "What emerges from this imbalance is a reading that either has Jonathan's passion unrequited or at least unconsummated or perhaps David playing out a lover's role only so far as it suits him to keep Jonathan's affections strongly alive."[85] In Fewell and Gunn's interpretation, then, the hierarchical nature of the relationship is not simply a question of political rank, but one in which unequal power dynamics are expressed at the most intimate level insofar as David effectively manipulates Jonathan for his own ends.

Susan Ackerman similarly notes how the eroticized treatment of Jonathan and David's relationship functions to put Jonathan in the role of a wife, but focuses less on the characterization of David than on the ideological functions of the relationship. She notes that the explicit account of political dynamics in the biblical presentation of the David and Jonathan relationship imperfectly fulfills the need the narrative expresses to depict David's ascendancy over Jonathan, a need that the eroticized treatment of the relationship expresses more adequately.[86] Indeed, Ackerman here breaks with Fewell and Gunn's characterization of David insofar as she sees the narrative as indicating that Jonathan does not feel mistreated in David's ascent

---

84. Noll, *The Faces of David*, 55 and 93.

85 Fewell and Gunn, *Gender, Power, and Promise*, 150.

86 Ackerman, *When Heroes Love*, 220.

to the throne, "and thus David cannot be accused of malevolently usurping the Israelite crown from Jonathan."[87]

The fact that non-erotic and erotic readings of David and Jonathan's relationship are possible means that the clear prohibitions of Leviticus, the negative construal of homoeroticism as violence in Genesis and Judges, and the association of homoeroticism with idolatry in Romans have only an ambiguous counterweight in the biblical canon. This imbalance requires that strategies be found to strengthen queer connections with the David and Jonathan story. I suggest that musical practices offer one way to do so. The fact that biblical laws and narratives similarly have an ambiguous relation to political ideals of egalitarianism demands that the musical practices under discussion be interrogated for their relation to specific political agendas and structures.

---

87 Ibid., 221.

CHAPTER 3

Queer Musicology and the History of Biblical Interpretation

THE INTERPRETIVE CONFLICT GENERATED by the ambiguities in the Jonathan and David stories means that whatever solace queer religious people may find in the biblical depiction of love between two men will always be vulnerable to attack or compromise once the interpretive context shifts from private personal affirmation to securing social conditions—especially within ecclesial bodies—that will contribute to flourishing of queer persons.[1] Many queer people are as tired of "being debated" as we are of being explicitly attacked, a fatigue expressed in John Fortunato's piece, "The Last Committee on Sexuality (Ever)."[2] The recent introduction of "Third Way" churches in the Baptist tradition continues the ecclesial commitment to "discuss" and "agree to disagree" on the full inclusion of queer members. Because such "discussion" can take a spiritual and psychological toll, queer people who are invested in biblical religions would do well to sidestep the rancor of exegetical strife and anchor our relation to the text in a different way. Experiencing the story through music offers one such approach. A queer musical experience of the Jonathan and David story can strengthen, or even create, a connection between queer identity and biblical faith. The

1. On the inadequacy of private affirmation and the need to move to social analysis, see Christ, *Diving Deep and Surfacing* and Ruether, "Spirit and Matter, Public and Private."

2. Fortunato, "The Last Committee on Sexuality (Ever)." See also Gilson, *Eros Breaking Free*, 1–2.

approaches of public debate in religious communities and private appropriation are not mutually exclusive. The identity formed in such an experience can be a starting point for different dialogues with religious communities or it may simply be a form of creating a "spiritual, but not religious" relation with a particular biblical narrative.

This chapter will advance a double approach to using music to sidestep the problems associated with engaging in the exegetical stalemate around the biblical narrative. Two aspects of musical experience—its sensuality and its historicity—make it an ideal medium with which to explore a queer identification with Jonathan and David in a way that takes the fluctuating and provisional status of the interpreted text into account. Attention to this dual aspect of musical practice broadens the focus of the argument in two ways. First, it shifts attention to a different historical period; second, it shifts attention to a different medium. By opening the frame in this way, the argument brings greater attention to the inevitably contextual nature of interpretive acts. The multiplication of contextual foci means that, from a relational theological perspective, one can achieve a better awareness of the multi-layered aspect of mutual relations. Attention to these layers can foreground the sheer variety of possible relations to the past.[3] Music's sensuality helps us re-embody past patterns of perceiving and knowing, making for a tighter link between relational theology's sensual and historicist angles.

The current debate over Jonathan and David is an episode of the ongoing interpretive activity of readers of the Bible.[4] Whether read through the hermeneutical principles of the allegorical method in patristic or medieval approaches, humanist text-critical approaches in the Renaissance

---

3. See discussion of Heyward's relational understanding of history in chapter 1.

4. For an overview of the issues in the history of biblical interpretation see, Grant, *A Short History of the Interpretation of the Bible*; Parris, *Reception Theory and Biblical Hermeneutics*; Burrows and Rorem, *Biblical Hermeneutics in Historical Perspective*; and Gössmann, "History of Biblical Interpretation by European Women." For an overview of the history of biblical interpretation as part of an argument about the proper role of Scripture in Reformed theology, see Rogers and McKim, *The Authority and Interpretation of the Bible*. Some important accounts of specific historical eras include Dawson, *Allegorical Readers and Cultural Revision in Ancient Alexandria*; Smalley, *The Study of the Bible in the Middle Ages*; Shuger, *The Renaissance Bible*; and Katz, *God's Last Word*. For an overview of how David and Saul, respectively, appear in the history of interpretation, see Frontain and Wojcik, *The David Myth in Western Literature* and Ehrlich, *Saul in Story and Tradition*. See also Ewbank, "The House of David in Renaissance Drama." See also Thompson, *Writing the Wrongs* for another approach to balancing current feminist insights with historical data.

and Reformation, historical-critical methods relating to Enlightenment perspectives, or through a variety of postmodern resisting strategies, the interpretive activity over time contributes to the meaning of the text, and, at some stages, even literally determines the text, as material culture analysts have noted.[5] This ongoing interpretive activity binds any meaning of a biblical text to historicist limitations and means that even the most liberating readings are provisional interpretations subject to new insights in the future. Attention to the historicity of interpretation prevents queer readings from lapsing into a kind of biblicism that obscures the necessary interplay of text and interpreter.[6]

From the perspective of upholding a religious tradition, the cumulative, if generally delimited, interpretive activity over time has the weight of authority and is a theological resource in its own right.[7] From this angle, ongoing interpretive acts provide continuity between the text's origin and its modern contexts. From a historicist perspective, however, the "ongoingness" of a tradition's interpretive activity must be understood as a construction after the event by subsequent readers. From this angle, it is not the continuity, but the ruptures in thought processes that are of primary interest. While theorists since Marx frequently focus on historical ruptures to denaturalize an oppressive structure that appears "naturally given" or "commonsense," both decisions—focusing on continuity or rupture—are precisely decisions, acts, more or less conscious, by someone in the present to interpret the past in a certain way. As the historian Eviatar Zeruvatel notes, this tension between "lumping" and "splitting" the past is intrinsic to all historical inquiry.[8] This dynamic relationship between continuity and rupture means that historical change offers both queer and religious identities flexibility in articulating needs and norms. Liberal theological positions from Schleiermacher forward have explored the productive tension between tradition understood as a continuous connection to the past and historicity as exposing radical changes.[9]

5. On material culture approaches to readers determining the text, Eisenstein, *The Printing Press as an Agent of Change*, 303–450 and Ferrell, *The Bible and the People*.

6. For the interplay from a liberation theological perspective, see Croatto, *Biblical Hermeneutics*.

7. See particularly, Ebeling, *Kirchengeschichte als Geschichte der Auslegung der Heiligen Schrift*.

8. Zerubavel, *Time Maps*.

9. Some explorations include Harvey, *The Historian and the Believer* and Braaten, *History and Hermeneutics*. See also Soelle, *Thinking About God*, 7–21, for an engagement

Attention to various interpretations of biblical texts across history helps pinpoint where contemporary entailments of a given position are contingent on a variety of factors. That is, the mapping of biblical narratives to extra-biblical realities varies in different historical and cultural situations. For example, Jonathan Boyarin provides a detailed analysis of how people in various times and places have used the Exodus narratives in ways that confound contemporary expectations of how the narratives "should" function ideologically.[10] His analysis ranges from the use of Exodus in Saxon historiography to contemporary disputes about Zionism. He notes that in an exchange between Michael Walzer and Edward Said, both writers assume continuity between the ancient Israelite Exodus and modern Zionism. While formal parallels between the two instances are undeniable, Boyarin finds that close attention to the work of the early Zionist Theodor Herzl reveals only one reference to Exodus, and one that specifically denies that nineteenth-century Jews can reproduce the conditions of the Exodus, at that.[11] A formal parallel is no guarantee of a meaningful parallel in any given situation. The parallel must be supplied with meaning by interpreters. A formal parallel that seems obvious given the cultural assumptions of one historical era may not surface given other historical and cultural assumptions.

Thus, different sets of formal parallels may be at work in different periods. In the contemporary debate, Jonathan and David hold a central place in the discussion about the relation of biblical narratives to modern homoerotic identities. However, in the Renaissance, visual artists linked David to homoeroticism with a very different story: the story of David and Goliath.[12] Renaissance artists such as Donatello and Caravaggio depicted David's slaying of Goliath in a manner that highlighted the beauty of David's body. This fact opens room for contemporary art historical disputes about the function of that beauty, disputes that lay bare the variety of ways in which art historians and cultural critics understand both the historical malleability of sexuality and their own relation to history.[13] Within the positions

with the interplay of orthodox, liberal, and liberationist paradigms of theology, each having a different understanding of the relation of history and tradition.

10. Boyarin, "Reading Exodus into History."

11. Ibid., 539.

12 A Google search for "David Jonathan queer" turns up approximately 614,000 hits, in comparison to the search field "David Goliath queer," which yields approximately 8,350 hits. Search performed September 12, 2009.

13. Schneider, "Donatello's Bronze David" and "Donatello and Caravaggio," Frontain,

taken up, one interpretation asserts that Renaissance depictions of David and Goliath construe the artist as Goliath felled by the beauty of the young model, an interpretation strengthened by the fact that Caravaggio's Goliath is a self-portrait. While Raymond-Jean Frontain notes that the twentieth-century artist Paul Cadmus took up this Renaissance trope of using David and Goliath to visually explore the relation of the artist and his model and/or lover, this strand of interpretation in the visual arts has not had a major impact on the discussion of queer relations to narratives about David in the contemporary discussion.[14] The use of a sixteenth-century trope by one twentieth-century artist does not reverse the general trend that since World War II, Jonathan and David, not David and Goliath, has been the primary site of queer identification.

Just as past artists mapped homoeroticism onto a biblical narrative that is to contemporary theologians not an obvious candidate for that mapping, past readers of Jonathan and David's love likewise did not map it neatly onto the categories contemporary readers might expect. Rabbinic commentaries construe the relation between David and Jonathan in terms of the application of *halacha*.[15] The commentaries present Jonathan and his son Mephiboshet as a deep Torah scholars; Mephiboshet is even David's teacher in Torah.[16] One commentator, Baraita de-Yeshua, has a more negative reading of Jonathan, using him to show how actions performed with resentment delay messianic salvation, as Jonathan regrets his kindness to David as opening space for David's designs on Saul.[17] The lengthy farewell between Jonathan and David in 1 Samuel 20 discussed in chapter 2 as an instance of possible homoeroticism is an opportunity for the rabbis to engage in deep ethical reflection—but not on sexual ethics. Rather, the rabbis fault Jonathan with failing to provide David with provisions, a failure

"The Fortune in David's Eyes." Counter-arguments, based on the idea that seeing homoeroticism in early modern depictions of David and Goliath imports a modernist homosexuality into them, can be found in Fulton, "The Boy Stripped by His Elders" and Bersani and Dutoit, *Caravaggio's Secrets*.

14. On Cadmus, see Frontain, "The Fortune in David's Eyes." Incidentally, the cover of a recent anthology of queer musicological writings, Fuller and Whitsell, eds., *Queer Episodes in Music and Modern Identity*, uses a picture by Cadmus on the cover.

15. Ginzberg, *The Legends of the Jews*, vol. 4, 76; vol. 6, 244; vol. 6, 253. For an overview of David in early Jewish commentary, see Pomykala, "Images of David in Early Judaism."

16 Ginzberg, *Legends of the Jews*, vol. 4, 76; vol. 6, 244, n. 108, n. 111.

17 Ibid., vol 6, 244, n. 109.

which leads through a series of events to the debacles of massacre of the priests of Nob, the exclusion of Doeg from the community of the pious, and the deaths of Saul and his sons. The lesson from the grim repercussions of Jonathan's forgetfulness is that "refraining from giving a departing guest the necessary provisions for his journey is accounted to one as a deliberate sin," even in the case of forgetfulness.[18] The two foci of homoeroticism and hospitality do not preclude each other, but in the act of reading, which details receive the weight of attention can make for major differences in how readers make meaning from the text.

One could easily multiply examples of interpretive strategies across the centuries from the Jewish and Christian traditions, as well as from secular sources, a task which would be crucial in a work of historical theology.[19] Because my focus is not on the tradition itself, but on the significance of historical difference within the tradition for contemporary gay theology, it is appropriate to select from the range of interpretations to focus on more a more particular set of differences. The specific examples in the following chapters will be seventeenth- and eighteenth-century musical interpretations from England. To provide some preliminary context for the analyses in subsequent chapters, and to continue the present discussion of the fluctuating nature of the history of biblical interpretation, I will turn to interpretations from the mid-sixteenth and early-eighteenth centuries.

The first example comes from the reformer John Calvin, who was an important source of theological reflection in early modern England. In a series of sermons on the books of Samuel preached in Geneva in 1562 and 1563, Calvin discusses the lament at some length.[20] Perhaps to modern expectations, the most surprising aspect of Calvin's sermon is that he is insistent that the love of David and Jonathan was akin to that between a husband and wife.[21] However, Calvin also asserts that their love was a chaste love.[22] While Calvin construes the love of Jonathan and David as marriage-like,

---

18 Ginzberg, *Legends of the Jews*, vol. 6, 253.

19. For an exemplary example of this line of inquiry, see Harding, *The Love of David and Jonathan*.

20. Calvin. *Sermons on 2 Samuel*, 16–47. For context, see Torrance, *The Hermeneutics of John Calvin* and Puckett, *John Calvin's Exegesis of the Old Testament*.

21. Calvin, *Sermons on 2 Samuel*, 45.

22. On Calvin's discomfort with female sexuality generally, see Bouwsma, *John Calvin*, 52–53; for his celebration of marriage and sexual desire, see 136–37. For medieval antecedents to sexual renunciation within marriage, see Elliott, *Spiritual Marriage*. Primary documents on Genevan attitudes to marriage can be found in Witte and Kingdon, *Sex, Marriage, and Family in John Calvin's Geneva*.

the emphasis on chastity in marriage precludes Calvin, and the community which took him as a moral authority, from using the matrimonial understanding of Jonathan and David as a warrant to affirm homoerotic monogamy, as the Genevan couple Pierre Jobert and Thibaud Lesplingly learned with lethal results in 1562, when they were executed for sodomy. The execution took place in the very year in which Calvin preached on 2 Samuel.[23] The stark juxtaposition of an assertion of homosocial marriage in preaching and sodomy executions makes dramatically clear both how differently early modern people could see the entailment of an interpretation, and the stakes involved.[24]

The central point, however, to which Calvin returns repeatedly in his sermon is the inappropriateness of David's "excessive" expression of grief. For Calvin, David's extravagant lament signals that David's emotions were too locked into attachment to the creaturely, rather than accepting of the order and plan of the creator. Calvin uses this point not only to drive home the ethical demand to honor the creator over the creation, but also to point out that even God's elect are not immune from committing sins in this life. From a contemporary perspective, this insistence on emotional restraint would seem to be fundamentally at odds with the impulse to set this text to music, as Romantic notions of music as a form of self-expression persist in popular culture. However, early modern composers could easily take Calvin's exhortations into account when setting the text of the lament, as a prominent strand of early modern musical thought emphasized music's ability to harmonize the soul with the cosmos rather than its ability to express an autonomous self.[25] Music, in such an understanding, attunes singers precisely to the larger order, giving them the perspective to see one's sorrow in the scheme of things, rather than letting the heart turn in on itself.

The point here is not to show Calvin as a direct source of understanding on the part of early seventeenth-century composers; rather it is to show one significant Reformed interpretation and its different entailments from contemporary ones. Because, in England, Calvin's thought was largely mediated by the perspective of Theodore Beza, a sermon of Calvin can only contextualize seventeenth-century English music as one option in a range

23. Naphy, "Sodomy in Early Modern Geneva," 101–2.

24. This juxtaposition raises questions for Boswell's *Same-Sex Unions in Premodern Europe.*

25. See, for example, Tomlinson, *Music in Renaissance Magic.*

of Reformed positions.[26] That caution must be taken to extrapolate from Calvin to English Calvinism can be seen in the fact that the Geneva Bible, a sixteenth-century English translation heavily glossed with Calvinist inflected commentary, is more relaxed on the matter of what kind of love Jonathan and David shared, considering the love of wives for husbands or mothers for children equally acceptable modes of interpreting the passage, in contrast to Calvin's insistence on one understanding.[27]

Nearly a century and a half after Calvin's preached his sermon in Geneva, the English proto-feminist Mary, Lady Chudleigh's examination of love gives Jonathan and David pride of place. Her writings are removed from Calvin's both in time and by genre. Calvin's sermon is explicitly theological; Chudleigh's essays pertain to secular matters. Chudleigh was one voice in early Enlightenment feminism that reached its apogee in the writings of Mary Wollstonecraft.[28] Her writings then participate in a historical shift toward an analysis of women's oppression that was a precondition for the feminist, and later lesbian/gay, theologies discussed in chapter 1. Where Calvin shows what was conceivable within the Reformed trajectory of Reformation thought that was a strand in the Jacobean setting of the music discussed in chapter 4; Chudleigh shows some changes in gender politics with which George Frederick Handel, the composer discussed in chapter 6, contended.

In 1710, the year Handel arrived in London, Chudleigh published her *Essays upon Several Subjects in Prose and Verse*. Her essay on love builds to an extended poetic paraphrase of David's Lament over Saul and Jonathan, first passing through several examples of friendship in Greek mythology.[29] Her essay thus highlights the importance of Jonathan and David for an understanding of love by using Greek mythology as foil to Jonathan and David understood as historical figures, and by creating contrast between prose and poetry, reversing a perhaps more expected mapping of prose with history and poetry with myth. The way Chudleigh reconfigures Greek and Hebrew literary antecedents, then, provides an example of the way people continually refigure the past for present purposes.

---

26. See Kendall, *Calvin and English Calvinism to 1649* for an account of Calvin's influence in English Protestantism and its mediation through Beza.

27. See the comment on 2 Samuel 1:27 in *The Geneva Bible*.

28. Smith, *Reason's Disciples* and Lerner, *The Creation of Feminist Consciousness*.

29. Chudleigh, *The Poems and Prose of Mary, Lady Chudleigh*, 352–62.

Whereas the most heated dispute in the contemporary discussion around Jonathan and David has to do with genital contact, the interpretive difference between Calvin and Chudleigh revolves around two very different issues. One issue centers on the value of marriage, with Calvin drawing David and Jonathan into discourses of marriage, while Chudleigh divorces them from said discourse and draws them into discourses of friendship. The essay immediately preceding that "On Love," is on friendship, setting a context of friendship, not marriage, for love. Chudleigh's first publication, "The Ladies Defence: Or the Bride-Woman's Counsellor Answer'd" was a ringing indictment of the kind of patriarchal marriage Calvin saw as integral to good social order. It was also an attack on a non-conformist preacher from the perspective of an Anglican.

The other point of conflict arises in relation to how they value emotional expression. While for Calvin, David's wallowing in expression of grief was an example of impiety, Chudleigh praises precisely David's ability to express emotion.[30] "O! In what pathetick Language does he speak his Grief, how elegantly tell his Sorrow!" Where Calvin sees the lament as an example of emotion out of control, Chudleigh ties this "elegant lament" precisely to David's ability to control his emotions in the face of Saul's injustices: "The Injuries he did him never raised his Passion, or made him do an unbecoming Action . . . Full of Concern for both [Saul and Jonathan], full of the tenderest Sentiments that Grief could cause, or Love inspire, he thus express'd his Thoughts, and paid the noblest Tribute to their Fame."[31]

In relation to contemporary interpretations, neither Calvin nor Chudleigh connect the various topics raised by the lament in a way that modern gay theologians would, for neither would be comfortable with the extent to which relational theology insists on God's mutability and immanence. Calvin, like some modern theologians and biblical commentators, sees David and Jonathan as a married couple, but not in the sense that this marriage would be consummated, whereas gay people now would take a conjugal understanding as a warrant for affirming same-sex eroticism. One can differentiate Chudleigh's feminism from that of contemporary feminist theologians insofar as late-seventeenth- and early-eighteenth-century English feminists largely had Tory sympathies, a way of positioning feminism at odds with the socialist views held by Heyward and others.[32] Indeed, the

---

30. For an in-depth analysis of the relationship between eighteenth-century English sensibility and ideologies of gender, see Barker-Benfield, *The Culture of Sensibility*.

31 Chudleigh, *The Poems and Prose of Mary, Lady Chudleigh*, 358–59.

32. On the Tory tendencies of early modern English feminists, see Smith, *Reason's*

polemical situation of "The Ladies' Defense" pits sex against class, insofar as she argues from an established church position against a non-conformist. Furthermore, her attack on women's subordination closes with an argument for the appropriateness of wives' subordination to *reasonable* husbands.

What these examples show is that the past, like the present, is internally differentiated. The internal differentiation of the past means that one can not assume an absolute break between the past and the present, for some aspects of the past may continue to inform present assumptions relatively undisturbed.[33] However, the terms over which people contended in the past may or may not be the same as those which people in the present do. That is, the overlap between past and present interpretive conflicts must be assessed on a case-by-case basis; one can neither assume absolute difference nor unmitigated continuity.

To take the meaning of biblical texts as inherently bound to the historical changes of interpretive activity means that one must face up to the fact that current queer interpretations may in the future give way to interpretive norms that will configure meaning on terms that contemporary queer people may find unrecognizable. Not only the interpretive disputes in the present (discussed in the previous chapter), but the ongoing historical limits of any interpretive move make it difficult to secure an identity-based reading from the Bible. The meaning-making processes readers bring to the biblical text indicate that biblical meaning can never be fixed into a definitive statement. For some, this fact is a cause for anxiety that leads to a more rigorous attempt to fix the meaning. Others see this fact as liberating insofar as the reader is not beholden to an external authority, but can relish in the agency of reading. Either way, close attention to a variety of interpretations and their historical contexts shows the indeterminacy of textual meaning to be a fact which must be reckoned with.

Because queer identities are sexual identities, however, simply eroticizing the meaning of the text will go far toward bringing it to a position that is productive of queer possibilities, rather than a position where queer identities and the hermeneutics supporting those identities are called into question by ecclesial authorities. Eroticizing the text is a way of empowering queer identities, hard-won through social struggle, both secular and

---

Disciples, 3, As Mack summarizes the two competing historical narratives, which make a socialist-feminist narrative difficult to sustain: "It is as automatic for feminists to point to a decline for women in the early modern period as it is for Whig historians to see progress," *Visionary Women*, 412.

33. Contra Skinner, "Meaning and Understanding in the History of Ideas."

religious.[34]A vital link between the biblical text and queer identities in this respect is the fact that the Bible is a record of historical struggle. To the extent that biblical faith is a protest against injustice and oppression, the queer experience of violence and marginalization demands that queer people eroticize the text in our quests for full flourishing in the social sphere because our experience of oppression is precisely a denial of our ability to express our sexuality without social sanction. This struggle is ongoing and meets new challenges as society changes.

The queer identities that seek to eroticize the biblical text must, therefore, maintain connection with subversive histories and radical edges of activism. For example, the legacy of Stonewall must be as much a legacy of people of color, drag queens, etc. as it is of "homosexuals." In the current context, queer identities must engage trans activism as the most potent edge of queer revolution. The demand to keep the radical edge of queer activism will meet up with a severe historical discrepancy in my argument, as the history I engage is early modern English music, as opposed to, for example, House Music, with which African-American gay men established cultural power. The centrality of the narrative of classical music—and my love for it—can only blunt a genuinely queer subjectivity of struggle unless itself thoroughly historicized.

Queer eroticizations of biblical texts can provide queer people a clearer understanding of how our religious and sexual desires interact, and why we may be loathe to compromise on either count. The task of eroticizing the text does not replace the need to engage it in communal deliberation in contexts where queer identities are still under attack on biblical grounds. Rather, it provides a complementary approach, in which queer people can maintain a life-giving relation to biblical texts on our own terms. From a Protestant theological perspective, the eroticization of the text gives queer people a means by which to proclaim faith—with the strongest sense of confidence—in the biblical witness as part of the regenerative work of God.[35]

34. I follow Schüssler Fiorenza here, in shifting the terms from biblical authority to social struggle. "Although I am writing as a Christian theologian, I am neither attempting to persuade women to remain members of biblical religions, nor am I arguing that they should read the Bible, or why. Rather, I seek out a process and method for a feminist political reading that can empower women, who, for whatever reasons, are still affected by the Bible to read "against the grain" of its patriarchal rhetoric." *But She Said*, 7.

35. Phillip Melanchthon's *Loci Communes Theologici* is a rich resource from which to explore connections and tensions between Protestant and queer understandings of faith as trust and confidence grounded in the biblical witness, though queer theologians will of necessity think through what is revealed in the Law differently than Melanchthon and

Although I write out of a commitment to Protestant spirituality, the practice of eroticizing the Bible can shift the context for reflecting on Jonathan and David in such a way that homoeroticism, rather than biblical religion, is the field in which one seeks connections. This recontextualization opens room for inter-religious dialogue, multi-faith hermeneutics, and renegotiations of sacred/secular divisions as homoerotic identities exist across such divides.[36]

A crucial shift from interpretation to identification is at stake in the task of eroticizing the biblical text.[37] The questions are not simply, "what is the indeterminacy of the text, how do the meaning making structures work, how do people in different historical eras make different meanings from the parameters of the biblical text?" The question is also "how can queer people find life, not death in these narratives and this history?" Life will always be subject to flux and historical relativity; this does not mean we do not need provisional resting points to articulate where we are and where we have been before moving on to consider where we might be going.

The internal problems associated with reading Jonathan and David as a model for erotic friendship are far less significant, however, than the problems associated with reading the text as part of a community that includes people who want to exclude the possibility of any affirmation of queer people. If reading Jonathan and David as "gay" allows for a queer subject to identify with the biblical text, the identification secured by this interpretation recognizes its insecurity as it meets up with contradictory interpretations. It is at this point that the consolations of music prove effective. Not in guaranteeing identity, but in pulling a blanket around a wounded body, that can sink into a sonorous embrace and heal. As I will explore, the consolations of music cannot guarantee identity because music is just as subject to multiple interpretations and historicist relativization as is the biblical text. Furthermore, the musical examples I choose invite identification with a particular Eurocentric history that the liberation theologies that motivate my argument challenge.

Music provides one forum in which the eroticization of the text can be made explicit, and shared publicly. The arts have always been a medium

---

other reformers did. See Pauck, *Melanchthon and Bucer*.

36. For multi-faith hermeneutics, see Kwok, *Discovering the Bible in the Non-Biblical World*. Important renegotiations of sacred/secular understandings include Bellah, *Beyond Belief* and Jakobsen and Pellegrini, *Secularisms*.

37. I would like to thank Candace West for helping me see the importance of this point.

in which Christian spirituality connects with the erotic in a way not always sanctioned by official doctrine. Leo Steinberg's *The Sexuality of Christ in Renaissance Art and Modern Oblivion* is one sustained study of this dynamic.[38] In the nineteenth and twentieth centuries, as art often supplanted religion, the exploration of biblical themes for erotic content even becomes an area in which the Bible is effectively secularized, as in Oscar Wilde's and Richard Strauss's explorations of Salome from the Gospel of Mark.[39]

Cross-culturally, people have related music and sexual desire in several ways. The slogan "Sex, Drugs, and Rock and Roll," encapsulates one historical moment when music was an integral part of a cultural movement to "unchain" sexual desire. From the 1980s forward, the popular singer Madonna has continuously explored musical representations of female sexual desire in an often deliberately provocative way.[40] Frequently, attempts to prescribe "appropriate" forms of musicking are part of a more general regulation of sexuality or gender identity. These prescriptions range from the use of gendered and sexual metaphors in arguments about music to rules about musical conduct. For example, early modern female singers had to contend with a cultural understanding that women's public speech indicated sexual availability, an assumption that generated major conflicts around the control of nuns' musicking in seventeenth-century Bologna, where the ecclesiastical control of chastity and nuns' musical-liturgical practices frequently collided.[41]

One salient approach to this juxtaposition or connection of music and sexuality can be found in Susan McClary's investigations of music using the "mapping of patterns through the medium of sound that resemble those of sexuality."[42] For McClary, the history of tonality is a way to chart the history of sexuality, providing one concrete model of how to connect the sensuality of musical experience to the inevitability of social change. McClary notes how tonal and rhythmic musical patterns raise and channel libidinal energy, either delaying or driving toward expected climaxes. She links the tonal conventions of the "common practice era"—in music history approxi-

38. Steinberg, *The Sexuality of Christ in Renaissance Art and Modern Oblivion*.

39. On art as a secular substitute for religion from the nineteenth century onwards, see Dahlhaus, *The Idea of Absolute Music*, 78–102 and Levine, *Highbrow/Lowbrow*. On Salome, see Kramer, "Culture and Musical Hermeneutics."

40. See Schwichtenberg, *The Madonna Connection*.

41. For women's public speech as indicating sexual availability, see Jones, *The Currency of Eros*. On nuns' musicking in Bologna, see Monson, *Disembodied Voices*.

42. McClary, *Feminine Endings*, 8.

mately from 1750 to 1900—with a particularly masculine pattern of sexual tension and release, that in which tension builds up toward a single goal and releases in a climax. She construes the standard history of tonality as a masculine quest to find ways to prolong tension and make climaxes more violent in a quest for transcendence. She also probes music by women and gay composers for alternative modes of experiencing pleasure, ones that do not strive toward transcendence beyond climax but allow for various forms of lingering in the moment.[43] While this strategy of paying attention to gender difference has earned her charges of essentialism,[44] she still provides a valuable service in drawing attention to various ways in which constructions of musical desires can easily correlate with patterns of sexual activities.

Shortly after the publication of McClary's *Feminine Endings,* queer musicologists began to probe a different method of analyzing music's relation to sexuality. In lieu of an introduction, the inaugural anthology of queer musicology, *Queering the Pitch: The New Gay and Lesbian Musicology* opens with a "posy of definitions and impersonations" by the literary critic Wayne Koestenbaum. His first anecdote about a lesbian's desire to study Clara Schumann illustrates the insight, "My musical and sexual passions are not necessarily identical, but I wish to assume no distinction between them."[45] This statement, then, sets the tone for the entire volume, which takes up a range of approaches to the relation of music to queer experience and/or identity. Its first-person voice is significant, for a central methodology of queer musicology, at least as practiced in the 1990s, was to plumb one's own subjectivity in the search for parallels and relations between musical and sexual desires, known intimately in the body, the senses, and personal experience, and thus difficult to distill to abstract ideas known through the distancing procedures of detached observation of others' activities and reports.[46]

---

43. For McClary's examinations of women composers, see *Feminine Endings,* 112–47 and "Different Drummers." For her discussion of gay composers, see *Feminine Endings,* 53–79 and "Constructions of Subjectivity in Schubert's Music."

44. See especially Barkin, "Either/Other," and Taruskin, "Material Gains," 463–65.

45. Koestenbaum, "Queering the Pitch" 2.

46. The confessional approach of early queer musicology has become much less prominent in recent years. Thanks to Nadine Hubbs and Fred Maus for confirming my impressions on this front. For an attempt to unpack "lesbian reading" in a manner that resists some of the unstated assumptions queer musicologists seem to share, see Johnson, *The Feminist Difference,* 157–64. Johnson resists the idea that reading "as a lesbian"

In using this confessional methodology, queer musicology shows the interaction between music and subjectivity. Koestenbaum's *The Queen's Throat: Opera, Homosexuality, and the Mystery of Desire* was one of the first works to explore the interrelation of music and subjectivity.[47] His argument begins with a series of memories, not organized to make a logical argument, but juxtaposed to evoke the quality of remembering disparate experiences, which come together in not entirely willed ways to create a sense of self. The turn to memories, independent of an organizing narrative format, highlights the contingencies to which people are subject, a fact that already shows how attention to music's sensuality opens doors to understanding the historicity of musical and sexual experience. This sense of memory of disparate experiences opens room for exploring ways in which people identify with music in ways that go beyond finding analogies. For Koestenbaum, both "homosexuality" and "opera" are constitutive of his subjectivity, but the connections he seeks are not the sort of homologies between sexual and musical gestures that McClary explores. Rather, he notes connections at a very different level, pointing to discrepancies at the more local level:

> I discovered, long ago, that I had a taste for records. Some time later, I discovered I had a taste for mens's bodies. . . . I knew about taste before I knew about homosexuality. And so when homosexuality arrived in my body, I could understand it as just another taste, albeit a grimy and forbidden one—unlike records, which were clean and wafer-thin. . . . The category of "homosexuality" is only as old as recorded sound. Both inventions arose in the late nineteenth century, and concerned the home. Both are discourses of the home's shattering: *what bodies do when they disobey, what bodies do when they are private.*[48]

Koestenbaum here makes a distinction between his experience of the cleanliness of recordings and the dirtiness of sex; but sees both aspects as constitutive of gay identity, both because his gayness manifests as much in

---

is possible without being caught up in prefabricated media images of what constitutes "lesbianism." Her attempt to "catch herself" in the act of identifying "lesbianally" with literature and film leads her to an impasse between her erotic and her political desires.

47. Koestenbaum, *The Queen's Throat*. Around this time, Mitchell Morris also explored the listening practices of opera queens as productive of meaning, but with a more ethnographic, rather than subjective, voice. See "On Gaily Reading Music," where he lays out a gay reader-response theory for music with opera queens as a prime example, and "Reading as an Opera Queen."

48. Koestenbaum, *Queen's Throat*, 46–47.

fussiness as in sexual activity[49] and because recording and homosexuality are manifestations of late nineteenth-century historical developments. Similar explorations of gay male subjectivity, with a similar affirmation of the contingencies of experience, can be found in Kevin Kopelson's discussion of piano playing and D. A. Miller's investigation of the Broadway musical.[50] In "Love Stories," Fred Maus relates several experiences that connected attentive listening to music to various aspects of sexual and gender identity.[51]

Philip Brett's article, "Piano Four-Hands: Schubert and the Performance of Gay Male Desire" is both an extended meditation on the interrelation of musical performance and sexuality and an intervention into an academic debate on the interpretation of Schubert's biography.[52] The musicologist Maynard Solomon made a case for Schubert's homoerotic desires, to which several scholars responded.[53] Like the relation of Jonathan and David, Schubert's identity became the rope in a game of tug-of-war between those who read Schubert as having homoerotic inclinations and those who did not. This process of deliberating over the proper interpretation of the evidence about Schubert's life spilled over into a musicological listserv, in which the tensions between gay people and straight people were especially explicit. Brett's turn to how gay men experience Schubert's music, rather than engaging in the game of tug-of-war, not only added a missing queer voice to the debate, but allowed him to explore connections between homoeroticism and Schubert's music from his own performances of it to its presence in the film *Carrington*. Brett's article, read in relation to the academic debate preceding it, thus offers a useful model for my larger argument about Jonathan and David. In both cases, detailed attention to musical experience shifts the focus from an area in which queer identities are contested to those in which they can be, at least provisionally, established.

Brett proceeds by first laying out the political context of the Schubert debate, and then going into a detailed, evocative description of his performances of Schubert's Grand Duo, and finally analyzing the film score of

49. Ibid., 58.

50. Kopelson, *Beethoven's Kiss* and Miller, *Place for Us*.

51. Maus, "Love Stories."

52. Brett, "Piano Four-Hands."

53. Solomon, "Franz Schubert and the Peacocks of Benvenuto Cellini." Responses include Steblin, "The Peacock's Tale," Solomon, "Schubert," Muxfeldt, "Political Crimes and Liberty," Gramit, "Constructing a Victorian Schubert," Agawu, "Schubert's Sexuality," McClary, "Music and Sexuality," Webster, "Music, Pathology, Sexuality, Beethoven, Schubert," and Winter, "Whose Schubert?"

Carrington, to show how popular culture shows evidence of associations of Schubert with homoeroticism. He notes the opportunities of physical proximity, with both keyboard players sitting on a single bench, for erotic tension, an opportunity already heralded by Rossini's instructions for one of his piano four-hands pieces from his *Péchés de Vieillesse*, in which Rossini encourages playing "with love" involving the hands and the knees.

For many queer and feminist musicologists, the way in which musical and erotic desires intermingle implies that practices and understandings of musical and erotic experiences that keep the two separate are mainly a result of repression and anxiety.[54] Both the connection of music to eroticism, and anxious attempts to control both, are well-attested to over history. However, it is not at all clear to me that the separation of music and sexuality necessarily has to be a result of anxiety and control. In some cases, definitions of "music" or "sexuality" may align easily, whereas in other instances, what counts as either term may simply not overlap with what is designated by the other term.

Listeners and performers often find that non-queer specific music awakens or constructs queer identities. In her attentiveness to the music of Kate Bush, PJ Harvey, and Tori Amos, Jennifer Rycenga explores ways in which a lesbian listener can imagine sisterhood across a lesbian/straight divide. Based on its marginal status in the operatic canon, its original performance in a girls' school, and imagined dynamics between female characters in Purcell's *Dido and Aeneas*, Judith Peraino identifies with the opera itself, the product of a heterosexual composer, not with a particular character.[55] The converse is also true; straight people can identify with explicitly queer music, as evidenced by the huge cross-over appeal of Melissa Etheridge, whose coming out had no noticeable impact on her sales. Still, queer musicians will often engage in a kind of double-coding to maintain crossover appeal.[56] D. A. Miller notes how a turn to explicit representation of gay themes in the Broadway musical actually dilutes the potential for queer modes of identification with the genre.[57] What this inexact fit between production and reception across gay/straight distinctions means

54. Brett, "Musicality, Essentialism, and the Closet," Maus, "Masculine Discourse in Music Theory," McClary, "Terminal Prestige," Cusick, "Gender, Musicology, and Feminism."

55. Peraino, "I Am An Opera."

56. Maus, "Glamour and Evasion."

57. Miller, *Place for Us*, 124–37.

for the subsequent chapters is that the task is not primarily to prove that any of the composers in question were reading Jonathan and David as an erotic couple—the task is to discern how queer people might identify with the music said composers produced.[58]

Queer reflection on music as analogous to sexual experience, however, shows that the "unassailably queer" aspect of a musical experience is irreducibly subjective. Just as two people who both identify as queer may find very different qualities and persons erotically stimulating, so the eroticization of and identification with music on queer terms follows no set patterns. The fact that Koestenbaum focuses on opera, Kopelson on piano music, and Miller on the Broadway musical highlights the fact that there is not an inexorable route from a given form of music to identification. Rather, these disparate foci show that the paths from music to identification are many. A clear example of how this may work can be found in two queer interpretations of the music of Yes. Jennifer Rycenga postulates that aspects of Yes's music provide a queer alternative to the masculinism of Led Zeppelin, especially as articulated in "The Battle of Evermore."[59] I, on the other hand, note ways in which Yes conforms to a heteronormative masculinity and explore Led Zeppelin's "No Quarter," as a means of queering the terms I find problematic in Yes's "Close to the Edge."[60]

These queer musicological writings show continuity between the theological perspectives explored by Comstock and Heyward and cultural self-understandings outside of the religious sphere. Suzanne Cusick's essay "On a Lesbian Relation with Music," while not explicitly theological, blends seamlessly into these theological arguments.[61] First, her very title signals a common emphasis on relation as key to queer identity. Her treatment of music and women as similar in their capacity to be lovers with her mirrors Comstock's sense of treating both Scripture and people as friends. Most profoundly, because feminist theologians have to a large degree rejected concerns with an afterlife as appropriate for religious concern, Cusick's statement—with its inclusion of conventionally religious terminology—

58. For a detailed study of straight/gay relations in production and reception, see DeAngelis, *Gay Fandom and Crossover Stardom*.

59. Rycenga, "Tales of Change within the Sound."

60. Von der Horst, "Precarious Pleasures." For a thorough analysis of gender in the music of Led Zeppelin, see Fast, *In the Houses of the Holy*.

61. Cusick, "On a Lesbian Relation with Music." See also Epstein's incorporation of Cusick's thought in *Melting the Venusberg*, 130–34. Also helpful is Detels, "Autonomist/Formalist Aesthetics."

that her understanding that music's beauty lies in its capacity to awaken "the transcendent joy of being alive, not dead, and aware of the difference," blends in perfectly with the tenets of feminist theology.[62] And significantly, in light of relational theologians' commitments to transnational justice, Cusick has more recently turned her attention to the use of music as torture in the "Global War on Terror."[63]

Jennifer Rycenga pursues a similar sense of relationality in musical contexts, but with more explicit religious guiding principles, prominently that of the relation of the One and the Many derived from the neo-Platonist philosopher Plotinus.[64] As a lesbian composer, she probes the work of creating mutual relations among composers and performers, a process that breaks down a long-standing hierarchy between composers and performers.[65] In her approach to describing music, like Cusick, she shies away from score-based analysis, preferring to focus on a "tactility" of sound. But in contrast to the relational theologians discussed here, Rycenga values a tension between monism and pluralism that distinguishes her perspective from theirs. She differs from Heyward and Cusick in that she is not willing to reclaim the word "transcendent" as spiritually valuable.

MUSIC AND HISTORICITY

Temporality and embodiment of experience connect both queer musicology and relational theologies to historicist understandings of reality. The performance of music from the past in the present exemplifies questions of historicity and embodiment that are central to the argument of the dissertation. The historical mediation of experience is a fact that pertains to

62 Cusick, "Lesbian Relation," 69. Feminist critiques of the afterlife include Gilman, *His Religion and Hers*, Ruether, *Sexism and God-talk*, 235–58; Carol Christ, "Reverence for Life;" Jantzen, *Becoming Divine*, 128–43.

63 Cusick, "Music as Torture/Music as Weapon."

64. Rycenga, "Lesbian Compositional Process" and "Sisterhood." In contrast, other queer and feminist musicological positions explicitly distance themselves from a religious sensibility, see especially Peraino, *Listening to the Sirens*.

65 Rycenga, "Lesbian Compositional Process," 276–78. This concern with performers as embodied agents is also a crucial aspect of Cusick's lesbian-feminist musicology, see "Gender and the Cultural Work of a Classical Music Performance" and "Feminist Theory, Music Theory, and the Mind/Body Probem." Another feminist critique of the superordinate position of the composer can be found in Citron, *Gender and the Musical Canon*. Citron emphasizes the composer/listener relationship as opposed to the role of the performer in music.

religion, music, and sexuality. In her essay "'Experience,'" Joan Scott notes how what seem like immediate experiences are inherently bound up with social scripts.[66] While many arguments assume that the social and historical mediation of experience undercuts religious claims to experiential authority, affirmation of the historicity of experience is at the heart of liberal theological proposals from Schleiermacher forward. Both musical and religious experience often share a *sense* of immediacy that critical analysis shows to be mediated. Musical meaning-making processes are contingent on historical and cultural factors.[67]

Musical experience cuts through the either/or of "discursive constructions" and "bodily immediacy." In contrast to the widespread notion that music is "the universal language," musical perception is in fact highly mediated by cultural and linguistic factors that vary cross-culturally and over time.[68] One of the most basic building blocks of musical space—the interval—has been construed in very different ways over history. In the middle ages, a shift in the classification of consonant and dissonant intervals occurred, while expressive associations of major and minor thirds changed over the course of the sixteenth to the nineteenth centuries.[69]

Queer musicology offers some specific ways in which such historicist insights function in musical theorizing. Wayne Koestenbaum draws attention to the temporal aspect of musicking in several ways. He notes how one is able to compare Maria Callas's performances over time, and how the passage of time makes for different effects in the performance, the later performances have a darker tone, but a more subdued register, the latter of which he reads as a sign of her imminent departure from operatic performance.[70] Koestenbaum's attention to various performances, and his emotional investment in the entire career of a singer, binds his musical con-

---

66. Scott, "'Experience,'" 22–40.

67. Levy, "Covert and Casual Values in Recent Writing About Music," Subotnik, *Developing Variations*; Stefani, "A Theory of Musical Competence," Hamm, "Privileging the Moment of Reception," Rabinowitz, "Chord and Discourse," Blacking, "The Problem of 'Ethnic' Perceptions in the Semiotics of Music," Robison, "Somebody is Digging My Bones."

68. For a succinct statement of this fact, see Hood, "The Challenge of Bi-Musicality," 55–59.

69. For medieval classifications of dissonance, see Crocker, "Discant, Counterpoint, and Harmony," 7. On the expressive function of thirds, see Bianconi, *Music in the Seventeenth Century*, 55.

70. Koestenbaum, *Queen's Throat*, 146. See also page 32 for attention to the importance of the changeability of the voice.

struction of queer subjectivity to temporal processes rather than to a fixed reference point. This attention to effects of temporality in very localized contexts opens room for more subtle insights about the fundamental reality of change that can be applied to a larger sense of historical change.

Queer musicologists are also clearly rooted in present perspectives, as shown by the use of contemporary literary theory by Koestenbaum, Kopelson, and Miller. While all of these authors deliberately probe their subjective desires and autobiographies, they do not simply assume experience yields direct knowledge of the self. Rather, they understand experience to be linguistically and culturally predetermined. It is not a transhistorical gay subject that emerges from a sense of self that is conceptualized through the insights of Michel Foucault and Roland Barthes, but a specifically postmodern subject. This particularity of this mediation of experience means that questions must be engaged about what analogies between the queer musicological insights they advance and the music from the past they engage work.

Historicist elements in queer musicology warrant "return to the composer," but on relational terms. Attention to experience is a deliberate shift away from a hierarchy in which the composer has pride of place, with the performer and the listener understood as passive vessels. While queer and feminist musicologists aim to dislodge the composer's *centrality* to musicological inquiry, this does not mean that attention to composers can be neglected. Some attempts to refigure engagements with composers in a new paradigm include Thomasin LaMay on the sixteenth-century madrigalist Madalena Casulana and Elizabeth Le Guin on the eighteenth-century composer Luigi Boccherini.[71] While such engagements with composers on new terms is a worthy endeavor, it is the practice of performance that ultimately mediates what a composer did in the ast and what people do in the present.

The development of performance practices informed by historical sources contemporaneous with compositions antedating 1750, as well as the increased attention to the sources themselves, began in the nineteenth century and blossomed into one of the most vibrant aspects of classical music culture in the late twentieth- and early twenty-first centuries.[72] The movement generally goes by the name of Early Music, though some prefer

71. LaMay, "Madalena Casulana;" Le Guin, *Boccherini's Body.*

72. For a general overview of the Early Music movement, without much by way of critical or analytic reflection, see Haskell, *The Early Music Revival.* Informative interviews with Early Music practitioners can be found in Sherman, *Inside Early Music.* See also Kerman et al., "The Early Music Debate," 113–30 and Shelemay, "Toward an Ethnomusicology of the Early Music Movement."

the term "Historically Informed Performance." Not only has this movement infused classical music cultures with new energy, but it has raised a number of intellectual and ethical challenges as well.

One of the prominent intellectual issues Early Music performance raises has to do with the relation between past and present. As noted in the first chapter, one of the major figures to push historicist insights to their logical conclusions is Friedrich Nietzsche. Early music performance provides a concrete example of the interrelation of two aspects of his thought—the necessary perspectivalism of all knowing and the importance of forgetting in the relation of knowledge and action. One glaring example of how Early Music performance reveals "forgetting" in Nietzsche's histori- cal sense can be heard in two very different recordings—by the Ensemble Guillaume de Machaut de Paris and by the Ensemble Project Ars Nova—of the fourteenth-century composer Guillaume de Machaut's "Joie, plaisance" from his *Remede de Fortune*.[73] While any two recordings will offer differ- ences to compare, it takes a bit of effort to hear these two recordings as performances of the same work. After listening to the two recordings side by side, it should be apparent that we have no idea what music sounded like in the fourteenth century; we have "forgotten" the sound. We can make educated approximations, but that is no substitute for a live fourteenth-cen- tury performance, access to which is an impossibility. Nevertheless, we can distinguish both performances as performances of Machaut, and not of an- other composer, say, Guillaume Dufay. The performances mediate knowl- edge *of Machaut*, not music in general. But, the fact that the performances sound nothing alike makes the perspectival aspect to knowing clear. Each performance mediates Machaut through a different set of decisions by the performers, decisions that commit the performers to one manifestation of the music to the exclusion of another. These performances, with their dis- tinct perspectives, can be compared, but not experienced simultaneously. (One could, conceivably, play both recordings at once, but that would not be the experience of synthesizing two historical mediations but of generat- ing a third experience that would be more akin to the music of John Cage than that of Guillaume de Machaut.) In this sense, performance in general and that of Early Music in particular is a particularly fertile area with which to explore the historicity of experience.

---

73. Ensemble Guillaume de Machaut de Paris, *L'art musical et poétique de Guillaume de Machaut*; Ensemble Project Ars Nova, *Remede de Fortune*.

None of the issues raised by the interactions between past and present in Early Music, however, negates the fact the music is still *performed*, with all of the positive implications for queer theorizing that performance carries. Since the publication of Judith Butler's *Gender Trouble*, the notion that gender is performed and that it in important ways precedes sex has been central to queer theorizing. Queer musicologists have seized on the connections between the performativity of gender and the performance of music to strengthen connections between queer identity and music.If the necessity of ignorance is a component of Early Music performance that highlights its connection to Nietzsche's perspectival radical historicism, the performers embodied enacting of past patterns, for example allowing past forms of notation to guide patterns of breathing,[74] connects Early Music performance to the relational understanding of history as explored by Heyward.

Attention to the fact that performers must make choices in their musicking brings out the ethical aspect of performance, which has been confronted with regard to Early Music from a variety angles.[75] In the 1950s, the German Marxist philosopher Theodor Adorno wrote a critique of the early music performance movement in his essay "Bach Defended Against his Devotees."[76] Adorno shares with queer musicologists a commitment to an ethical approach to music. His solutions, however, are radically different. Adorno charged early music performers of ceding their subjectivity to an objectivist ideal, betraying the kind of commitment to historical knowledge that Nietzsche had previously diagnosed as stifling of agency.[77] Adorno, as a Marxist dialectician, demands that performer's subjectivity not slavishly imitate the score, but wrestle a rooted subjectivity from the details of the score. Although Adorno sometimes does reflect on the agency of

74. Pérès, liner notes to Ensemble Organum, *Polyphonie Aquitaine du XII Siecle: Saint Martial de Limoges.*

75. On musicological distrust of ethical reflection, see Morris, "Musical Virtues," 45.

76. Adorno, "Bach Defended Against His Devotees." Some important exegeses of Adorno's ideas about music for context can be found in Subotnik, *Developing Variations*; Zuidervaart, *Adorno's Aesthetic Theory*; and Paddison, *Adorno's Aesthetics of Music*. A major aspect of Adorno's essay is to critique notions of Bach as restoring medieval notions of ontology in the modern age. For a similar "de-theologizing" of Bach in the interests of social analysis, see McClary, "The Blasphemy of Talking Politics During Bach Year."

77. Nietzsche, "Vom Nutzen und Nachteil der Historie für das Leben," 250. A particularly dreary performance of the sort lambasted by Adorno can be heard in the recording of Johann Hermann Schein's 1623 *Israelisbrünnlein* by the Rheinische Kantorei under the direction of Hermann Max.

performers, especially in his contrast of the conductors Arturo Toscanini and Wilhelm Furtwängler, in contrast to queer musicologists foregrounding of performers, Adorno shows his modernist preference for the agency of composers when he turns to orchestrations of Bach by the composers Anton von Webern and Arnold Schoenberg as ideal manifestations of how subjectivity can be wrung from a score.[78]

The performances of early music with which Adorno would have been familiar were deliberately amateurish and mechanical. However, as Early Music performers developed more compelling musical practices, the ideologies underlying the performance practice continued to value objectivism over subjectivism as critically analyzed by Lawrence Dreyfus and Richard Taruskin in the 1980s. Dreyfus notes that the idea of authenticity is the guiding thread of Early Music practice.[79] Dreyfus notes furthermore that a fundamental aspect of Early Music performance, as practiced until the early 1980s, is the repression of envy, which Dreyfus casts as a creatively productive virtue, rather than a vice. Where Early Musicians were experimenting with non-hierarchical models of musicking, Dreyfus saw an abdication of the pursuit of musical excellence, and a kind of *resentment* which Nietzsche similarly viewed as stifling the virtues of a creating self. In this respect, Dreyfus's analysis of early music again brings tensions between Nietzsche's and relational theologians understandings of historicism with their respective entailments to the surface, for the establishment of non-hierarchical relations desired by relational theologians are at odds with the demand for ultimate creativity sought after by Nietzsche and reiterated by Dreyfus.

The contemporary musicologist Richard Taruskin, writing after developments in Early Music performance, continued the ethical critique of Early Music along Adorno's lines, but was able to distinguish between the ideology and the practice of Early Music.[80] He launches a protest against neo-Platonist ideologies that privilege the eternal over against the ephemeral, noting that the ideology of Early Music performance boils down to "people are dirt." This striking phrase highlights the extent to which modern performers subordinate their desires, where Taruskin locates

78. Adorno, "Bach Defended Against His Devotees," 146. For contextualization, see Subotnik, "Toward a Deconstruction of Structural Listening."

79. Lawrence Dreyfus, "Early Music Defended Against Its Devotees."

80. Taruskin, "The Pastness of the Present and the Presence of the Past." A recent collection of Taruskin's writings, *The Danger of Music and Other Anti-Utopian Essays* provides a larger context for his musical and ethical priorities.

actual authenticity, to ideals of some kind of purity associated with the composer's intentions, which are fundamentally unknowable. Over the course of attacking this neo-Platonist undercurrent of Early Music ideology, he decisively makes the point that Early Music performance is in fact modern performance—noting that performances that strive for "historical authenticity" have a distinct tendency to become more uniform in tempo and dynamics and to aim for a 'cleaner' sound, regardless of the era from which the music originated.[81] When an Early Music style of playing makes the same kind of changes to approximate the historical origin of both fourteenth-century Paris and eighteenth-century Leipzig, it is clear that what is happening is not a return to earlier styles of playing, but the imposition of a modern idea of what constitutes authenticity on music of the past. Taruskin has no problem with the actual results of this form of musicking—he takes issue with the degree of self-deception and self-abnegation involved in pretending that one is being "faithful to the past" rather than using the past to further one's own musical desires.

One ethical issue that the performance of early music raises is how, and whether, to perform music that expresses ideals that modern people have come to find repugnant. In 1992, Lawrence Rosenwald, a Jewish English professor active in the early music scene, raised the issue with regard to the performance of medieval music expressing anti-Semitic sentiments.[82] A performance by Ensemble Alcatraz of a thirteenth-century cantiga, "Gran Dereit," in which the performers substituted "heretic" for "Jew" in a tale of a Jew who attempts to deface an icon of the Virgin Mary provided the impetus for his reflections on the matter. His view was that emendation of the text papered over, rather than confronted, the cantiga's anti-Semitism, and felt that the performance pressed him into colluding with it. Such invitation to collusion is present on Ensemble Alcatraz's commericial recording of the cantiga, on which a lengthy instrumental improvisation by a first-rate ensemble hooks the listener into enjoyment of the song before one hears the narration, raising the possibility that attachment on a musical level will

81. Taruskin, "Pastness of the Present," 155. He follows the analysis of Leech-Wilkinson in Taruskin et al., "The Limits of Authenticity," 14. More recent investigations of early music include Butt, *Playing with History* and Haynes, *The End of Early Music*.

82. Rosenwald, "On Prejudice and Early Music." Another musicologist who has made anti-Semitism a central concern in the performance of Early Music is Marissen. *Lutheranism, anti-Judaism, and Bach's St. John Passion*. Marissen also debated the issue with regard to Handel's Messiah: Oestreich, "Hallelujah Indeed."

preclude critical engagement of the text.[83] The journal that published Rosenwald's essay also published a number of responses, which ranged from appreciative to defensive.[84]

In contrast to the arguments that performing music "authentically" will leave modern audiences enthralled to ethically abhorrent perspectives rightly shed long ago, Judith Pickering examines a variety of ways in which Early Music practices may reintroduce limitations on women's musical agency which have largely been shed as a result of the women's movement's impact on musical institutions.[85] A vivid example of a musical practice not resurrected for the sake of historical authenticity is the use of *castrati* in Baroque opera.[86] Here, Early Music performers universally agree that modern ethical sensibilities trump the quest for historical authenticity. However, as Pickering notes, while the discontinuation of castration opened room for female singers to expand their repertory, the rise of professional countertenors to sing roles originally composed for castrati is closing that room again. Thus, questions of power and gender resurface as ethical questions within a collective decision to preempt the ethical dilemma posed by the *castrato's* challenge to historical authenticity.

These aspects of musical historicity show that the inevitable gap between past and present opens room for new uses for past music, including deliberately celebrating music's erotic power in connection with modern cultural, political, and religious struggles to forge queer identity. Thus, music from any era is a potential resource for eroticizing a biblical text. What

83. Ensemble Alcatraz, *Visions and Miracles*. Of course, the behavior of individual listeners will go in many different directions while listening to the recording. There is nothing to say that a listener would not be reading the lyrics of the forthcoming narration during the improvisation. The most sustained argument that proceeds from the suspicion that musical seduction staves off critical engagement of ideologically and ethically problematic texts is Clement's *Opera, or Undoing of Women*.

84. Ensemble Alcatraz et al., "Responses to 'On Prejudice and Early Music,'" and Sanford et al., "More Responses to 'On Prejudice and Early Music.'" The defensiveness reached its extreme in Sanford's response, "It is not enough apparently for an ensemble to be musically excellent and historically informed in its performing practices; now we must put all the texts we perform through a moral and political litmus test and practice revisionist editing to purge them of anything offensive to today's politically correct sensibilities." "More responses," 39.

85. Pickering, "*Mulier in ecclesia taceat.*"

86. Some literature on the question of modern performance of castrato roles includes Miller, "*Farinelli's* Electronic Hermaphrodite and the Contralto Tradition," Cathcart, "*Do di petto,*" and DeMarco, "The Fact of the Castrato and the Myth of the Countertenor." For a novelistic treatment of castrated singers in a modern context, see Amis, *The Alteration*.

eroticizing the text through music will not do, however, is fix the meaning of the text unequivocally in such a way that queer people can turn to the Bible to prove the morality of queer existence. The conjunction of biblical interpretation, music, and social practices of friendship and sexuality in musical settings of Jonathan and David brings into focus how multiple discourses interact to destabilize meaning because each discourse has its own historical dynamics.[87] While all three fields continually interact with one another, making an absolute distinction between them impossible, they are autonomous enough for their relations to shift over time. Furthermore, disciplinary practices governing the study of the Bible, music, and sexuality have their own dynamics, mediating knowledge of the three fields in ways that don't always align easily. With regard to the contemporary debate, this "destabilization of meaning" applies to all approaches to reading the text including both the queer and the heterosexist readings of the Jonathan and David stories discussed in chapter 2.

Because music can constitute queer identity independent of representational aspects, the process of interpreting the text musically can connect a disputed text to an experience that is unassailably queer. These experiences can be relativized by historical analysis, showing where said experiences are contingent on various historical vagaries. All experience is limited and finite, grounded in a particular place and time. But the relativity of experience does not equal the falsity of experience. This inability to falsify an erotic experience is what anchors the homoerotic interpretation without going back to an insistence that the "gay" reading of the text has to correspond to the intention of either the biblical authors or the composer of the text in question. Describing the limits of an experience simply acknowledges its inherent historicity. It is also precisely the limits of experience that allow us to differentiate between experiences, and thus to relate to others, rather than narcissistically seeking the self in the other. The following chapters will engage with some of these other people from the past.

---

87. See, especially, Foucault, *The Archeology of Knowledge.*

CHAPTER 4

Retrieving the Past and Making a Self
Recording Technology and the Mediation of Jonathan and David

How, PRECISELY, CAN MUSIC offer an alternative approach to the David and Jonathan stories than an exegetical approach that gets mired in debate over what happened, or what was imagined to have happened, millennia ago? Contextualized within cotemporary queer musicological insights and modern recording technology, early modern English musical representations of Jonathan and David offer an erotic understanding of their love that allows for queer people to identify with the narratives without being drawn into the stalemate of exegetical arguments. The issue of contextualization is important and in the following chapter, I will recontextualize the music in question by examining the historical setting of their composition, in which the potential eroticism of the musical interpretations would not have been as explicit. In this chapter I examine how contemporary recordings of compositions by Thomas Weelkes (1576–1623) and Thomas Tomkins (1572–1656) that depict the love of David and Jonathan provide opportunities for queer identification. A recording of a hymn on David's Lament by Orlando Gibbons (1583–1625) will raise questions about what kind of relations between the past and the present a musical engagement with David's Lament can offer. These pieces are part of a larger number of seventeenth-century anthems on David's lament over Jonathan, including anthems by Robert Ramsey (died 1644), John Milton, Sr. (1563–1647), William Bearsley, and four anonymous settings.[1] All of the composers who wrote anthems on David's lament over Jonathan also composed anthems on David's lament over Absalom, which have received considerably more scholarly attention than the Jonathan laments. The selection of the anthems by Weelkes and Tomkins and the hymn by Gibbons is based on the fact that they have been recorded by modern performers, allowing for a detailed description of the kind of interaction with sound mediated by technology that is central to contemporary musical experience.[2] The privileging of recorded works thus locates the anthems in a kind of canon largely delimited by the norms of classical music performance and further limited by the economic forces that make certain works more marketable than others.[3]

Following the lead of the queer musicologists discussed in the previous chapter, particularly Wayne Koestenbaum's argument in *The Queen's Throat*,[4] this chapter will focus on my own listening practices as a gay man at the beginning of the twenty-first century. This method best allows me to probe the inherently subjective nature of the experience of sexual and musical desire. There is a strong risk of reifying a public/private dichotomy in this approach, but it remains the approach closest to my own experience. Other, more communal, forms of musicking will open very different possibilities for meaning and resistance than the experience I discuss here. In other instances, worship may even incorporate a musical queering of the story as an integral part of the experience.

The shift in voice also marks the transition noted in the previous chapter from the interpretation of the biblical text to dynamics of identification with it. Furthermore, I will privilege recordings over scores, simply to account for the experience of everyday listening pleasures that give rise to said identifications.[5] This not to say that score reading is unimportant—it is vital for getting at the distinctions between listening for pleasure and study-

1. See Godt, "Prince Henry as Absalom in David's Lamentations," 329–30.

2. See Théberge, *Any Sound You Can Imagine* and Katz, *Capturing Sound*.

3. For canonical issues as delimiting musical meaning, see Bergeron and Bohlman, *Disciplining Music*. That marketability plays a role here is apparent in the fact that Robert Ramsay's anthem "How Are the Mighty Fallen" has been recorded by Magnificat, directed by Philip Cave. The recording, however, is out of print and difficult to find.

4. Koestenbaum, *The Queen's Throat*.

5. See Maus, "Learning from 'Occasional' Writing," for some approaches to non-score-based writing and thinking about music.

ing for knowledge or preparing for performance. But score-based reading mediates perception in a particular way that shifts attention to different aspects of music than the everyday experience of hearing with machines does. This focus on recordings—at the outset at least—also differentiates my experience as a listener from the experiences of performers, who have a very different embodied relationship to the music in question, as well as having different relationships to the score.

My experience of music is primarily a negotiation of a conflict between internalization and critique of the ideals and tenets of absolute music—the notion that music is a non-discursive mediator of pure form, a notion rooted in German Enlightenment and Romantic thought and the dominant paradigm of classical music performance through the twentieth century.[6] Although all of the pieces discussed in this chapter were composed about two centuries before people formulated the idea of absolute music, the discourse of absolute music is pertinent because the performers through whom I first became aware of the tradition of renaissance polyphony, the Tallis Scholars, explicitly recontextualize it according to the norms of absolute music, arguing that said norms do greater justice to the aesthetic integrity of the music than the liturgical contexts for which it was written.[7] Furthermore, both absolute music in general and the performances of the Tallis Scholars were a means by which I self-enforced the closet in adolescence, as I found in both a way of delving into disembodied pleasures, even ecstasy. Seventeenth-century music, in particular Venetian opera, on the other hand, provided musical norms that I could not easily reconcile with the desires for musical/sexual purity I sought elsewhere in music. Thus, the interrelation of absolute music and seventeenth-century music pertains to both historicist insights into the various ways in which musical performance relates past to present and to a personal narrative of erotic self-definition.

I internalized absolute music largely through regular symphony concert attendance in my childhood and youth. When I started to seek connections between radical politics and music, I found in the thought of

6. On absolute music, see Dahlhaus, *The Idea of Absolute Music* and Chua, *Absolute Music and the Construction of Meaning*. For absolute music as the protocol of classical music, see Kingsbury's ethnographic study, *Music, Talent, and Peformance*.

7. Phillips, *What We Really Do*, 216–18 for Phillips' preference for modern concert halls over ecclesiastical venues and 219 for his preference for treating polyphonic masses in the manner of multi-movement symphonic works rather than integrated into a liturgical context.

Theodor Adorno both a thoroughgoing Marxist ethical sensibility and a kind of formalism that to a great degree maintained the ideals of absolute music, which Adorno synthesized into an understanding of the social value of autonomous music as a space from which real social critique was possible.[8] However, later in life I came to experience several dissonances with those ideals and tenets, both in terms of the fading of the cultural capital of absolute music and queer critiques of said music.[9] This internalization of various cultural forces means that my interrogation of my own listening practices is not simply solipsistic indulgence, but an opportunity to examine how the subject is of necessity constituted by cultural forces, and how selves negotiate incompatible cultural narratives.[10] I expect readers to find points of similarity and difference between their experience and mine.[11] The point of attending to personal experience is to stimulate readers to interrogate their own experiences, to bring into clearer focus how they negotiate the conflicting cultural codes that bring subjects into being.[12]

Examining personal experience as a negotiation of cultural codes is inherently a historicist endeavor because it locates the subject not as an autonomous Platonic soul, but as a process bound to the flux of historical change. The fact that I am discussing CDs, and not MP3s, already highlights the ephemeral quality of experience.[13] A CD or LP has a physical status like

8. Adorno, *Introduction to the Sociology of Music*. For a succinct exegesis of Adorno's relation to the formalism inherent in discourses of absolute music, see League, "Radical Formalism and the Working Class." See also Subotnik, *Deconstructive Variations*, 148–76.

9. On the "crisis" of classical music, see Lebrecht, *Who Killed Classical Music* and Horowitz, *Classical Music in America*. For queer critiques of the tenets of absolute music, see especially Cusick, "Gender and the Cultural Work of a Classical Music Performance." For a partial defense and reconstruction of many aspects of absolute music in light of postmodern critiques, see Kramer, *Why Classical Music Still Matters*.

10. McClary similarly notes that she begins with a belief that her own reactions to music are "legitimate," and do not simply reflect her quirks, but are the result of lifelong contact with music and other cultural media, *Feminine Endings*, 21–2. I aim to take McClary's approach another step by treating the reactions as legitimate, but also interrogating them further.

11. That this point needs to be elaborated was brought to my attention by Moore's review of my essay "Precarious Pleasures." "I found it a very difficult essay, because . . . I was unable to identify with the author . . . Hitherto, I guess I had found it important to insist that we had to jettison our putative objectivity, but when that fails to communicate, perhaps we have a problem," "Review of *Progressive Rock Reconsidered*," 296.

12. For the subject as the product of the "conflict of interpellations," see Smith, *Discerning the Subject*.

13. On MP3s, see Sterne, "The MP3 as Cultural Artifact."

a book, which sets one clear contextual constraint. While listeners may in fact listen to a CD or LP in a variety of ways—focusing on a single track, for example—the producers of a CD or LP have put at least some thought into putting musical works into a specific sequence, which is at minimum visually inescapable on the recording's jacket. The rise of iPods and YouTube creates a technological context for musical reception in which deracination from context is intensified. For example, a CD will generally preserve the sense of a multi-movement work as a whole, at least in terms of the default sequence and visual appearance on the jacket. While someone listening to a CD *may* skip tracks, the i-Pod *encourages* hearing single movements out of sequence in a mix of various kinds of music, thus making the kind of structural listening to which someone steeped in absolute music takes for granted unlikely. My lifespan encompasses this technological shift, marking the musical practice—listening to CDs—I most readily envision when I think of "music" as a sign of my own aging process and my historical location as a subject formed largely in the late-twentieth century First World.[14] Even though I now experience much music through YouTube, the fact that I still imagine a CD collection as the primary manifestation of the "imaginary museum of musical works" shows that my experience is one step closer to the cultural norms of absolute music than those of a younger generation. However, the way in which recording technology implicates any subject in historical change also highlights the fact that it opens room for agency in the musical experience.[15] By deracinating music from a fixed context of origin, recording technology creates a wider spectrum of contexts for musical meaning.

Not only technology, but also contemporary thought mediates the experience of hearing music in a queer context. As discussed in the previous chapter, an aspect of current musicology is the eruption of queer and feminist voices in academic writing on music. One aspect of this writing that emerges as particularly pertinent to queer listening strategies is the exploration of polyphonic textures as analogous to bodies in love-making. Susan McClary's description of seventeenth-century trio sonatas, in which

14. For a description of one Third World manifestation of cultural identity formed through modern recording technology, see Manuel, *Cassette Culture*.

15. Benjamin, "The Work of Art in the Age of Mechanical Reproduction," Mowitt, "The Sound of Music in the Era of Its Electronic Reproducibility," Silverman, *The Acoustic Mirror*; and Koestenbaum, *The Queen's Throat*, 46–83. For a more negative view of recording technology as creating an illusion of disembodiement, see McClary, *Feminine Endings*, 136.

"two equal voices rub up against each other, pressing into dissonances that achingly resolve only into yet other knots, reaching satiety only at conclusions," is a particularly vivid example of such a description of polyphonic textures as analogous to erotic desire.[16] McClary not only brings attention to the erotic quality of the Italian trio sonata, but also to the historicity of this understanding of eroticism through recourse to Stephen Greenblatt's investigation of Galenic understandings of desire as they play out in Renaissance dramatic conventions.[17] According to McClary, the rise of common practice tonality can be explained in part by the scientific discovery that female arousal is not necessary for procreation, leading to models of desire more strictly oriented to male patterns of tension and release. Such mappings also occur in other historical contexts, for example, consider the notion of "copula" and its semantic closeness to "copulation" in twelfth-century polyphonic music.[18]

Suzanne Cusick also explores intricate polyphonic textures as a way to explore reciprocity in lesbian desire, a way to refuse the question "who's on top?" in a lesbian relationship.[19] For Cusick, however, the exploration does not consist of seeking out a homology between sonic gestures in music and tactile gestures in love-making.[20] Rather, her explanation of her love for playing Bach's *Canonic Variations on "Vom Himmel hoch"* relates to her desire to reveal hidden, complex relationships to listeners.[21] Her desire to perform in order to reveal complex musical relationships manifests a more general refusal on her part to separate mind and body, a refusal that echoes feminist theological critiques of mind/body divisions.[22]

The anthems "O Jonathan" by Thomas Weelkes and "Then David Mourned" by Thomas Tomkins are a good source to explore the importance

16. McClary, *Feminine Endings*, 37. For a fuller investigation, see Dell'Antiono, "The Sensual Sonata."

17. See Greenblatt, *Shakespearean Negotiations*, 66–93.

18. Holsinger, *Music, Body, and Desire in Medieval Culture.* For a critique of Holsinger's reading of copula, see Peraino', "Review of *Music, Body and Desire,*" 381–82.

19. Cusick, "On a Lesbian Relation with Music," 74–78. It seems to me, though, that gay male culture has moved more decisively toward accepting divisions into "top" and "bottom" roles than was the case twenty years ago. For an early musicological critique of egalitarianism as an erotic norm in lesbian musicking, see Peraino, "'Rip Her to Shreds.'"

20. Cusick, "On a Lesbian Relation," 76.

21. Ibid., 77–78.

22. Cusick, "On a Lesbian Relation," 76. See especially Ruether, *Sexism and God-talk: Toward a Feminist Theology*, 72–92.

of polyphonic textures in feminist and queer theorizing because they are part of a body of works in which polyphonic techniques are prominent. Where I find the most obvious example of how early modern music can elicit a queer relation to the Jonathan narratives is in the compositional choices of Thomas Weelkes in his anthem "O Jonathan."[23] Weelkes' anthem, alone among the settings under consideration, sets precisely the segment of the biblical text that is the *locus classicus* for a queer appropriation of the Jonathan and David stories, 2 Samuel 1:26–27, in which David speaks of Jonathan's love for him.

As with many works in this genre, Weelkes's compositional rhetoric advances through the anthem by changing the musical texture to highlight changes in text. Where I lock in most unambiguously to a queer relation to the anthem is at the words "thy love to me," where the texture creates a kind of rocking motion, as voices pass the words back and forth. My identification with the anthem as fulfilling the kind of desire the Jonathan and David stories spark coalesces around the way Jonathan's love becomes the occasion for an undulating and caressing gentleness, which then blossoms into a cadence (musical resting point) on the word "wonderful," a cadence that stands out in the anthem because it is the only place in the anthem where a cadence marks tonal movement away from the final. Following the cadence, the music moves through a figure in which the voices overlap each other on the words "passing the love of women." Here, various voices enter on a high note, and then drop below another voice and ascend through what another voice is singing. "Passing the love of women" here means that voices, like limbs, intertwine.

Two recordings bring out different ways in which the recontextualization of the anthem in the present may or may not further queer desires. The anthem is available on recordings by The Consort of Musicke, directed by Anthony Rooley, and the Winchester Cathedral Choir, directed by David Hill.[24] While both recordings primarily feature sacred anthems, the former recording also incorporates madrigals, some of which are on themes of erotic desire, while the latter recording only includes sacred works. The way in which the Consort of Musicke recording contextualizes the anthem can encourage an erotic hearing, as it brings madrigals (secular music, often

23. Modern editions refer to this piece as a "sacred madrigal," rather than an anthem. However, nomenclature is a matter of modern categorizing. See diGrazia, "Funerall Teares or Dolefull Songes?" 555, n. 1.

24. Weelkes, *Madrgigals and Anthems* and *Cathedral Music*, excerpted on *The English Orpheus*.

with erotic texts) and anthems (sacred music for performance in cathedral settings) into a common context of a single recording, ideally to be heard as a whole sequence. In contrast, the Winchester Cathedral Choir situates the anthem squarely among Weelkes' sacred output, a decision that does not foreclose the possibility of erotic investment in the piece, but which does make an erotic identification with the anthem less likely. In particular, the inclusion of Weelkes's verse anthem, "If King Manases [sic]," sets a tone of free-floating contrition that is inimical to the kind of opening of sensual receptivity celebrated by Audre Lorde and the relational theologians who follow her definition of the erotic. The text, by the Jesuit poet Robert Southwell, opens with a comparison of King Manasses's restoration after repenting of his sin and the possibility of a lowly worm to earn such grace and moves to an expression of the inability of the poem's subject to mend his will.[25] Throughout the verse anthem, this sense of contrition—with no specification of what the nature of the offense is—persists unabated until an eleventh-hour expression of desire for reconciliation with Jesus Christ at the closing of the anthem. The anthem also provides another way in which early modern English composers mobilize the historical narratives of the Hebrew Bible: Here King Manassas becomes a figure for the individual's repentance. However, the general sense of repentance and the tropes of self-abnegation that fuel the impetus toward repentance create an overall context for "O Jonathan" that does not bring out its erotic potential.

Another contrast between the two recordings is that the Consort of Musicke sings one on a part, in contrast to the larger cathedral choir. The smaller ensemble encourages one to identify with a more intimate setting, a situation that allows for closer awareness of distinct interpersonal relations within a group, rather than the larger setting where the singers' relations to each other are mediated more explicitly through a single figure of the director. It was this contrast between intimacy and lack thereof that I experienced acutely as a violist, finding in chamber music performance an opportunity for exploring intimate relations in chamber music and in orchestral playing sheer alienation. In Heyward's view, "intimacy is the deepest quality of relation."[26] In light of the relational theology that Heyward develops as the basis for rethinking queer identities in biblical religions, then, the Consort of Musicke provides a model of identification with dynamics of a key element of the vision at the heart of queer theology.

25. Cited in liner notes to Weelkes, *Cathedral Music*.
26. Heyward, *The Redemption of God*, 44.

However, the lack of intimacy in the Winchester Cathedral Choir performance does not mean that it does not provide other means of erotic identification. The choir sings the anthem "O Jonathan" with a warmth and suppleness that, if I hear it on its own rather than as part of the whole sequence of anthems presented by the recording, actually provides a much greater opportunity for erotic identification than does the Consort of Musicke's recording. Furthermore, the slower tempo of the former recording allows me to linger in the moment; in comparison, the Consort of Musicke rushes me through the experience.

The second anthem under consideration is Thomas Tomkins' "Then David mourned with this lamentation." Tomkins' textual choices seem initially far less promising for a queer identification than do Weelkes'. Where Weelkes hones in on precisely the elements of the lament that give rise to speculation about homoeroticism in the Jonathan and David stories, Tomkins' text is a laconic statement that David mourned over Saul and Jonathan. Simply comparing the choices Weelkes and Tomkins make in regard to text selection would indicate that it is more likely for "O Jonathan" than "Then David mourned" to provide an opportunity for a homoerotic identification with the music and the narrative behind it. However, musical procedures are not identical to textual procedures, and recordings show very different ways of making the music speak of erotic desire, or not.

Where the Consort of Musicke and the Winchester Cathedral Choir show interpretive choices that intensify or downplay a visibly potential homoeroticism in Weelkes' text selection, the recordings of Tomkins' anthem show more radically that eroticism in music can be a matter of performance, *rather than* a matter of composition. Two recordings of Tomkins' anthem that confirm the suspicion that "Then David mourned" de-eroticizes David's lament are by the Choir of St. George's Cathedral and Tallis Scholars.[27] The fact that the Choir of St. George's Cathedral uses children who have difficulty maintaining intonation creates a simple aesthetic block to full engagement with the anthem. In the instance of the Tallis Scholars, however, such technical problems are not at issue. Rather, the entire musical event—my listening to a recording of the Tallis Scholars performing an anthem by Thomas Tomkins—is fraught with layers of meaning before I even put the CD in the CD player, as the Tallis Scholars were a prominent means by which I attempted to escape sexual desire before coming out. Their performances epitomize a "clean" sound—a sound they developed in

27. Tomkins, *Cathedral Music by Thomas Tomkins* and *The Great Service.*

relationship to the emerging dominance of CDs that occurred in tandem with their early recordings. According to the director, Peter Phillips, "our music does seem to have been associated right from the beginning with the clarity the CD can produce, which is very fortunate for us. Fortunately, our sound, and the actual method of the music, were suited to this ultra-clear sound of the CD, and we got to be associated with it."[28] This clean sound modeled a desire for beauty unencumbered by the messiness of the physical world, which in turn reinforced desires to flee sexual desire into a pure realm of disembodied perfection.[29] The degree to which I fused Tallis Scholars recordings and sexual repression in late adolescence continues to leave me somewhat conflicted in my continued love of their musicking, years after I came out.

The Tallis Scholars' recording of Tomkins' anthem is consistent with their general clear vocal production and emphasis on the audibility of individual melodic lines. While the result is certainly beautiful, it is a performance that initially failed to have much of an impact on me, in comparison to their performances of other works. This sense of "being left cold" on an initial hearing shows how this performance decidedly did not provide an opportunity for identification, erotic or otherwise, with the dynamics of the text. Furthermore, the Tallis Scholars' long-term phrasing of the anthem is a steady retreat from an imbalanced and overpowering entrance by the upper voices, which echo the lower voices' initial statement of "Then David mourned."[30] David's activity is the focus, downplaying the relations with Saul and Jonathan that occasioned the activity.

I had considered settled, on the basis of the recordings that I had heard and Tomkins's textual choices in his anthem, that "Then David mourned" must be heard, from a queer perspective, as a musical example of the suppression of homoeroticism in the Jonathan and David stories. Then, simply out of a sense of intellectual responsibility to hear multiple recordings of the anthem, I made a point to listen to the Oxford Camerata's recording.[31] My experience was one of astonishment, both at how the performance gen-

28. Quoted in Brown, "The Tallis Scholars, Gimell, and Peter Phillips," 94.

29. In this respect, my experience is rather different from that of Koestenbaum, who experienced the desire for the cleanliness of records as a model for desire in general. He interpreted later desires for grimy bodies as a contrasting manifestation of desire in general, not as a contradiction. *The Queen's Throat*, 46.

30. This sense of imbalance created at the entrance of the upper voices is uncharacteristic of Tallis Scholars' performances.

31. Tomkins, *Choral and Organ Music*.

erated a radically different sense of the overall sense of the anthem, and at the depth to which that sense was an erotic one. Of all the recordings under consideration, the Oxford Camerata's performance of Tomkins' "Then David Mourned" is the most enthralling performance in terms of releasing the erotic potential of a musical composition in a way that encourages desire for Jonathan as central to the music's meaning. The ensemble achieves this effect by drawing the phrasing throughout the anthem toward the rhythmic change on the word "Jonathan," such that the name Jonathan becomes the occasion for sonic patterns that suggest a series of waves breaking. Here, the release of tension is diffused through reiterations of Jonathan's name, each reiteration prolonging a fusion of desire and release. By phrasing through the entire text, to bring the overall motion to focus on "Jonathan," the performance stresses David's relation to Jonathan over against David's relation to Saul. Neither the Tallis Scholars nor the Choir of St. George's Chapel come anywhere close to performing the music with this sense of smooth phrasing right into the word "Jonathan," nor do they allow the change in rhythm to function as the culmination of built-up tension. In these performances, in contrast to the Oxford Camerata's, Saul and Jonathan are presented as parallel figures, rather than Saul being simply the occasion to heighten the significance of Jonathan. The mere existence of the Oxford Camerata's performance, however, establishes in fact an eroticized interpretation of David's desire for Jonathan, which queer people can turn to as incontrovertible evidence that the biblical text opens spaces for homoerotic desires. Unlike an exegetical argument, which can be refuted by further research, the presence of non-eroticized performances does not falsify the existence of an eroticized one.

A final setting of David's lament over Jonathan is Orlando Gibbons' "Thy Beauty Israel," from *Hymns and Songs of the Church*, first published in 1623, and recorded by Tonus Peregrinus in 2006.[32] Tonus Peregrinus forecloses more opportunities for queer identification with David's lament than it opens. The most salient aspect of this foreclosing is the fact that when the text turns from David's description of Saul to David's description of Jonathan, male voices give way to female voices, a decision by performers given the format of Gibbons' score. This performance decision means that at the point in the text that I hone in on as the point of identification, the performers introduce a gender difference that shifts from the sonic enjoy-

---

32. Wither, *The Hymnes and Songs of the Church*. Gibbons, *Hymns and Songs of the Church*.

ment of male voices to the mediation of Jonathan's love for David through women's voices. Thus, my erotic desire for male bodies as manifested and imagined through male voices is deflected at the precise moment I expect its fulfillment. On the other hand, this performance decision could also be celebrated as breaking down narrow understandings of gay identity, pushing toward a more fluid sense of gender identity, or toward gay/straight solidarity. I also catch a glimpse of erotic potential in Tonus Peregrinus's performance in the way the stress on the words "beauty" and "pleasure" makes them stand out as important and connected despite the fact that they are separated in time.

Cuts in the text also foreclose possibilities for homoerotic identification, though this is not something that would be apparent to a casual listener. "Thy Beauty Israel" is a strophic song in which the text consists of five sections, each having two stanzas. Tonus Pereginus performs only the first stanza of the first section and the entire fourth section, cutting the majority of the text entirely. The fifth section, however, contains the crucial verses that describe the love of Jonathan for David and specifies that it was in every way that this love surpassed the love of women.[33]

Like the Geneva Bible commentary mentioned in chapter 3, Withers' text emphasizes multiple possibilities for the comparison of Jonathan's love to womens' love. Withers' text is even more inclusive—emphasizing "every way," not simply the obvious choices of mothers or wives. Here is a case where a homoerotic subtext *may* have been present in the seventeenth century, given the dedication of *Hymns and Songs of the Church* to King James, whose attachment to royal favorites was a matter of open record.[34] Whether or not a seventeenth-century singer or listener would have made the connection, though, for a twenty-first century listener, "every" comparison of a man's love to a woman's love certainly includes sexual expressions of love, and may even be the dominant comparison.

The Tallis Scholars pursue, from the performer's standpoint, a secularization of polyphonic religious music. The performance practice of the Tallis Scholars deliberately moves Renaisssance polyphony from a liturgical setting to a concert setting, which in turn provides a stronger sense of continuity between their live performances and their recordings. The director, Peter Philips explicitly acknowledges that it is not the sound of

33. Wither, *The Hymnes and Songs of the Church*, 7.

34. See Bergeron, *King James and Letters of Homoerotic Desire* and Young, *King James and the History of Homosexuality.*

sixteenth-century choirs he attempts to recreate, but the achievements of the Berlin Philharmonic, particularly as it pertains to a kind of blended sound and attainment of a standard of beauty.[35] His attempt to match the beauty of the Berlin Philharmonic in his approach to Renaissance polyphony furthermore is one aspect of his agenda of performing the music according to the protocols of absolute music, rather than in the liturgical contexts for which the music was written.[36]

In contrast to the Tallis Scholars, Tonus Peregrinus maintains some continuity with liturgical traditions and function. For example, rather than treating Gibbons' "work" as an inviolable text, Tonus Peregrinus freely rearranges the order to make it reflect contemporary needs. This rearranging, however, relates to a sense of continuity with the overall tradition, rather than a radical or subversive recontextualization. The 1623 publication of *Hymns and Songs of the Church* was a series of lyrics by George Wither, adapting songs from the Bible, with music by Gibbons, possibly conceived as a competitor for the popular Sternhold and Hopkins Psalter.[37] Wither arranged his paraphrases in the order that they occur in the canonical Bible. To follow this ordering would make the *Hymns and Songs of the Church* a commentary on the sweep of the biblical narrative, an approach that could highlight the roots of historicist theology in the biblical narration of Israelite history. Tonus Peregrinus, however, rearranges the hymns according to affect. Rather than connecting the performance to historicism, it connects more easily to desire.

The form of Gibbons' composition demands a different kind of interplay between composer and performer than do the anthems by Weelkes and Tomkins, as the inner voices are deliberately left to the performer's realization. In the recording in question, the performers explore a variety of ways of approaching these realizations, "from unadorned melody via pastiche to exuberantly postmodern counterpoint."[38] The group extends this freedom to include the introduction of a musical "Amen" sung at various points throughout the recording—an "Amen" that connects the performance to modern, personal experience rather than historically-norms

---

35. On Phillip's view of the "undesirability" of the sound of sixteenth-century music, see Phillips, "Performance Practice in 16th-Century English Choral Music," 195. On the Berlin Philharmonic as an aesthetic ideal, see Sherman, *Inside Early Music*, 123.

36. Phillips, *What We Really Do*.

37. Harley, *Orlando Gibbons and the Gibbons Family of Musicians*, 153.

38. Pitts, liner notes to Gibbons, *Hymns and Songs*.

as it is an "Amen" that was sung before meals in the director's family.[39] By sharing this information publicly, the performer invites the listener to share in the director's personal history, divorcing the music from the kind of pure formal sound that absolute music strives for. The recording also intersperses some original compositions throughout Gibbons' hymns. This free approach to including modern compositions and counterpoint in the context of Gibbons' work is more in the spirit of ongoing tradition than historical objectivity. A connection through the broad tradition of Anglican liturgical music allows the ensemble to "modernize" in a way that stresses a sense of continuity, even if the sonic results are often jarring to expectations of seventeenth-century compositions.

The Tallis Scholars and Tonus Peregrinus, then, mobilize very different manifestations of the sacred in their performances, allowing one to probe different theological possibilities. The director of the Tallis Scholars explicitly severs the connection between the polyphonic music he directs and the Christian theology it expresses: "Although I find many of the details of the Christian story ridiculous, and the mystification of them in Spanish Catholicism sinister, the compositions of [Tomas Luis de] Victoria come over as supremely powerful, because he believed passionately in the texts he chose and was able to turn that belief into passionate music. But it is the music which communicates to me, not necessarily the words."[40] The sacrality that the Tallis Scholars—unintentionally, perhaps, but with stunning success—substitute for a liturgical expression of Christian theology is a neo-Platonic aura of the sort critiqued by Walter Benjamin.

Where the Tallis Scholars offer an escape from embodiment, Tonus Peregrinus sanctifies the domestic sphere, connecting the performance to the comforts and nurture of family. From a Queer perspective, however, both options are fraught with danger, as desires for Platonic purity negate the affirmation of bodily pleasures and the discourse of family has been one of the prime tools with which heterosexism has been enforced.[41] Nevertheless, forging alternative understandings of family has been a task of queer struggle as much as the struggle to hold non-familial bonds in esteem.

The performances of the Consort of Musicke, the Oxford Camerata, and Tonus Peregrinus of early seventeenth-century compositions about

39. Pitts, liner notes to Gibbons, *Hymns and Songs.*

40. Philips, *What We Really Do,* 219.

41. Ruether, *Christianity and the Making of the Modern Family.* For a queer revisioning of family see Weston, *Families We Choose.*

Jonathan and David are clearly specific interpretations of early modern music that cannot have the final word on what these texts mean. Nevertheless, some of these interpretations offer viscerally inescapable queerings of the love of Jonathan and David. Weelkes' intertwined voices on "passing the love of women," especially as sung by the Consort of Musicke, and the Oxford Camerata's lush release of tension on the word "Jonathan" both pull my experience of this text into an undeniably erotic realm These moments of identification with specific musical performances have a brute facticity that shifts the interpretive problem for the text from "did Jonathan and David sleep together?" to "what do specific musical experiences of Jonathan and David's relationship do for contemporary queer subjects?" These performances and the extent to which they invite queer identification simply are an integral part of the interpretive history of the biblical text. By drawing a distinction between the visceral and the unmediated, it is possible to position the erotic identification with these musical moments as historically relative, but undeniably real. It is this reality of queer identification with Jonathan and David through music that cannot be contested in the reception of these biblical stories.

CHAPTER 5

Weelkes's "O Jonathan" in Early Modern England

THE PREVIOUS CHAPTER DEALT with how the musical mediation of David's lament over Jonathan through recording technology can deepen queer engagement with the lament. Attending to the experience of identifying with David's lament through an intensified sensuality allowed us to explore the erotic side of relational theology. However, Heyward's relational theology is not simply an erotic theology, it is a historicist theology. To do justice to the range of Heyward's thought, it is important to attend to the music's context of origin.

In this chapter I recontextualize "O Jonathan," by Thomas Weelkes in its historical context, with special attention to factors that would make the hearing of the anthem different. By focusing on *heard* differences, I maintain the privileging of embodiment crucial to writing sexual theology and not just theology about sexuality. However, by attending to heard *differences* I will explore a range of possible meaning-making aspects of Weelkes's piece, not all of which will reinforce an erotic understanding of Jonathan and David. In addition to the heard differences, I will also address some cultural, political, and religious differences that will further shift our understanding of the possibilities and constraints in thinking through what Weelkes's piece may have done in its historical context.

The primary historical difference between contemporary and early modern views is the universality of sodomy prohibition in the medieval and early modern world. Whatever cultural affirmations of homoeroticism existed in early modern England, this proscription foreclosed an explicit theological affirmation of same-sex desire. The anthems under discussion were all written during the reign of King James I & VI, who has become an object study in how a subject might negotiate a proscription of sodomy and homoerotic desires. In *Basilikon Doron*, James forbids the tolerance of sodomy. However, James's homoerotic desires were an open secret—secretive enough to make firm historical pronouncements difficult, but open enough for there to be general consensus that James preferred erotic activity with men. Indeed, the difficulty in thinking through early modern homoeroticism rests on such slippages between what people said and what people did.

One institution that exposes this discrepancy between what people said about sodomy and what people did is the role of the favorite, or a special friend of the king. Widely recognized as an erotic relation, the favorite confounds contemporary relational theology's insistence on friendship as the exploration of equality. As noted in chapter 2, the biblical narrative slips between describing David as Jonathan's servant and as Jonathan's friend. The way these two terms relate is one major area of historical difference. In contemporary American society, these two terms would be conceived as antithetical. Likewise, Aristotelian descriptions of friendship presume equality between friends. In early modern England, however, the position of the favorite relates "servant" and "friend" in a very different way than either Aristotle or capitalist ideology do.

These general assumptions about sexuality, friendship, legality, and sin go far in forcing us to reconsider how we might hear the anthems by Weelkes, Tomkins, and Gibbons in their historical context. But from a musical perspective, there are much more direct differences in how we might think about historical difference here.

Not only patterns of identification, but more basic patterns of perception go through such mediations. Musical meaning is the result of finding coherence in sonic patterns, a process that depends to an extraordinary degree on historical, cultural and linguistic contingencies.[1] One clear example of how linguistic templates shape musical perception is the existence of two incompatible narratives about sonata form. Sonata form is a widely-used form for classical music compositions in which an exposition presents two themes in different keys, a development plays with the themes and expands

---

1. For a particularly astute study of how such linguistic contingencies shape musical perception, see Levy, "Covert and Casual Values in Recent Writing about Music."

on tonal instability, and a recapitulation re-establishes the first key, and which presents the themes from the exposition in that key. While both themes and keys are intrinsic to sonata form, narratives focusing on one or the other create either a story of *return* to idyllic harmony (the thematic story) or of *resolution* of initial conflict (the key story). Different listeners may hear the same performance in opposed ways, one taking for ground what the other takes for figure.[2] Because language can shape musical perception so profoundly, it is crucial to attend to the ways in which linguistic and musical conventions shift over the course of history.

To illustrate the historicity of perception in relation to the anthems discussed here, I will return to Weelkes' "O Jonathan." At a fundamental level of perception, modern listeners are generally attuned to the bass as a reference point for understanding tonal motion in music, whereas until the seventeenth century, the tenor was the basic reference point.[3] At the outset of "O Jonathan," a musical detail highlights what is at stake in this distinction. After the first exclamation of "O Jonathan," the bass comes in alone on the word "O," singing a chromatically altered note (measure 4). My own hearing of this moment has changed over time from a sense informed more by common practice harmony as a reference point to a sense informed more by early modern counterpoint. From a harmonic standpoint, what I heard was a slight slip in the bass that is especially significant because of its isolation. The bass moves down a half-step, creating a sense like the Doppler effect. During my initial hearings of the piece, I always heard the music that followed strictly in reference to that unusual G-sharp. Although the music re-establishes equilibrium quickly after that moment, my ear stayed stuck on the oddness of that Doppler effect, only catching up to the subsequent flow of the music much later. With repeated listening, looking at the score, and attention to early modern musical theory, I came to hear the subsequent music more in light of the central pitch of the anthem, E, to which the tenor holds doggedly throughout this section, giving the moment a greater sense of stability than disruption. What I heard in my initial responses was a sense that the bass's G-sharp was pulling me into a new space, like turning to enter a new room. The second way of hearing allows the G-sharp to add a different color to an established space, more like changing the wallpaper

2. Rabinowitz, "Chord and Discourse," 49–52.

3. In England, the first musical theorizing that shifts from the tenor to the bass is in a text by Thomas Campion, most likely published in 1613. Wilson, ed., *A New Way of Making Fowre Parts by Thomas Campion and Rules How to Compose by Giovanni Coprario.* On the dating of the publication, 4.

than entering a different room. This attention to a small detail of the music's unfolding shows that what initially seems uncontrovertibly direct is a matter of intense historical conditioning.

This difference between hearing the G-sharp at the beginning of "O Jonathan" as "turning to enter a new room" or "changing the wallpaper," is significant for understanding the meaning of any potential eroticism of the anthem. The "turning to a new room" way of hearing the music connects well with McClary's reading of Franz Schubert, in which she interprets pivoting to distant harmonic areas as a way in which he explored a countercultural homoerotic subjectivity.[4] Her argument contrasts a conventional masculine understanding of identity as one requiring clear boundaries and opposition to a feminine Other to identities that that accept fluid boundaries and resist closure. At the outset of the anthem, the music heard through modern conventions evokes the possibility of a pivot to distant harmonic areas, but does not follow through with it. But the presence of this suggestion very early in the piece can allow for sitting with the implications of a pointing toward genuine otherness that would link homoerotic desire with a strong sense of transgressiveness. However, the "changing the wallpaper" hearing eliminates the possibility of a listening strategy attuned to arguments about the sexual politics of tonal difference and with it a strong sense of the anthem as communicating transgressiveness.

Attention to early modern theory brings other aspects of the anthem's meaning-making process into account. These differences are apparent in Weelkes' use of hexachords and his setting of the tenor's melodic line. Hexachords were a pedagogical tool for teaching singing. Identical syllables, ut-re-mi-fa-sol-la, could denote different notes of the scale, depending on where one placed "ut." The three common tones "ut" could describe were C, G, and F. These different starting places made for a "natural" hexachord on C, a "hard" hexachord on G, and a "soft" hexachord on F. These various descriptions of the hexachords meant that composers could play with associations of "hardness" and "softness" in setting texts. In his study of hexachords in late renaissance music, Lionel Pike notes that Weelkes hardens the hexachordal space at the end of the phrase, "passing the love of women."[5] Pike contrasts Weelkes's use of a harder hexachord to common

---

4. McClary, "Constructions of Subjectivity in Schubert's Music." For a study of early modern England with a similar understanding of the semiotics of masculinity, see Johnston, *Beard Fetish in Early Modern England.*

5. Pike, *Hexachords in Late Renaissance Music,* 38.

uses of hard hexachords to express bitterness or to evoke "anti-pastoral" at-titudes, suggesting rather that it "'caps' various passages in the piece where Weelkes has set up a pattern of expectancy only to break out of that pattern for an expressive purpose."[6] For Pike, the specifics of the expressive purpose at this point are left uncommented. However, there are a number of ways one could interpret the use of the harder hexachord at this specific moment in the text. In a historical sense, one could turn to the gendered associa-tions of "hard" and "soft" in the renaissance to note how "passing the love of women" meant a turn to a more explicitly masculine space. Here, male friendship explicitly displaces the presence of women and masculinizes the subject by disassociation with the feminine. This interpretation could apply equally well to an eroticized or non-eroticized understanding of the rela-tionship of Jonathan and David. However, one could also hear this move to a harder hexachord in erotic terms—as the music makes clearer that the love of Jonathan passes the love of women, the music literally gets hard. This interpretation would lend support to the view that sacred art served as a opportunity for explicit, hard-core homoerotic imagery in Renaissance culture.

The melodic activity of the tenor over the course of the anthem dif-ferentiates between David's address to Jonathan and his relationship with Jonathan, as the tenor always either holds on to the note E, or moves down by step and back to E, the final (the appropriate note for a melody's ending in a modal framework), when intoning the name "Jonathan," but explores the range of either the fifth or the octave when expounding on aspects of the relationship between David and Jonathan. Thus, the melodic motion of the tenor contrasts the immobility caused by grief with the dynamic activ-ity engendered by relating with a living partner, while keeping both aspects of experience within the bounds of the Phrygian mode, a mode commonly used for lamenting. This aspect of the tenor's melody may be imperceptible to the modern listener of a recording, as the tenor voice may be "lost" in the overall sound of the polyphonic texture. Close attention to the norms of early modern compositional technique brings out an aspect of the music that would not be prominent in the contemporary reception of listening casually to a CD.[7]

6. Pike, *Hexachord in Late Renaissance Muiscs*, 38.

7. Furthermore, while all these concrete details point to the historicity of musical meaning, one must imagine them within another more fundamental sonic difference, as explored by Smith, *The Acoustic World of Early Modern England* and Cockayne, *Hubbub*.

While we can establish, on the basis of historical evidence, some parameters of clear-cut differences in perception, training oneself to hear "historically" gives one a better, but not an indisputable sense of what actually happened in an early modern performance of the music. The fact that the Tallis Scholars and the Oxford Camerata present such radically different approaches to Tomkins' anthem is a reminder that we do not know what the music sounded like in its seventeenth-century setting. The contrast is not as radical as that of the Machaut example in the previous chapter, given that all of the performances work within a narrower range of performance practices. Nevertheless, the extent to which seventeenth-century performers opened or closed possibilities for relishing in the sensuality of music remains a matter of conjecture.

Not only musical perception, but social contexts and ideological implications of music are subject to historicist differences. In the case of the anthems in question, the fact that my *primary* question is "how can they ground modern queer identities" connects them unambiguously to erotic experience—and to erotic experience defined more precisely with specific entailments by voices such as Audre Lorde's, at that—places the anthems within a intertextual web that both includes and is fundamentally at odds with the anthems' intertextual web in the early seventeenth century.[8] Taking the basic semiotic dictum that signs function according to their relative position as a starting point, intertextual approaches locate meaning in contexts. Thus, modern performances generate meaning in relation to both present contexts and historical ones. But the past context did not include the present.

It is impossible to draw a strict line between contemporary queer celebrations of music as productive of erotic desire and early modern understandings of the matter because early modern English writings are not in agreement as to whether or not music is an erotic power. Thomas Morley's 1597 treatise *A Plain and Easy Introduction to Practical Music* evokes a sense disparate views at the outset of his treatise:

> Master: I have heard you so much speak against that art as to term it a corruptor of good manners and an allurement to vices, for which many of your companions termed you a Stoic.

---

8. On intertextuality as a theory of meaning production, see Kristeva, *Revolution in Poetic Language*, Foucault, *Language, Counter-Memory, Practice*, 113–38, Worton and Still, *Intertextuality*; Clayton and Rothstein, *Influence and Intertextuality in Literary History*, and Frow, *Marxism and Literary History* 125–69.

Philomathes: It is true; but I am so far changed as of a Stoic I would willingly make a Pythagorean, and for that I am impatient of delay; I pray begin even now.[9]

To be sure, the pedagogical function of the dialogue form accounts for this exposition of differing views, but a range of positions was evident in early modern England. Sixteenth- and seventeenth-century English perspectives on music ranged from the condemnation of public musicking as arousing "filthie lust" by Phillip Stubbes in the *Anatomy of Abuses*, to an understanding of music as a properly decorous inducement to piety by the anonymous author of *The Praise of Music*, to a frank direction of how to compose music to accentuate various past-times including hunting, drinking, and "amorizing," by Thomas Ravenscroft in *A Briefe Discourse of the true (but neglected) use of Charact'ring the Degrees*.[10] Morley's tension between "stoicism" and "Pythagoreanism" bespeaks a tension between a view that is distrustful of music for eliciting passion and one that celebrates music for illustrating mathematical order—neither of which celebrate music's ability to stimulate erotic passion. However, Morley's music-theoretical writings must be held together with his contributions to the madrigal, a genre often quite frank in its celebration of erotic delight.

Regardless of the range of opinion, no early modern writer would have been able to make the explicit connections between the sensuality of music and political struggle for queer identity that is constitutive of queer musicology.[11] One writer's views reveal a particularly clear contrast between queer musical writings and possible ways of hearing the music in its historical context. For if queer theorists in the present look to complex polyphony as analogous to bodies in lovemaking, this was not necessarily the case in early modern England. In a sixteenth-century musical theoretical text, Andreas Ornithiparcus lays out a number of procedures for how to create polyphonic music. The lutenist and composer John Dowland translated this work into English in 1609, making it a contemporary source

9. Morley, *A Plain and Easy Introduction to Practical Music*, 10. For the significance of stoicism in seventeenth-century England see, Barbour, *English Epicures and Stoics*.

10. *The Praise of Musicke*, Ravenscroft, *A Briefe Discourse Of the true (but neglected) use of Charact'ring the Degrees*.

11. This claim is somewhat different than asserting that the attempt to discern the role of homoeroticism in pre-modern settings is futile or necessarily anachronistic. Rather, it is an acknowledgement that the ability to make the connection between music and queer political struggles explicit makes a great deal of difference for meaning-making possibilities.

for seventeenth-century understandings of music.[12] In contrast to the queer understanding of polyphony as enticing one to the pleasures of bodily desire, Ornithiparcus sets up his theoretical treatise with a moralizing story from antiquity, in which the Greek character Clytemnestra was able to maintain chastity because a musician played music for her in modes that encouraged chaste desires. The story demonstrates the irresistible power of music by telling how Clytemnestra's suitor Aegisthus was able to finally break down her resistance and seduce her after murdering the musician. Thus, where contemporary queer musicologists find a technique with which to explore explicitly erotic desires, at least some early modern theorists are positing the exact same technique as a means of delivering chaste desires.

Not only the perception of compositional technique—either mediated through linguistic frameworks or musical expectations based on familiarity with various repertoires—but also the embodied context of hearing the music is radically different in the present than it was in the seventeenth century. Foremost, the recording technology through which the music is now mediated did not exist. Thus, the music can now be connected to a private, domestic sphere for which it was not intended. Rather, as music for the church, the music inevitably took a position within social and ecclesial tensions that had political consequences far beyond whatever disputes local congregations might have over liturgical propriety today.[13] The use of music to express theological tensions were particularly apparent in an episode at Canterbury Cathedral in 1641, in which congregants frustrated the clergy's opening of the Divine Office by singing the twenty-two sections of a metrical version of Psalm 119, as opposed to simply the first one that had been selected as the opening of the service.[14] The political implications of such tensions are most evident in the fact that in the 1645, Parliament replaced the *Book of Common Prayer* with the *Directory for the Public Worship of*

---

12. Ornithoparcus, *Andreas Ornithoparcus his Microlgus.*

13. For a solid treatment of the various liturgical positions in early modern England, see Davies, *Worship and Theology in England, Volume 2.* More recent scholarship, however, has shown that the divisions into "Anglican," "Catholic," and "Puritan" that Davies uses uncritically were not nearly as fixed and clear-cut as implied by Davies' argument. See, for example, Smith, "Catholic, Anglican, or Puritan?" and Questier, *Conversion, Politics, and Religion in England, 1580–1625.* Recall Weelkes' setting of a poem by a Jesuit for performance in a Church of England service, for example.

14. Owens, "Introduction," 15.

God, a decision that ended cathedral music of the sort composed by Weelkes and Tomkins.[15]

The scholarly consensus since the 1970s has been that the most plausible historical context for the composition of some of the works under discussion is the death of Henry Frederick, Prince of Wales, son of King James I, in 1612.[16] Because none of the anthems explicitly state that they were composed for this purpose, this case has to be made from inferences and coincidences in the historical record. The case for this context was made by Irving Godt on the basis of a number of facts. Most prominently, the text "When David Heard," does not appear in the English liturgy; a number of compositions by a disparate group of contemporaries on a common text suggests a special occasion. The text selected is most appropriate for the death of a patron's son. Godt notes that the uniformity of text suggests a matter of national importance; his case is strengthened by the fact that it would be unlikely for thirteen different composers to have one common patron aside from the king. He furthermore pointed to very disparate compositional choices, especially noting different tonal plans, to argue that the composers came to this text independently, not following each other as models.[17]

This theory is attractive because it would provide a concrete setting that would allow for an event-centered analysis, locating the anthems specifically at memorial services for a royal figure. Furthermore, Prince Henry represented ideological factions in significant tension with King James, making the cultural activity around his death a rich source for interrogating cultural, religious, and political tensions in the early seventeenth century.[18]

However, it is now clear that the older scholarly consensus that the death of Prince Henry was the most probable impetus for the composition of the anthems on David's laments rested on insufficient evidence. In an

15. Owens, "Introduction," 16.

16. Most explicitly spelled out by Godt, "Prince Henry as Absalom in David's Lamentations." This analysis does not pertain to Gibbons' "Thy Beauty Israel," clearly a later work. Previous scholarship that worked with the death of Prince Henry as the most probable occasion for the anthems in question includes Monson, "Thomas Myriell's Manuscript Collections," Duckles, "The English Musical Elegy of the Late Renaissance," Brett, "The Two Musical Personalities of Thomas Weelkes," Walls, "London, 1603–49," 296.

17. Godt, "Prince Henry as Absolom in David's Lamentations," 326.

18. Some investigations of these tensions include Williamson, *The Myth of the Conqueror*; Strong, *Henry, Prince of Wales and England's Lost Renaissance*; Badenhausen, "Disarming the Infant Warrior," McCullough, *Sermons at Court*; and Wilks, *Prince Henry Revived.*

article published in *Music and Letters*, Donna diGrazia provides a compelling case for an alternative scenario for the composition of the anthems on David's laments over Absalom and over Saul and Jonathan.[19] After examining the tenuousness of the evidence connecting the anthems with Henry's death, she provides a stemmatic analysis of the manuscripts, showing that the compositions most likely do not date primarily from 1613, but rather extend from possibly as early as the 1590s into the 1620s. One telling piece of textual evidence is that composers consistently inserted the phrase "When David heard" at the beginning of their anthems on David's lament over Absalom, a phrase that is present several chapters earlier in the books of Samuel (2 Samuel 3:3), but not at the lament in 2 Samuel 18. If, as Godt argued, the composers' independence of musical choices indicates that they resorted to this text independently as an obvious biblical passage to express grief for a royal figure, the consistency of this insertion would strain credulity.[20] Rather, the consistency of the textual juxtaposition of either an independent phrase or a borrowing from 2 Samuel 3:3 and 2 Samuel 18 points to a single model on which several composers based their compositions. DiGrazia locates a pair of anthems by the composer William Bearsley as this model, and notes that they could have been composed as early as the 1590s.

Given diGrazia's argument, a contextualization of the anthems in the seventeenth-century must content itself with more general observations. To begin, what sort of tensions or continuities exist between modern queer understandings of the anthems and those of seventeenth-century performers? Because we can not go back in time to hear the music as performed in the seventeenth century and because early modern theorists generally did not generally highlight the erotic power of sacred music, it is impossible to know to what extent choirs would have highlighted or downplayed elements of the music that lead to erotic identification with it. But even to ask the question is to think about the place of homoeroticism in the early Stuart church in a way that would most likely have confused early modern people. Indeed, as Alan Bray notes, one consistent feature of self-understandings of homoeroticism in early modern England is a major gap between a universal acknowledgement that sodomy is among the most heinous of crimes, and a general bewilderment on the part of people who engaged in homoerotic

---

19. DiGrazia, "Funerall Teares or Dolefull Songes."

20. Ibid., 562–64.

acts that they were being charged with sodomy.[21] That early modern ecclesiastical figures could have same-sex desires is made clear from Archbishop
Laud's diaries, in which he describes his desire for Buckingham.[22] But these
desires did not translate into a conceptual defense of the sort that modern gay liberationists would recognize. Indeed, for some gay liberationist
voices, this impasse can only be described as hypocrisy, and the hoisting of
ecclesial figures on their own homophobic petards is cause for posthumous
celebration.[23]

However, enough evidence of homoeroticism in early modern England exists to warrant speculation on the possibility that early modern composers or listeners may have intended, perceived, or desired homoeroticism
in music.[24] The historiographical problem is how to interpret this evidence.
Recalling both the examples of Renaissance art, where Goliath, rather than
Jonathan, is the character that may have allowed early moderns to imagine
David in homoerotic terms, and Ornithiparcus' insistence that polyphonic
music can enforce chastity rather than erotic desire, it is obvious that mappings between culture and homoeroticism took different forms than in the
present.

The role of the favorite in literature reveals one site of homoeroticism
in early modern England that related to social structures in a very different
way than relational theologians propose.[25] The favorite was a particularly
close friend to a monarch in early modern England, who received personal
benefits from the friendship. While such friendships were not necessarily
sexual, in the popular imagination, the favorite was often conceived of as
"sexually omnivorous." This understanding of the favorite's sexuality was
furthermore associated with a range of problems, including religious apostasy, cowardice, skill in dancing to the detriment of skill in martial arts,
dependence on the whims of the monarch, treachery, and sorcery.[26] What

---

21. Bray, *Homosexuality in Renaissance England*.

22. MacCulloch, *The Reformation*, 500.

23. See Norris, "Homosexual People and the Christian Churches in Ireland," 33–34,
on the execution of Bishop John Atherton in 1640: "There is a particular spice in the
spectacle of a prelate hoisted by the petard of his own prejudice and it is one of the
peculiar rewards of the Scholarships in the area of homosexual persecutions that such
pleasures are comparatively frequent."

24. See Smith, *Homosexual Desire in Shakespeare's England*; Goldberg, *Sodometries*,
Traub, *The Renaissance of Lesbianism in Early Modern England*.

25. Perry, *Literature and Favoritism in Early Modern England*.

26. Ibid., 2.

the literary critic Curtis Perry observes most acutely, however, is that the favorite exposes tensions in the structure of a constitutional monarchy, with
the favorite representing an antithesis to reasoned law and common good,
showing the particularity of the monarch's pleasure.

Where relational theologians connect homoeroticism to the ethics of a
multicultural, socialist resistance to transnational capitalism, the discourse
of favoritism in early modern England reveals fault lines within England's
constitutional monarchy, fault lines that would erupt with violent force in
the 1640s, with the civil war. Yet, at this point it becomes particularly clear
that the historical narratives that contemporary relational theologians pursue are at odds with the historical reality of Early Modern England. The
English Civil War assumes a heroic position in current Marxist interpretation of English history, which explores implicit and explicit parallels to
social upheavals and anti-authoritarian expressions of egalitarianism.[27] It
was in the upheavals of the 1960s that Heyward explicitly made the connections between the knowledge of God and social movements for justice.[28]
Keeping in mind the caveat that in actual practice, the dividing lines between religious factions were not as neat as suggested by the clear typology
of Anglican/Puritan/Catholic, one can still note that broadly speaking, the
music of Weelkes and Tomkins participated in a high liturgical style that
was discontinued during the interregnum. Thus, to turn to these specific
anthems is to open imaginings of the relation of homoeroticism to social
stratification in ways that do not match the egalitarian vision of Heyward
and Comstock. Early modern discourses of friendship likewise point to
tensions between early modern views and contemporary understandings
of homoeroticism. Where modern theological understandings of erotic
friendship point to struggles for gender equality, in the early modern era,
male friendship was often seen in patriarchal terms.[29]

A final more specific examination of these differences can be explored
through one of the sources that preserves the anthem. Although "O Jonathan" is on a biblical text and suitable for church singing, all the surviving
manuscripts are from secular sources.[30] One of the manuscript sources for
Weelkes's "O Jonathan," is the collection *Tristitiae Remedium* by the clergy-
man Thomas Myriell, who held ecclesiastical positions at Chichester and

27. Hill, *The World Turned Upside Down* and Holstun, *Ehud's Dagger*.

28. Heyward, *Staying Power*, 13.

29. Hutson, *The Usurer's Daughter*; Callaghan, "The Terms of Gender."

30. Brown, *Thomas Weelkes*, 147

Norfolk, and died in 1629. *Tristitiae Remedium* is a partbook, a manuscript that lays out the notation of a composition so that people can sit around a table and each sing his or her melodic part. The manuscript preservation shows that "O Jonathan" would have been sung in a domestic setting at Myriell's home. In this sense, the Consorte of Musick's recording of "O Jonathan" among madrigals reflects the nature of the sources we have better than do those recordings that contextualize the anthem among compositions more clearly meant for church services. Myriell is known for reprinting a 1617 sermon, "The Stripping of Joseph" by Robert Wilkinson.[31] The occasion for the reprinting was King James I's response to the Amboyna massacre, a massacre of English traders by the Dutch in Indonesia in 1623. Myriell's preface to the sermon stressed how the Dutch were no less cruel to the English than Joseph's brothers were to him.[32] This comparison aimed to generate outrage against James' policy of working through diplomatic rather than military channels to resolve the tensions between the two countries after the massacre. What we know of Myriell's political sympathies, then, puts him squarely at odds with the pacific views of James I. What we know of Myriell's politics puts the contextualization of Weelkes's anthem in Myriell's collection in a stark contrast to anti-imperialist tendencies that relational theologians derive from liberation theologians. While Comstock contextualizes Jonathan and David in light of his solidarity work with an HIV+ Puerto Rican man, Myriell's politics favored an English patriotism that sought to maintain national honor over against peaceable relations with neighbors. Thus, even if any or all of the singers experienced "O Jonathan" in erotic terms, their performance could not have done the same ideological work as that explored in my identifications with the piece in light of Comstock and Heyward's relational theology.

While the agency of historians means that historical reconstructions of cultural, sexual, and religious issues in Stuart England open a variety of possible ways of imagining the relation of past and present, musical performances mediate that relation in concrete ways. In particular, as performances of English sacred music, they open room for experiencing homoerotic desire in a sacred context, clarifying possibilities for queer relational *theology* and not simply queer desires, simply because their status as liturgical works *a priori* places them in the discursive realm of the sacred. Clarifying these possibilities is not as straightforward as it might

---

31. Willetts, "The Identity of Thomas Myriell," 432.

32. Chancey, "The Amboyna Massacre in English Politics, 1624–1632," 588.

appear, though. Since at least the nineteenth century, the question of to what extent the sacred is simply a social category and to what extent it is an occasion of revelation is open to dispute. Theologians have had to wrestle with Ludwig Feuerbach's insistence that religion is psychological projection or Emile Durkheim's theory of religion as a social construction.[33] Heyward's relational theology grew out of the attempt by the Death of God movement to radically refigure the relations between sacred and secular.[34] Performances offer different negotiations of this shift between current and the early seventeenth-century understandings of the sacred and the secular. From a relational perspective, however, it is precisely these negotiations of identity across difference, more than the ability to situate the music firmly in the sphere of the sacred, that brings the theological importance of exploring differing possible relations between the past and the present to the surface.

33. Feuerbach, *The Essence of Christianity*, Durkheim, *The Elementary Forms of Religious Life*.

34. Heyward, *The Redemption of God*, xvii-xviii.

CHAPTER 6

Handel's *Saul* and Ironies of Identification

IN THIS CHAPTER, THE object, George Fredrick Handel's oratorio *Saul* (1738, first performance January 16, 1739), raises very different issues in terms of relating to Jonathan and David in the vector of homoerotic identification and historicist relativization than do the anthems and hymn discussed in chapter 4. It depicts the relation of David and Jonathan from the perspective of an established Enlightenment English nationalism, a perspective that aligns more easily with modern, academic, secular perspectives and the liberal theological positions that take modern scientific and philosophical challenges seriously than does the music written in the ecclesiastical tensions of early Stuart England.[1] It is also part of the "common era" of classical music, that standard repertory of music from about 1700 to about 1900 that forms the bulwark of widely performed classical music, and which uses a musical syntax most readily grasped by modern listeners. For these reasons, there is a smaller historical gap to cross between Handel's

---

1. For a description of how the trends of the oratorio's libretto are toward desacralization of the biblical narrative and the replacement of a particular, Israelite deity with a a a universal deity, see Perlitt, "Händels *Saul.*" Narrating the historical differences between early Stuart and eighteenth-century renditions of David's lament over Jonathan would bring another layer of analysis to my argument. The interplay between contemporary appropriation of the past through music and the historical "development" of music over time in relation to musical settings of David and Jonathan is an avenue for future research.

music and that discussed in the previous chapter. Yet, the relative smallness of the gap does not negate the significance of the fact that real historical differences maintain their significance.

Furthermore, from the perspective of the history of sexuality, eighteenth-century England saw the rise of Molly Houses, widely recognized as the first distinguishable homosexual subculture in the English-speaking world.[2] Thus, whereas the discourses of favoritism and sodomy of the early seventeenth century point to radical differences in the construal of homoeroticism when comparing early modern approaches and contemporary ones, the eighteenth century offers a lineage for gay subcultures, the sort of which have supported gay identity formation in contemporary times. Again, however, the flow of historical change makes this comparison tenuous, as younger generations increasingly accept gay, lesbian, bisexual, and transgendered identities as "normal," rather than "queer." With this increasing acceptance, energy in queer communities is shifting from the articulation of separate spaces for subcultural identities to a classically liberal struggle for equal rights in the legal sense.[3] While this shift manifests a combination of losses and gains for queer identities, it points to new opportunities and challenges arising that again situate the experience of reception and performance of music in the present in changing social dynamics that make fixed pronouncements impossible.[4]

In this chapter, I continue exploring my visceral and sensual responses to the music, while looking for areas in which historical difference highlights the contingencies of the experience of those responses. However, the dynamics of the experience is different in the case of Handel than with the early Stuart examples in chapter 4. There is an irony at the heart of my relation to Handel's oratorio *Saul*: While historical evidence points to the probability that Handel's personal preferences were homoerotic, his musical representation of Jonathan and David is one with which I have had a great deal of difficulty identifying.

---

2. Bray, *Homosexuality in Renaissance England*, ch. 4, "Molly," 81–114, and Norton, *Mother Clap's Molly House*.

3. For a critique of this shift, see Warner, *The Trouble with Normal*. Peraino discusses musical ramifications of this shift in the career of Melissa Etheridge in *Listening to the Sirens*, 135–43.

4. One might also reference Alix Dobkin's elegiac song expressing a desire for lesbian separatism, "Living with Lesbians," on *Living with Lavender Jane*, as a musical expression of the unfulfilled need for separatist spaces in the heyday of separatist arguments.

Two scholars in particular have made compelling arguments for Handel's probable homoerotic personal preferences. At the very least, it is indisputable that he participated in social circles—both in Italy and England—where homoeroticism was prominent. Moving toward a definitive statement that Handel was drawn to these settings because he found his own desires reflected there is a more difficult historical claim to prove.

Gary C. Thomas opened the question in an essay that asked the question both bluntly and ironically: "'Was George Frederick Handel Gay?'"[5] The scare quotes around the question signal that Thomas's argument raises critical questions around the very question he poses so starkly. His argument consists of three separate avenues of inquiry: a historiographical study, a material-cultural biographical sketch, and a concluding section raising larger theoretical questions. First, Thomas notes that Handel biographers from the eighteenth-century until the time of his writing struggled to reconcile Handel's presumed heterosexuality with the absolute dearth of evidence of any romantic relationship between Handel and a woman—or even evidence of any romantic interest on Handel's part. Thomas notes four recurring strategies musicologists have used to bring this lack of evidence in line with the presumption of heterosexual universality. First, historians have flat-out invented romantic interests and liaisons. A second, psychological, approach stresses Handel's relationship with his mother as leading to disinterest in other women. Thomas notes how given the prominence of mother fixation in clinical accounts of homosexuality, this theory simply introduces the possibility of a homosexual Handel at the moment historiographers seek to deflect it.[6] A third approach posits a celibate Handel. A final approach asserts that the entirety of Handel's erotic energy was directed into the creative process.

In contrast to these studies that seek to find a way to incorporate Handel into heterosexual norms, Thomas situates details of Handel's biographies with what we know about social circles in Italy and England where homoerotic behavior was practiced. In particular, Thomas gives a great deal of attention to Handel's residence at Burlington House, the home of Richard Boyle, Earl of Burlington.[7] He cites a letter from Alexander Pope

5. Thomas, "'Was George Frederic Handel Gay?"

6. I might part ways with Thomas here slightly. It is not clear to me to what extent the historians using this explanation are trying to stave off a homosexual Handel, or simply trying to account for a failed heterosexual Handel—which is not quite the same thing.

7. Thomas, "'Was George Frideric Handel Gay?'" 177–80.

describing the milieu: "I am to pass three or four days in high luxury, with some company, at my Lord Burlington's. We are to walk, ride, ramble, dine, drink, and lie together."[8] However, Thomas also resists a popularizing gay historiography that seeks to establish as many certifiably gay historical figures as possible. Thus, he takes issue with Marion Ziegler, author of an essay on gay composers in a 1977 sourcebook for gay facts, for supposing a romantic/sexual relationship between Handel and the German singer and theorist Johann Mattheson without providing corroborating evidence.[9]

Thomas concludes his essay with a section that explores an ambivalence that is strongly akin to a primary tension of this book.[10] On the one hand, he explores the political utility for queer struggle of a "gay Handel." On the other hand, he relishes in the freedom opened by the indeterminacy of an incomplete historical record and the possibilities of further historical changes in queer identity. In particular, he desires a complete escape from gender, which he sees as a necessary precondition of sexual liberation. Thomas is explicit that the conceptual entailments of the latter line of inquiry makes it impossible to "prove" Handel was "one of us," mitigating the political strength of the first line of inquiry.

Where Thomas took on the whole field of Handel studies, Ellen Harris's *Handel as Orpheus* approaches the question with a very different method and very different subject position.[11] It is primarily a study of Handel's contribution to a specific genre—the cantata—in which elucidation of homoeroticism is a means to an end, namely placing the cantatas in their historical social setting. She explicitly aligns herself with an eighteenth-century woman, Mrs. Delaney, who privately shared her knowledge of incidents of homoerotic activity between men—in a spirit of "amusement," and that her addressee "might not be ignorant in the ways of the world," though

---

8. Cited in ibid., 178.

9. Ibid., 175.

10. I am not sure to what extent I am indebted to Thomas for the extent to which I probe the historicity of sexuality in this book. I had read Thomas's essay about two years before I thought of the topic of musical representations of David and Jonathan, and seven years before I started graduate school. It is possible that Thomas's formulation was influential. However, Thomas's argument is one among many works that explored the prospects and difficulties of a historicized or even relativized understanding of homoeroticism, and his essay at the time struck me as an elegant approach to a question I was already familiar with from such queer theorists as Eve Kosofsky Sedgwick and Judith Butler.

11. Harris, *Handel as Orpheus.*

Harris connects her inquiry with the spirit inherent in the latter statement, not the pursuit of amusement.[12]

Harris notes that into the eighteenth century, the episode at the end of the story of Orpheus in Ovid's *Metamorphoses* in which Orpheus invents homosexual desire was well-known.[13] As an example of how this aspect of the Orpheus story was openly connected to current events, she cites the 1772 mock-eclogue by William Kenrick, in which he refers to Isaac Bickerstaff, who had fled England on account of sodomy charges, as Orpheus.[14] She furthermore proposes that it is this episode, in addition to Orpheus's musical powers, that is suggested in references to Handel as Orpheus. Handel's second opera, *Nero*, had a prominent role for Anicetus, Nero's lover (described exactly that way in the libretto).[15] Of particular importance to her argument is the patronage by Cardinal Pietro Ottoboni (1689–1740) and Cardinal Benedetto Pamphili (1653–1730), both of whom she sees as having homoerotic attachments. Pamphili wrote lyrics for Handel, some of which are homoerotically suggestive.

Harris's book, while generally well-received—it won two awards—has also been the subject of defensive criticism that has often distorted her argument.[16] She also notes that the publication of *Handel as Orpheus*, unlike her previous research, has garnered extensive speculation about her personal identity, leading to a number of *ad hominems* that are generally unusual in responses to academic arguments. It is the steady questioning of her motives, over against factual and conceptual issues, that made the response to this work different than that to work she had published previously. Thus, her simple description of a possible homoerotic subtext was enough to render her suspect in the eyes of scholars and members of the popular press. This difference in tone in the evaluations of a publication by an established, senior scholar makes for a remarkable case study illuminating the challenges scholars devoted to queer theory still face. She cites James Saslow's description of a standard sequence of arguments against queer studies in the arts: "1) There's insufficient evidence; 2) Even if there were enough evidence, it's embarrassing, even shameful, to consider it at all; and 3) Even if it were not morally objectionable, it doesn't matter anyway

12. Ibid., 19, 24.

13. See Ovid, *Metamorphoses*, 227.

14. Harris, *Handel as Orpheus*, 34.

15. Ibid., 40.

16. Harris, "Homosexual Context and Identity."

because it falls outside the scope of our profession."[17] This attempt to silence discussion of homoeroticism in biographical studies is strikingly revealed by the concluding sentence of Thomas McGeary's review of Harris's book: "Not proven."[18] The terseness and finality of the statement cuts off discussion, rather than opening further inquiry. It also misses the epistemological framework Harris evokes in her quotation of Stephen Hawking at the outset of her argument: "In general quantum mechanics does not predict a single definite result for an observation. Instead, it predicts a number of possible outcomes and tells us how likely each of these is."[19] While McGeary's point that Handel was not the object of the charges of various forms of sexual perversion aimed at the opera house between 1724 and 1736 lends some strength to his point that the evidence does not point toward homoeroticism, other points he makes simply show his obliviousness to the dynamics of the closet. His objection that homosexual activity would not have been treated with silence because "vicious and libelous assaults in the public press" were common and that the Society for the Reformation of Manners kept sodomy in public discourse betrays a severe blindness to the fact that these social dynamics are precisely those that would demand that actual homoerotic activity be kept under wraps, rather than spoken of freely.[20]

The popular and critical response to Harris' book recapitulates the dynamics at stake in the scholarly and ecclesiastical furor over homoerotic interpretations of Jonathan and David. In both cases, as with the example of Franz Schubert in chapter 3, the attempt to find a mirror for gay identity in a past historical figure leads not to a successful consolidation of identity, but rather leads into deeper engagement with social forces that are hostile to queer existence. On the other hand, the anti-academic responses from the gay press show how the historicist side of the equation can be unsettling to gay audiences. These resistances also show that escape from biblical religions is hardly a guarantee of escape from heterosexist dynamics. Again, these debates show the wisdom of Brett's decision to by-pass the "Schubert debate" and directly engage Schubert's role in the formation of various homoerotic identities.

Despite the resistance described by Harris, what she and Thomas have done is to shift the burden of proof to any scholar who wants to make an

17. Ibid., 53.
18. McGeary, "Review," 612.
19. Hawking, *A Brief History of Time.* Cited by Harris, *Handel as Orpheus*, 25.
20. McGeary, "Review," 612.

argument that presumes a heterosexual Handel. As Thomas asks, "In light of the composer's extensive and intimate association with demonstrably homosexual men and/or milieux, the question becomes this: on what basis can or ought one argue that Handel was everywhere he went an exception?"[21]

As evidence that some scholars have accepted that a "homosexual Handel" makes more sense than a "heterosexual Handel," one could look at a recent theoretical and historical synthesis of music through the lens of queer musicology. Judith Peraino develops Harris's analysis to point more directly at the interrelations Handel forges between music, homoeroticism, fantasy, and power.[22] She interprets Handel's Italian cantatas to texts by Pamphili as evidence that "music helped in an erotic game of power between two unmarried men, patron and artist."[23]

Harris and Peraino discuss homoerotic identity in relation to Handel's Italian cantatas, all composed early in his career. The composition in which Handel set David's lament, however, is an oratorio written later. From the perspective of the production of the oratorio, politics surrounding genre already reveal problems with a homoerotic identification with Handel's setting. The genre of the oratorio in eighteenth-century England was not only implicated in the development of nationalist identities, but also was a commercially successful alternative to Italian opera, which critics successfully feminized.[24] Handel arrived in England as a composer of Italian operas, a genre which met with considerable hostility, and became a vehicle through which critics lobbed charges of the introduction of sodomy to England via Italian cultural influence. These charges led to the commercial necessity for Handel to compose English texts on sacred themes. The very genre in which Handel sets a possible moment for homoerotic identification, then, represents a capitulation to homophobic discourse. This capitulation furthermore undermines the kind of historical narratives of progress, in which gay history points teleologically toward Stonewall as a defining event. Rather, Handel's shift to the genre of the oratorio bespeaks a cyclical vision of "gay history," in which periods of relative openness can be followed by severe repression. This alternative narrative finds a modern analogy not

21. Thomas, "'Was George Frideric Handel Gay?'" 180.

22. Peraino, *Listening to the Sirens*, 195–227.

23. Ibid., 209.

24. On political and national identity, see Smith, *Handel's Oratorios and Eighteenth-Century Thought*, on the feminization of Italian opera in England, see McGeary, "Gendering Opera."

in Stonewall as a triumphal watershed of liberation, but more tragically to the crushing of a nascent gay liberation movement in Weimar Germany by the rise of the National Socialist Party in the Third Reich, though the level of violence in the Third Reich pushes the analogy to a limit. Furthermore, the social patterns here call into question Comstock's view of a parallel between economic contraction and sexual repression. While the evidence he marshals explains twentieth-century United States dynamics and possibly the formation of Leviticus, here the silencing of a musical genre through anti-sodomitical rhetoric goes hand-in-hand with the growth of a middle class in eighteenth-century England. Just as his tendency to jump directly from the Bible to a modern context led him to overlook the importance of the Song of Songs in the history of biblical interpretation, so here the same tendency leads him to make firmer parallels between the social patterns generated by economic activity and sexual ethics.

Handel's oratorio differs from the works discussed in chapter 4 in that it is a dramatic work covering a number of episodes from 1 and 2 Samuel, rather than an isolated verse. Because of this, reading the oratorio in light of the general reception of Jonathan and David means that one must deliberately foreground their friendship, as opposed to other aspects of the oratorio.[25] One study of the oratorio's representation of friendship in its historical context has been offered by Ruth Smith.[26] Smith contextualizes her discussion of the depiction of friendship in *Saul* with an eighteenth-century rewriting of William Shakespeare's *The Merchant of Venice*, George Granville's *The Jew of Venice* (1701). One can chart a significant change in understandings of homoeroticism and male friendship over the course of the seventeenth century in this rewriting, as Granville downplays elements in the friendship of Antonio and Bassano that might be read as sexual. In contrast, Michael Radford's 2004 film adaptation of the play interprets the friendship explicitly as a sexual one. Thus, *The Merchant of Venice* provides a clear example of how experiences of friendship and erotic desire have been separated and aggregated at the key moments discussed in this book: aggregated casually in early Stuart England, separated in the eighteenth century, and reconnected in the present.

Smith argues that the libretto of *Saul* participates in the general trend noted in Granville's rewriting of Shakespeare, namely the suppression of

25. For an interpretation of the oratorio in the context of the reception of the figure Saul, see Bartelmus, "Handel and Jennens Oratorio 'Saul.'"

26. Smith, "Love between Men in Jennens' and Handel's *Saul*."

material that could be seen as homoerotic. She dwells on the farewell in 1 Samuel 20 as an erotic scene that is absent from the oratorio. The most pertinent fact about the libretto for the purposes of this argument is that Jennens supplied an aria for Jonathan to express directly his affection for David.[27] Handel composed music for the aria, but in the end marked it for omission. This is the textual moment that would link the oratorio most unequivocally to the terms laid out by Comstock in chapter 1. It is a clear and unequivocal expression of the bond, which Comstock identifies as Yahweh, between the two men. The deletion of this aria, then, presents the clearest example of how the oratorio denies an opportunity for a homoerotic identification with Jonathan and David.

The deletion also raises questions about what it means to relate the oratorio to a "gay Handel" as explored by Thomas and Harris. Given contemporary expectations of gay identity, the fact that the aria was deleted shows that even if Thomas and Harris are correct in their suspicions that Handel "was gay," he did not express it in the ways that conform to modern ideas of gay expressivity. However, the deletion does fit well with Harris's notions of musical self-silencing as a strategy Handel used during his London years.

Despite the fact that the text downplays potentially erotic elements of the relationship between Jonathan and David, it still gives enough prominence to Jonathan that a hearing of the oratorio could coalesce around him as a point of focalization. It is this focalization that could be eroticized for a given listener or in a given hearing, based on various factors, including familiarity with the biblical background, personal attraction to a given singer, or a simple psychological need for confirmation of desires.

Indeed, the music and the text raise independent desires that pull my experience of the oratorio in very different directions. I turn to this oratorio because of a *text* that deals with the relation of Jonathan and David. Handel's *music* on the other hand draws me into David's subjectivity independent of Jonathan, and leaves me alienated from Jonathan as a character. Of course, the extent to which this is my experiences depends on performances *and* is a matter of the temporality of (erotic) experience. I find that the more I engage the oratorio, the more I find productive possibilities for homoerotic identification with it. This "slipperiness" of experience is one of the greatest challenges to writing the kind of subject-oriented analyses I follow queer musicologists in pursuing here. As I further engage the oratorio, what may

27. Cited by Smith, "Love between Men in Jennens' and Handel's *Saul*," 229.

emerge will be a story of seduction, in which Handel's oratorio slowly convinces an unwilling listener to surrender to its charms. For the purposes of writing under time constraints, I am writing from the subject position of one still resisting its advances. However, this instability generated by a subjective, rather than an attempt at an objective reading of the text, shows in microcosm what is at stake in historicizing interpretations. Just as my personal experience inevitably shifts over time, so do collective experiences go through changes.

Generally, when I listen to *Saul*, my attention sharpens particularly at David's aria "O Lord, whose mercies numberless." An intensification of musical beauty at this point elicits this sharpened attention, an experience that makes this moment a kind of musical focal point for the oratorio. However, this focalizing point does not align with the points I expect to have desire heightened based on the narrative. Text and music work at cross-purposes. Jonathan's aria "Birth and Fortune I despise" should be the point to which I gravitate, based on text, but David's aria "O Lord whose mercies numberless" is the point at which Handel's music anchors subjectivity. This dynamic of Handel's music drawing me into identifying with narrative dynamics very different than those I would expect given the text is also present in his 1752 oratorio *Jephtha*, where my interest is primarily in the subjectivity of Jephthah's daughter. However, Jephthah's aria "Waft her, angels, through the skies" is where musical beauties become irresistible to the point that they become the fulcrum of the oratorio. But this aria expresses his sorrow at losing the daughter he will sacrifice, not a critique of his vow to sacrifice her. Thus, the perpetrator of violence, rather than its victim, is the bearer of a subjectivity with which I cathect in hearing the oratorio. The disjunction of desires raised by narrative and musical elements in *Saul* is not nearly so stark, or so disturbing, as in *Jephtha*. After all, David is the person to whom Jonathan's affections are directed. Yet, the narrative situates David primarily in relationship to Saul, not Jonathan, in this aria. One could, and some may, experience the expressive strength of the communication of David to Saul in light of homoerotic interpretations of the relation of David and Saul. However, I do not. Like Comstock, despite my awareness of the exegetical weakness of this approach, I approach the text and its interpretations with a strong desire for the kind of egalitarian, companionate, fraternal, and erotic relations that form a particular ideal of gay relationships.

In one respect, however, the narrative placement of David's aria is pertinent to its role in being a musical moment that distracts from narrative desires, insofar as it highlights music's power. The aria is the point at which David deliberately sings to soothe Saul's madness. Whereas in most of the oratorio, actual singing represents a kind of heightened speech, here singing is simply singing.[28] Thus, the text draws attention to music at the precise place where music is most explicitly eroticized.

In the context of the oratorio as published, Jonathan expresses his desire most unambiguously in the aria, "Birth and Fortune I despise." This aria is one point where one can examine the ways in which Handel aligns music and text, in keeping with the Baroque emphasis on matching music to text. Handel's exemplary predecessors in this regard were Henry Purcell in the English context and Heinrich Schütz in the German context in which Handel received his early training under Friedrich Zachow.[29]

Jonathan's aria moves between two prominent *figurae*, an initial ascending arpeggiation of the tonic triad followed by a step-wise descent with each pitch punctuated by repetition (first appearance measure 1) and a simple sung motif that ascends and descends by step and is echoed by the violins (first appearance measure 31)—the echo being an integral part of the overall *figura*.[30] The second motif sets only the words "of virtue." The second *figura* is marked adagio in contrast to the overall allegro of the aria. Contrapuntally, each *figura* has an initial brief exposition in parallel motion, followed by more varied contrapuntal procedures. The initial arpeggiation is in unison, whereas the stepwise motif moves in parallel thirds. The unison articulation of the opening arpeggiation is unmistakable because Handel scored the *figura* for both strings and winds—the differing colors would highlight that different lines are in unison. The contrapuntal procedure of contrasting between parallel unisons and parallel thirds reinforces the distinction between the arpeggiated and step-wise melodic motifs. Finally, in terms of harmony, the first *figura* establishes the tonic, while the second *figura* stretches out the dominant, resolving into the tonic with a return to the first *figura*. Thus, the phrase "from virtue let my friendship rise" has two different text-music relations. In the first relation, the word "virtue" is isolated, and the second *figura* becomes a musical signifier for the concept "virtue." In the second relation, the word "virtue" is folded

28. For a detailed and conceptually rich investigation of distinctions between the representation of speech and song in musical drama, see Abbate, *Unsung Voices*.

29. For the dynamics of German music pedagogy in the seventeenth century, see Butt, *Music Education and the Art of Performance in the German Baroque*.

30. Handel, *Saul*.

back into the overall sense of the phrase, as the resolution of the dominant and the return of the first *figura* sets the whole phrase "from virtue let my friendship rise."

How might one interpret this lingering on and sweetening of the word "virtue?" Returning to Mary, Lady Chudleigh's interpretation of David and Jonathan, a very straight-forward answer emerges. For Chudleigh, David's ability to express sentiment is of a piece with his ability to avoid any "unbecoming action" in the face of injustice. Thus, virtue and sentiment are part of a single *Gestalt* that expresses itself in a cultivated self. However, Handel's musical procedures isolate the word "virtue" from their general context in such an exaggerated manner that the possibility arises that this is a moment in which he codes Jonathan's desire as subversive, by treating the word "virtue" ironically. If this possibility was indeed the case, it would mean that Handel used music to double-code Jonathan's virtue. It would register as a simple continuity between sentiment and virtue to ears not clued into Handel's homoerotic social context, but as a message to those within that homoerotic *milieu* that he, in the voice of Jonathan, believes the notion of virtue to be subordinate to that of pleasure.[31] This latter interpretation maintains plausibility to the extent that one finds the arguments of Thomas and Harris about Handel's homoerotic identity convincing.

The difference between Jonathan's and David's arias also points to possible divergences between gender and eroticism. Jonathan's aria exhibits possibilities for gender subversion, with his stark juxtaposition between martial and feminine musical tropes, but not in this case much opportunity for erotic investment in that gender subversion.

Saul, like Handel's *Jephtha*, devotes considerable time to expanding suggestive passages in the biblical narrative to full-fledged expressions of eighteenth-century familial ideology. *Jephtha* goes so far as to devote the entire first act into the separation of characters into female characters in the domestic sphere and male characters in the military sphere. It is from this position of clearly demarcated gendered spaces that Jephtha' violence against his daughter proceeds.

A major way in which Jennens' libretto brings the biblical text into alignment with eighteenth-century notions of companionate marriage is through the characterization of Merab, Saul's oldest daughter. In the biblical text, Merab is strictly speaking an object. The narrative presents her strictly

---

31. On double-voiced utterance in music, see Brackett, "James Brown's 'Superbad' and the Double-Voiced Utterance," and Maus, "Glamour and Evasion."

in relation to men, as an object of exchange between Saul and David, and then to Adriel the Meholathite. Grammatically, she is never the subject of a sentence, but always an object, which reinforces her narrative function as a conduit of male power.[32] She does not speak, giving the reader no sense as to her preference of David or Adriel as a husband, or her desire for a husband at all. Jennens, however, changes the biblical narrative so that it is Merab who actively rejects David as a suitable husband, rather than Saul who peremptorily gives her to another man.

Merab, in Jennens characterization, furthermore acts as a foil to Jonathan. Where Jonathan argues on the basis of virtue, Merab argues on the basis of rank. One can see the text here setting up a tension between aristocratic notions of rank against friendship established by virtue. This opposition has been diagnosed as part of an ascendant capitalism in eighteenth-century England, with "virtue" being associated with the rising middle class. The oratorio neutralizes the tensions between aristocratic and capitalist modes of hierarchy by placing the tension within a narrative of royal succession.[33] Like relational theologians, then, the oratorio pulls the relationship of Jonathan and David beyond the strictly private realm into a moral/political argument. However, where relational theologians push beyond the mobile hierarchies of capitalism, the total context of Handel's oratorio was part of the establishment of a rising middle class and the commercialization of music.[34]

In light of the fact that Merab receives extended characterization that is completely absent from the biblical text, it is significant that Ahinoam, Saul's wife, is not present in the oratorio at all.[35] Her absence is furthermore striking given that in a later oratorio, Handel set a text which invented a wife for Jephthah, who is not present in the biblical narrative. Ahinoam's absence makes the oratorio at one level a story of the conflict between raw patriarchal authority and companionate marriage, with Saul representing the former and David and Michal representing the latter. Neither

32. 1 Sam 14:49; 18:17, 19, and 2 Sam 21:8.

33. Smith argues that Jennens' and Handel's characterization of David bypasses eighteenth-century associations of virtue with a rising middle class and that attention to musical drama would do much to dismantle the very idea that virtue and capitalist classes were firmly linked. "Love between Men in Jennens' and Handel's *Saul*," 233–34. I think this an overly narrow view of the nature of ideology in narrative.

34. Plumb, *The Commercialisation of Leisure in Eighteenth-Century England.*

35. See Feldman, "The Absent Mother in Opera Seria," for a discussion of the significance of the absence of mothers in eighteenth-century musical drama.

patriarchal authority nor companionate marriage as understood in the eighteenth century, as it turns out, are conducive to queer identity. As the narrative unfolds, Saul's madness, but not his marriage is represented. His primary interaction with another woman is the Woman at Endor—thus rather than depicting him as interacting with a wife, who would birth the children who would continue his line, he is interacts with the woman who foretells his death.

Handel's treatment of David's Lament consolidates the oratorio's failure to provide an means of identifying homoerotically with the relation of David and Jonathan. As one of the pleasures of listening to the oratorio is following large scale narrative movement, as with an opera, the Lament occupies a space in which narrative movement ceases and the text and music draw out a single moment for a lengthy period of time. My impatience here with the lack of narrative development, however, contrasts with other queer and feminist musicological voices, such as Susan McClary's for whom escape from the confines of narrative teleology is the essence of music's liberating power.

Furthermore, the Lament comes at the end of a lengthy work—in most recordings about two hours, in the recording directed by Paul McCreesh nearly three hours. By the time the performers reach the Lament, I have had generally had about as much Handel as I need for the time being and am ready to wash my ears out with something like Webern or Everything But the Girl. In contrast, the anthems from early Stuart England go right to the text I'm interested in.

Handel also disperses the text of the Lament, so that several singers sing it, shifting the emphasis to the broader social implications of the lament, rather than the more personal utterance. From the perspective of the relational theologians discussed in chapter 1, this compositional decision is laudable insofar as it refuses a public/private binary, showing how personal relations are imbricated in larger relational patterns in society. On the other hand, the compositional decision interferes with a desire to hear the utterance "Great was your love for me" as a deep-felt personal expression of intimacy.

Handel's oratorio exemplifies my relationship to Handel in general in that it elicits musical desires that are opposed to textual desires. Generally speaking, my preference for the Hebrew Bible over the Christian New Testament continually pulls me toward Handel, who wrote many oratorios on narratives on the Hebrew Bible, over against his contemporary Johann

Sebastian Bach, whose music I find more satisfying aesthetically, spiritually, and erotically, yet whose sacred music manifests a Pietist focus on Christ that I find less interesting than the exploration of the variety of narratives available in the Hebrew Bible. What draws me to Bach is his tendency to evade clear-cut cadences, extending phrases contrapuntally into an ongoing flow of motion, whereas Handel has a much greater tendency toward clear-cut periodization. Handel's tendency toward periodization, however, also frees him to explore silence in a musically meaningful way, which might allow for cross-historical explorations of the relation of silence and homoeroticism as manifested in the aesthetics of John Cage.[36] Furthermore, just as Handel's textual preferences draw me into music I find less satisfying than those of Bach's, Handel's biography suggests that I "should" be more drawn to his music than Bach's, given that my life mirrors more closely that of a geographically mobile man with probable homoerotic preferences than it does that of a local church musician and family man.

Interestingly, reception here mirrors production insofar as Handel and the librettist for *Saul*, Charles Jennens, were not on the best of terms. For example, Jennens took pride in the fact that Handel attributed his coming down with an illness in 1743 to Jennens' criticisms.[37] In a letter dated September 19, 1738, Jennens also objected to Handel's addition of a Hallelujah finale to *Saul* by describing Handel's head as "more full of Maggots than ever," and describing the proposed Hallelujah as nonsense.[38] Obviously, the tensions apparent here did not prevent Jennens and Handel from successfully collaborating to create the end product. Similarly, to point out that text and music can work at cross-purposes is not to assert that they do not complement each other or work in tandem overall.

The relation between music and text, moreover, is a factor in production and perception of music that shows why historicism is imperative to keep in mind. Despite the fact that, as recent neurological studies show, music and language are processed very similarly, they remain different semiotic systems.[39] From a historicist perspective, it is the semiotic difference

36. On Handel's silences, see Harris, "Silence as Sound." For comparison, see Cage, *Silence*.

37. See Harris, *Handel as Orpheus*, 47. Handel's relationship to Jennens thus offers a challenge to theoretical explorations of the erotics of literary collaboration, such as Masten, *Textual Intercourse* and Koestenbaum, *Double Talk*.

38. Cited by Hicks, "Handel's *Saul*," 248.

39. On the music/language relation from a neurological perspective, see Patel, *Music, Language, and the Brain*. For semiotic analyses of music and text see Steiner, *The Sign in Music and Literature*, Scher, *Music and Text*.

between musical and linguistic systems of signification that needs to be kept in focus, because it allows for charting historically variable ways of relating the two. The notion that music should somehow mirror text was a sixteenth-century invention, largely derived from the ideas of the literary theorist Pietro Bembo.[40] A clear contrast between this approach and earlier, medieval approaches can be seen in Aegidus of Murino, writing around 1400, who instructs composers of motets to write the music, and then "put the words over . . . the music as best you can."[41] Dissatisfaction with such a gap between musical and textual desires were a driving force in the creation of Baroque musical aesthetics, as seen in the theoretical writings and musical compositions of Giulio Caccini and Claudio Monteverdi.

This emphasis on congruence of words and music led to a close association between music and rhetoric in Baroque aesthetics, to the extent that rhetorical procedures often determined musical form. In the early seventeenth century, the German theorist Joachim Burmeister wrote what is generally acknowledged as the first work of musical analysis, in which he applied rhetorical analysis to a motet of Lassus.[42] This rhetorical approach to musical structure was prominent throughout the Baroque era.[43] After Handel, the "emancipation of music from language"[44] was a crucial development in the formulation of the discourse of absolute music discussed in chapter 4. A pertinent example of how the historically contingent assumptions that inform musical perception in relation to the difference between Baroque music and absolute music can be seen in nineteenth- and twentieth-century approaches to Johann Sebastian Bach's *Musical Offering*. Bach scholars regularly rearranged the work in accordance with principles of absolute music—such as "symmetry"—showing how even those who spent their academic careers steeped in the dynamics of Baroque music could not shake off the frameworks of absolute music that informed their cultural norms.[45] However, a rhetorical analysis of the *Musical Offering* shows the ordering of the work left by Bach to have a logic consistent with

40. On the influence of Bembo, see Feldman, *City Culture and the Madrigal at Venice*, 87–96, 126–33.

41 Cited in Weiss and Taruskin, *Music in the Western World*, 67.

42. Burmeister, *Musical Poetics*, 204–7.

43. See, for example, Kirkendale, "Ciceronians versus Aristotelians on the Ricercar as Exordium, from Bembo to Bach."

44. Neubauer, *The Emancipation of Music from Language*.

45. See Kirkendale, "The Source for Bach's *Musical Offering*," 88–91.

the thought-patterns of the Baroque world, which the attempts to shoehorn it into the formal concerns of absolute music reveal to be very different than those of modernity.

Often, feminist and queer musicologists have turned their attention to ways in which music resists the patriarchal narratives it accompanies. In a discussion of Lucia di Lammemoor, Susan McClary notes various ways in which Donizetti's music colludes with a misogynist text, however, she also notes that the singer's high e-flat signifies power in a way not authorized by the text.[46] Jessye Norman's performance of Schumann's song-cycle *Frauenleben und -liebe,* goes against the grain of the misogynist text and music.[47] Her singing of "Er, der Herrlichste von Allen," is belabored rather than celebratory. In the case of Handel's *Saul,* however, the same dynamic queer people have explored in order to *resist* patriarchal hegemony creates a wedge between desires for the representation of homoeroticism and desires for musical beauty. Rather than finding in the music an escape from a patriarchal narrative, I find the music tells a different story than the one I want to hear.

In the 1990s, in a desperate gesture revealing insecurities both in classical music marketing and the formation of gay identity, RCA released a compilation of classical music under the title *Out Classics,* featuring music by known gay composers (bizarrely including Frederic Chopin, apparently on the basis of his relationship with Georges Sand), and adorned with a jacket cover showing a photograph of a bare-chested, highly built man.[48] The experience of interacting as a gay man with Handel's music I have described in this chapter should have dispelled the underlying assumptions in the creation of such a CD. The first assumption is that homoeroticism is a trans-historical constant, by means of which gay men can find mirrors for their identity regardless of historical difference. The second assumption is that the composer is the key agent in musical meaning, such that patterns of identification go directly from listener to composer without the mediation by performers and recording technicians playing a role. Rather, the experience of a failed identification with a representation of Jonathan and David by a composer whose biography leads me expect easy identification

---

46. McClary, *Feminine Ending,* 90–99.

47. Cusick, "Gender and the Cultural Work of a Classical Music Performance."

48. *Out Classics.* See also *Gay American Composers,* also featuring a bare-chested man on the cover.

points again to the inexact match between supposedly universal sexual categories and historical contingencies.

Conclusion

FOR MODERN QUEER FOLK who want to be reconciled to biblical religions, the relation of Jonathan and David is a crucial narrative in seeking to fulfill that desire. While tensions between biblical and queer commitments persist, the story of a man's constant love for another man in the biblical context will continue to provide a means to negotiate biblical faith and queer identity as long as Bibles are read. Jonathan and David allow queer people to connect to biblical visions of justice and hope without being forced to choose between biblical and queer identities. Whatever the exegetical weaknesses of arguments for a gay Jonathan and David are, their story has proven to inspire many queer people to claim the legacy of biblical faith. While exegetical arguments will certainly continue, the gay reading of Jonathan and David has already shown to have enough resonance in the text to be assured of it being a significant trajectory in the history of biblical interpretation.

However, people interpret and use the stories of the love of Jonathan and David in widely different ways. Shifting the terms from what the text says to how people use it is what allows us to speak of a *living* tradition, that which binds communities together in quest of common life. It is in people's ongoing activity, both work and play, both intentional and spontaneous, that a biblical story is transformed from the inert words on a page to a revelatory insight. This book has unearthed a variety of ways in which people have read the story. Relational theologians use Jonathan and David as a paradigm of their theological vision; biblical scholars study David and Jonathan to understand dynamics of the biblical text, and to intervene, more or less explicitly, in contemporary ecclesiastical debates about homoeroticism; rabbinic interpretations use them to delve into non-sexual ethics; early Stuart composers set David's lament over Saul and Jonathan to music in styles that showed options within liturgical tensions; Handel negotiated the end of Italian opera by turning to the oratorio, showing his setting of Jonathan and David to be predetermined by a homophobic frame of reference.

Because the object of study is not simply Jonathan and David, but rather the interrelation of these various approaches to them, it is impossible to tie all the threads together into a neat and coherent conclusion. Rather, the various vectors and axes that determine different interpretive conflicts, as well as the different trajectories that result from widely divergent interpretive priorities, disperse Jonathan and David into contexts that have little to do with each other. While these contexts share Jonathan and David as a common touchstone, finding ways to hold, say, rabbinic debates and Enlightenment musicking together strains against the stubbornness of historical particularity. Rather, bringing various interpretations into a common picture only highlights how completely different worlds emerge out of historical and cultural difference. A poignant expression of the difficulty—expressed with a strong doubt that the difficulty can be overcome— of bridging two of the worlds described in this book, the early modern and the contemporary, can be seen in Lucille Clifton's poem "Quilting," in which she juxtaposes two worlds, one in which a mother and her daughter quilt together to meet their needs, another in which alchemists mumble as they transform chemistry into science.[1] Clifton asks at the end of the poem if these worlds can coexist. Clifton speaks from a modern African-American experience that informs many of the relational theological insights of Comstock and Heyward. She describes the difference between early modern epistemologies and modern African-American survival as one of two worlds drifting apart, with no guarantee of reconciliation or synthesis.

However, what musical performance of past works accomplishes is a continual re-establishment of connection between past and present, between worlds lost and worlds in the making. While every musical performance is an inevitably temporal phenomenon which comes to an end, each performance provisionally synthesizes present needs and desires with the hard facts left from the past. Worlds may continue spinning away from each other, but musical performance offers the opportunity to bring them back into interaction. While the dispersal of the text into various interpretive contexts makes it impossible to speak of a simple story that reflects and matches current needs, musical performances can lead bodies into fresh engagement with unexpected insights about what Jonathan and David can do.

1. Clifton, *Quilting*, 3.

What we find in examining how music from the past can generate homoerotic identities in the present is that whatever people in the past were doing and thinking, their legacies can spark new insights in the present. A spark, however, is not a mirror. A flame dances differently as it interacts with a match, a candle, dry firewood, or the metal it turns red. We do not need to narcissistically seek the self in the other in the quest to forge identity in relation to the past. When we stop to listen and let the dead speak, we find that what we seek is not always what they offer. It is this difference that reveals *relation* rather than *identity* in the first place.

This sense in which we find relation, rather than identity, with our forebears means that the historical malleability of homoerotic experience is not a stumbling block to finding inspiration in homoerotic experience in widely different contexts. Comstock's selective reading of the Jonathan and David story reveals more difference than similarity between his theological vision and the biblical narrative with which he grounds that vision. Jonathan's love for David did not open into egalitarian and multi-cultural social visions, as Comstock's theology does. Rather, Jonathan's love does not challenge a number of ethical stances that Comstock sees as inimical to the task of gay liberation. By turning from theological appropriation to exegetical debate, the fact that there is not an identity between modern gay identity and biblical visions of love between men becomes apparent. Rather, some elements of the story manage to cohere in a contemporary queer context, making for a tenuous link between two worlds that are more different than alike.

Relating different interpretations to each other is a theological task, because ultimately it is a way of bringing the layers and variety of human relations to consciousness, the first task in transforming non-mutual relations into mutual relations, a task that Carter Heyward ably describes as "godding." To remember the dead is to give their lives continued effect beyond the limits of their bodily existence. To struggle to remember the dead in terms they would recognize is to respect their integrity. To learn from the dead is to be empowered in relation to them. While relational theology models a distinct way of understanding the world, it of necessity must relate people to one another across conceptual divides that make for very different worldviews. What relational theology affirms is that God is revealed in the activity of making new and mutual relations with whomever one can.

At the same time, mutual relation does not mean one party submitting to the demands of another, but of finding common ground amidst differences. In this sense, it is not simply the job of Early Music performers to recreate the worlds of the past as accurately as is possible within the constraints of the fact that they are present day performers and not time machines. Rather, as people in the present who interact with music from the past, we have our own needs, demands, and desires which we bring to the dialogue with the past. That these needs are real does not negate the fact that they may not correspond to those of those with whom we dialogue through musical recreation of past worldviews. A relational understanding of musical interaction with the past shows a tendency in the debates over "authenticity" in Early Music performance to fall back into a dualism, rather than a distinction, between past and present. But it is precisely the praxis of musicking that makes such a dualism impossible to sustain. Music's inescapable temporality must be allowed to unsettle the tendency to fix thought into exclusionary binaries, and to embrace the ambiguities brought on by the ephemeral quality of existence.

It is precisely this refusal to fall into the trap of a dualistic either/or that allows us to reclaim both the biblical and musical traditions as sources of self-constitution and self-critique, and that allow us to see the past both as autonomous and subject to ethical judgment from present day vantage points. The details of the musical mediation of past and present offer new ways of integrating fidelity to biblical traditions and critique of said traditions. It becomes possible to stand with contemporary queer revisions of the biblical past without falling into confusion about the real differences between that past and our present.

Taking the range of interpretations offered both by composers and performers into account ultimately frees our understanding of Jonathan and David—and by extension our understandings of the biblical construction of friendship, politics, eroticism, and fidelity—from being a narrow prescription for action in the present. Rather, by exploring multiple possibilities, we find that turning to the past generates diversity rather than locking us into a tyrannical and authoritarian prescription that forecloses the possible futures new desires are always creating.

Bibliography

PRIMARY SOURCES

פירושים ל״ב עם גדולות מקראות. New York: Pardes Publishing House, 1951.

Berry, Lloyd E., ed. *The Geneva Bible, a facsimile of the 1560 edition.* "Introduction" by Lloyd E. Berry. Madison: University of Wisconsin Press, 1969.

Burmeister, Joachim. *Musical Poetics.* Translated by Benito V. Rivera. New Haven: Yale University Press, 1993.

Calvin, John. *Sermons on 2 Samuel: Chapters 1–13.* Translated by Douglas Kelly. Edinburgh: Banner of Truth Trust, 1992.

Campion, Thomas. *A New Way of Making Fowre Parts by Thomas Campion and Rules How to Compose by Giovanni Coprario.* Edited by Christopher R. Wilson. Aldershot, UK: Ashgate, 2003.

Chudleigh, Mary, Lady. *The Poems and Prose of Mary, Lady Chudleigh.* Edited by Margaret J. M. Ezell. New York: Oxford University Press, 1993.

Luther, Martin. *Die gantze Heilige Schrifft Deudsch, Wittenberg 1545.* 2 vols. Edited by Hans Volz. Munich: Rogner & Bernhard, 1972.

Morley, Thomas. *A Plain and Easy Introduction to Practical Music.* Edited by R. Alec Harman. New York: W. W. Norton, 1952.

Ornithiparcus, Andreas. *Andreas Ornithoparcus his Microlgus; or Introduction: containing the art of singing. Digested into foure bookes. Not only profitable but also necessary for all that are studious of musicke. Also the dimension and perfect use of the monochord according to Guido Aretinus. By John Dowland, lutanist.* London, Printed for T. Adams. Facsimile. San Marino: Huntington Library, 1940.

Ovid. *Metamorphoses.* Translated by A. D. Melville. Oxford: Oxford University Press, 1986.

The Praise of Musicke: wherein besides the antiquitie, dignitie, delectation & use thereof in civill matters, is also declared the sober and lawfull use of the same in the congregation and church of God. Oxenford: Joseph Barnes, 1586

Ravenscroft, Thomas. *A Briefe Discourse Of the true (but neglected) use of Charact'ring the Degrees.* A Facsimile of the London, 1614 Edition. New York: Broude Borthers, Ltd, 1976.

Sparks, H. F. D., ed. *The Apocryphal Old Testament.* Oxford: Clarendon Press, 1984.

Wither, George. *The Hymnes and Songs of the Church. Divided into two parts.* London, George Wither, 1623.

SECONDARY SOURCES

Abbate, Carolyn. *Unsung Voices: Opera and Musical Narrative in the Nineteenth Century.* Princeton: Princeton University Press, 1991.

Ackerman, Susan. *When Heroes Love: The Ambiguity of Eros in the Stories of Gilgamesh and David.* New York: Columbia University Press, 2005.

Adler, Rachel. *Engendering Judaism: An Inclusive Theology and Ethics.* Boston: Beacon, 1998.

Adorno, Theodor W. *Introduction to the Sociology of Music.* Translated by E. B. Ashton. New York: Seabury, 1976.

———. *Philosophy of Modern Music.* Translated by Anne G. Mitchell and Wesley V. Blomster. New York: Seabury, 1973.

———. *Prisms.* Translated by Samuel Weber and Shierry Weber. London: Neville Spearman Limited, 1967.

Agawu, Kofi. "Schubert's Sexuality: A Prescription for Analysis?" *Nineteenth-Century Music* 17:1 (1993) 79–82.

Alison, James. "The Gay Thing: Following the Still Small Voice." In *Queer Theology: Rethinking the Western Body,* edited by Gerard Loughlin, 50–62. Malden, MA: Blackwell, 2007.

Alter, Robert. *The Art of Biblical Narrative.* New York: Basic Books, 1981.

———. *The David Story: A Translation with Commentary of 1 and 2 Samuel.* New York: Norton, 1999.

Amis, Kingsley. *The Alteration.* New York: Viking, 1977.

Armour, Ellen T. *Deconstruction, Feminist Theology, and the Problem of Difference: Subverting the Race/Gender Divide.* Chicago: University of Chicago Press, 1999.

Attali, Jacques. *Noise: The Political Economy of Music.* Translated by Brian Massumi. Minneapolis: University of Minnesota Press, 1985.

Attinello, Paul. "Performance and/or Shame: A Mosaic of Gay (and Other) Perceptions." *Repercussions* 4:2 (1995) 97–130.

Bal, Mieke. *Death and Dissymmetry: The Politics of Coherence in the Book of Judges.* Chicago: University of Chicago Press, 1988.

———. *Lethal Love: Feminist-Literary Readings of Biblical Love Stories.* Bloomington: Indiana University Press, 1987.

Barbour, Reid. *English Epicures and Stoics: Ancient Legacies in Early Stuart Culture.* Amherst: University of Massachusetts Press, 1998.

Barker-Benfield, G. J. *The Culture of Sensibility: Sex and Society in Eighteenth-Century Britain.* Chicago: University of Chicago Press, 1992.

Barkin, Elaine. "Either/Other." *Perspectives of New Music* 30:2 (1992) 206–33.

Bartelmus, Rüdiger. "Handel and Jennens Oratorio 'Saul': A Late Musical and Dramatic Rehabilitation of the Figure of Saul." In *Saul in Story and Tradition,* edited by Carl S. Ehrlich, 284–307. Tübingen: Siebeck, 2006.

Begbie, Jeremy. *Theology, Music, and Time.* Cambridge: Cambridge University Press, 2000.

Benjamin, Walter. *Illuminations.* New York: Schocken, 1969.

Bennett, Harold. *Injustice Made Legal: Deuteronomic Law and the Plight of Widows, Strangers, and Orphans in Ancient Israel.* Grand Rapids: Eerdmans, 2002.

Berger, Peter, ed. *The Other Side of God: A Polarity in World Religions.* Garden City, N.Y.: Doubleday, 1981.

Bergeron, David Moore. *King James and Letters of Homoerotic Desire.* Iowa City: University of Iowa Press, 1999.

Bergeron, Katherine, and Philip V. Bohlman, eds. *Disciplining Music: Musicology and Its Canons.* Chicago: University of Chicago Press, 1992.

Berman, Joshua. *Created Equal: How the Bible Broke with Ancient Political Thought.* Oxford: Oxford University Press, 2008.

Bersani, Leo, and Ulysse Dutoit. *Caravaggio's Secrets.* Cambridge: MIT Press, 1998.

Bianconi, Lorenzo. *Music in the Seventeenth Century.* Translated by David Bryant. Cambridge: Cambridge University Press, 1987.

Biale, David. *Eros and the Jews: From Biblical Israel to Contemporary America.* New York: Basic Books, 1992.

Bird, Phyllis. "The Bible in Christian Ethical Deliberation Concerning Homosexuality: Old Testament Contributions." In *Homosexuality, Science, and the "Plain Sense" of Scripture,* edited by David Balch, 142–76. Grand Rapids: Eerdmans, 2000.

Blacking, John. "The Problem of 'Ethnic' Perceptions in the Semiotics of Music." In *The Sign in Music and Literature,* edited Wendy Steiner, 184–94. Austin: University of Texas Press, 1981.

Boer, Roland. *Knockin' on Heaven's Door: The Bible and Popular Culture.* New York and London: Routledge, 1999.

Boff, Clodovis. *Theology and Praxis: Epistemological Foundations.* Translated by Robert Barr. Maryknoll, NY: Orbis Books, 1987.

Borgerding, Todd. "Sic ego te dilegebam: Music, Homoeroticism, and the Sacred in Early Modern Europe" in *Gender, Sexuality, and Early Music,* edited Todd Borgerding, 249–63. New York and London: Routledge, 2002.

Boswell, John. *Christianity, Social Tolerance, and Homosexuality: Gay People in Western Europe from the Beginning of the Christian Era to the Fourteenth Century.* Chicago: University of Chicago Press, 1980.

———. *Same-Sex Unions in Premodern Europe.* New York: Villard Books, 1994.

Bouwsma, William. *John Calvin: A Sixteenth-Century Portrait.* New York: Oxford University Press, 1988.

Boyarin, Daniel. *Carnal Israel: Reading Sex in Talmudic Culture.* Berkeley: University of California Press, 1993.

Boyarin, Jonathan. "Reading Exodus into History." *New Literary History* 23:3 (1992) 523–54.

Braaten, Carl E. *History and Hermeneutics.* Philadelphia: Westminster, 1966.

Brackett, David. "James Brown's 'Superbad' and the Double-Voiced Utterance." *Popular Music* 11:3 (1992) 309–24.

Bravman, Scott. *Queer Fictions of the Past: History, Culture, and Difference.* Cambridge: Cambridge University Press, 1997.

Bray, Alan. *Homosexuality in Renaissance England, with a New Afterword.* New York: Columbia University Press, 1995.

Bredbeck, Gregory W. *Sodomy and Interpretation: Marlowe to Milton.* Ithaca and London: Cornell University Press, 1991.

Bibliography

Brett, Philip. "Music, Essentialism, and the Closet." In *Queering the Pitch: The New Gay and Lesbian Musicology.* Edited by Philip Brett, Elizabeth Wood, and Gary C. Thomas, 9–26. New York: Routledge, 1994.

———. "Piano Four-Hands: Schubert and the Performance of Gay Male Desire." *Nineteenth-Century Music* 21:2 (1997) 149–76.

———. *William Byrd and His Contemporaries: Essays and a Monograph.* Edited by Joseph Kerman and Davitt Moroney. Berkeley: University of California Press, 2007.

Brock, Rita Nakashima. *Journeys by Heart: A Christology of Erotic Power.* New York: Crossroad, 1991.

Brooten, Bernadette. *Love Between Women: Early Christian Responses to Female Homoeroticism.* Chicago: University of Chicago Press, 1996.

Brown, David. *Thomas Weelkes: A Biographical and Critical Study.* New York: Praeger, 1969.

Brown, Royal S. "The Tallis Scholars, Gimell, and Peter Phillips." *Fanfare* 15:6 (1992) 89–96.

Brueggeman, Walter. *Old Testament Theology: Essays on Structure, Theme, and Text.* Minneapolis: Fortress, 1992.

———. *A Social Reading of the Old Testament: Prophetic Approaches to Israel's Communal Life.* Edited by Patrick D. Miller. Minneapolis: Fortress, 1994.

Buber, Martin. *I and Thou.* Translated by Walter Kaufmann. New York: Scribner's Sons, 1970.

———. *Kingship of God,* 3rd edition. Translated by Richard Scheimann. New York: Harper and Row, 1967.

Burrows, Mark S., and Paul Rorem, eds. *Biblical Hermeneutics in Historical Perspective: Studies in Honor of Karlfried Froelich on His Sixtieth Birthday.* Grand Rapids: Eerdmans, 1991.

Butler, Judith. *Gender Trouble: Feminism and the Subversion of Identity.* New York: Routledge, 1990.

Butt, John. *Music Education and the Art of Performance in the German Baroque.* Cambridge: Cambridge University Press, 1994.

———. *Playing with History: The Historical Approach to Musical Performance.* Cambridge: Cambridge University Press, 2002.

Byatt, A. S. *Possession: A Romance.* New York, Random House, 1990.

Cage, John. *Silence: Lectures and Writings.* Middletown, CT: Wesleyan University Press, 1961.

Callaghan, Dympna. "The Terms of Gender: 'Gay' and 'Feminist' *Edward II.*" In *Feminist Readings of Early Modern Culture: Emerging Subjects,* edited by Valerie Traub, M. Lindsay Kaplan, and Dympna Callaghan, 275–301. Cambridge: Cambridge University Press, 1996.

Cathcart, Robin. "*Do di petto*: Covering the Castrato, the English Counter-tenor, and the Teachings of Manuel Garcia II." In *Sharing the Voices: The Phenomenon of Singing 2: Proceedings of the International Symposium, St. John's, Newfoundland, Canada, 1999,* edited by Brian A. Roberts and Andrea Margaret Rose, 51–59. St. John's: Faculty of Education, Memorial University of Newfoundland, 2000.

Champagne, John. *The Ethics of Marginality: A New Approach to Gay Studies.* Minneapolis: University of Minnesota Press, 1995.

Chancey, Karen. "The Amboyna Massacre in English Politics, 1624–1632." *Albion* 30:4 (Winter, 1998) 583–98.

Christ, Carol P. *Diving Deep and Surfacing: Women Writers on Spiritual Quest*. Boston: Beacon, 1980.

———. "Reverence for Life: The Need for a Sense of Finitude." In *Embodied Love: Sensuality and Relationship as Feminist Values*, edited by Paula M. Cooey, Sharon A. Farmer, and Mary Ellen Ross, 51–64. San Francisco: Harper and Row, 1987.

———. *She Who Changes: Re-Imagining the Divine in the World*. New York: Palgrave Macmillan, 2003.

Chua, Daniel K. L. *Absolute Music and the Construction of Meaning*. Cambridge: Cambridge University Press, 1999.

Citron, Marcia. *Gender and the Musical Canon*. Cambridge: Cambridge University Press, 1993.

Clark, Elizabeth A. *Reading Renunciation: Asceticism and Scripture in Early Christianity*. Princeton, NJ: Princeton University Press, 1999.

Clayton, Jay, and Eric Rothstein, eds. *Influence and Intertextuality in Literary History*. Madison: University of Wisconsin Press, 1991.

Clement, Catherine. *Opera, or Undoing of Women*. Translated by Betsy Wing. Minneapolis: University of Minnesota Press, 1988.

Clements, Ronald E. *Abraham and David: Genesis XXV and Its Meaning for Israelite Tradition*. Naperville, IL: Allenson, 1967.

Clifton, Lucille. *Quilting: Poems 1987–1990*. Brockport, NY: BOA Editions, Ltd. 1991.

Clines, David J. A. *Interested Parties: The Ideology of Writers and Readers of the Hebrew Bible*. Sheffield: Sheffield Academic, 1995.

———. *What Does Eve Do to Help? and Other Readerly Questions to the Old Testament*. Sheffield: JSOT Press, 1992.

Clines, David J. A., and Tamara C. Eskenazi, eds. *Telling Queen Michal's Story: An Experiment in Comparative Interpretation*. Sheffield: JSOT Press, 1991.

Cockayne, Emily. *Hubbub: Filth, Noise, and Stench in England, 1600–1770*. New Haven: Yale University Press, 2007.

Comstock, Gary David. *Gay Theology Without Apology*. Cleveland, OH: Pilgrim, 1993.

Cone, James H. *Black Theology and Black Power*. Maryknoll, NY: Orbis, 1997.

Conner, Randy P. *Blossom of Bone: Reclaiming the Connections between Homoeroticism and the Sacred*. San Francisco: HarperSanFrancisco, 1993.

Cook, Nicholas. *Musical Analysis and the Listener*. New York: Garland, 1989.

Cox-Miller, Patricia. "'Pleasure of the Text, Text of Pleasure': Eros and Language in Origen's Commentary on the Song of Songs." *Journal of the American Academy of Religion* 54:2 (1986) 241–53.

Craig, Clarence T. "Biblical Theology and the Rise of Historicism." *Journal of Biblical Literature* 62:4 (1943) 281–94.

Croatto, J. Severino. *Biblical Hermeneutics: Toward a Theory of Reading as the Production of Meaning*. Translated by Robert R. Barr. Maryknoll, NY: Orbis, 1987.

Crocker, Richard L. "Discant, Counterpoint, and Harmony." *Journal of the American Musicological Society* 15:1 (1962) 1–21.

Crompton, Louis. *Homosexuality and Civilization*. Cambridge: Harvard University Press, 2003.

Cross, Frank Moore. *Canaanite Myth and Hebrew Epic: Essays in the History of the Religion of Israel*. Cambridge: Harvard University Press, 1973.

Crossan, John Dominic. *Jesus: A Revolutionary Biography*. San Francisco: HarperSanFrancisco, 1994.

Bibliography

Cusick, Suzanne G. "Feminist Theory, Music Theory, and the Mind/Body Problem." *Perspectives of New Music* 32:1 (1994) 8–27.

———. "Gender and the Cultural Work of a Classical Music Performance." *Repercussions* 3:1 (1994) 77–110.

———. "Gender, Musicology, and Feminism." In *Rethinking Music*, edited by Nicholas Cook and Mark Everist, 471–98. Oxford: Oxford University Press, 1999.

———. "Music as Torture/Music as Weapon." *Transcultural Music Review/Revista transcultural de musica* 10 (2006). http://www.sibetrans.com/trans/trans10/cusick_eng.htm (accessed January 29, 2008).

———. "On a Lesbian Relation with Music: A Serious Effort Not to Think Straight." In *Queering the Pitch: The New Gay and Lesbian Musicology*, edited by Philip Brett, Elizabeth Wood, and Gary C. Thomas, 67–83. New York: Routledge, 1994.

Dahlhaus, Carl. *The Idea of Absolute Music*. Translated by Roger Lustig. Chicago: University of Chicago Press, 1989.

Daly, Mary. *Beyond God the Father: Toward a Philosophy of Women's Liberation*. Boston: Beacon, 1973.

———. *Gyn/Ecology: The Metaethics of Radical Feminism*. Boston: Beacon, 1978.

———. *Pure Lust: Elemental Feminist Philosophy*. Boston: Beacon, 1984.

Damrosch, David. *The Narrative Covenant: Transformations of Genre in Biblical Literature*. Ithaca, NY: Cornell University Press, 1987.

Darr, Katheryn Pfisterer. *Far More Precious Than Jewels: Perspectives on Biblical Women*. Louisville, KY: Westminster John Knox, 1991.

Davaney Sheila Greeve. "The Limits of the Appeal to Women's Experience." In *Shaping New Vision: Gender and Values in American Culture*, edited by Clarissa W. Atkinson, Constance H. Buchanan, and Margaret R. Miles, 31–49. Ann Arbor, MI: UMI Research, 1987.

———. *Pragmatic Historicism: A Theology for the Twenty-First Century*. Albany: State University of New York Press, 2000.

———. "Problems with Feminist Theory: Historicity and the Search for Sure Foundations." In *Embodied Love: Sensuality and Relationship as Feminist Values*, edited by Paula M. Cooey, Sharon A. Farmer, and Mary Ellen Ross, 79–95. San Francisco: Harper & Row, 1987.

Davies, Horton. *Worship and Theology in England, Volume 2: From Andrewes to Baxter and Fox*. Princeton, NJ: Princeton University Press, 1975.

Dawson, David. *Allegorical Readers and Cultural Revision in Ancient Alexandria*. Berkeley: University of California Press, 1992.

Dean, Winton. *Handel's Dramatic Oratorios and Masques*. Oxford: Clarendon, 1959.

DeAngelis, Michael. *Gay Fandom and Crossover Stardom: James Dean, Mel Gibson, and Keanu Reeves*. Durham: Duke University Press, 2001.

Dell'Antiono, Andrew. "The Sensual Sonata: Construction of Desire in Early Baroque Instrumental Music." *Repercussions* 1:2 (1992) 52–83.

DeMarco, Laura. "The Fact of the Castrato and the Myth of the Countertenor." *Musical Quarterly* 86:1 (2002) 174–85.

Derrida, Jacques. *Of Grammatology*. Translated by Gayatri Chakravorty Spivak. Baltimore: Johns Hopkins University Press, 1976.

diGrazia, Donna M. "Funerall Teares or Dolefull Songes? Reconsidering Historical Connections and Musical Resemblances in Early English 'Absalom' Settings." *Music and Letters* 90:4 (2009) 555–98.

Dinshaw, Carolyn. *Getting Medieval: Sexualities and Communities, Pre- and Post-Modern.* Durham: Duke University Press, 1999.

Douglas, Kelly Brown. *Sexuality and the Black Church: A Womanist Perspective.* Maryknoll, NY: Orbis Books, 1999.

Dreyfus, Lawrence. "Early Music Defended Against Its Devotees." *Musical Quarterly* 69:3 (1983) 297–322.

Duckles, Vincent. "The English Musical Elegy of the Late Renaissance." In *Aspects of Medieval and Renaissance Music: A Birthday Offering to Gustave Reese*, edited by Martin Bernstein, Hans Lenneberg, and Victor Yellin, 134–53. New York: Norton and Co., 1966.

Durkheim, Emile. *The Elementary Forms of Religious Life.* Translated by Karen E. Fields. New York: Free, 1995.

Eagleton, Terry. *The Ideology of the Aesthetic.* Oxford: Blackwell, 1990.

Ebeling, Gerhard. *Kirchengeschichte als Geschichte der Auslegung der Heiligen Schrift.* Tübingen: Mohr, 1947.

Eco, Umberto. "How Culture Conditions the Colors We See." In *On Signs*, edited by Marshall Blonsky, 157–75. Baltimore: Johns Hopkins University Press, 1985.

Edelman, Diana Vikander. "The Authenticity of 2 Sam 1, 26 in the Lament over Saul and Jonathan." *Scandinavian Journal of the Old Testament* 2:1 (1988) 66–75.

Edelman, Lee. *No Future: Queer Theory and the Death Drive.* Durham: Duke University Press, 2004.

Ehrlich, Carl S., ed. *Saul in Story and Tradition.* Tübingen: Mohr/Siebeck, 2006.

Eilberg-Schwartz, Howard. *The Savage in Judaism: An Anthropology of Israelite Religion and Ancient Judaism.* Bloomington: Indiana University Press, 1990.

Eisenstein, Elizabeth L. *The Printing Press as an Agent of Change: Communications and Cultural Transformations in Early Modern Europe.* Cambridge: Cambridge University Press, 1979.

Eisenstein, Zillah R., ed. *Capitalist Patriarchy and the Case for Socialist Feminism.* New York: Monthly Review, 1979.

Eliade, Mircea. *The Myth of the Eternal Return; or, Cosmos and History.* Translated by Willard R. Trask. Princeton, N.J.: Princeton University Press, 1971.

Ellens, Deborah L. *Women in the Sex Texts of Leviticus and Deuteronomy: A Comparative Conceptual Analysis.* New York: T. & T. Clark, 2008.

Elliott, Dyan. *Spiritual Marriage: Sexual Abstinence in Medieval Wedlock.* Princeton, NJ: Princeton University Press, 1993.

Emoff, Ron. *Recollecting from the Past: Musical Practice and Spirit Possession on the East Coast of Madagascar.* Middletown, CT: Wesleyan University Press, 2002.

Eng, David L., and Alice Y. Hom, eds. *Q & A: Queer in Asian America.* Philadelphia: Temple University Press, 1998.

Ensemble Alcatraz, et al. "Responses to 'On Prejudice and Early Music.'" *Historical Performance* 5:2 (1992) 73–83.

Epstein, Heidi. *Melting the Venusberg: A Feminist Theology of Music.* New York: Continuum, 2004.

Epstein, Julia, and Kristian Straub, eds. *Body Guards: The Cultural Politics of Gender Ambiguity.* New York: Routledge, 1991.

Ewbank, Inga-Stina. "The House of David in Renaissance Drama: A Comparative Study." *Renaissance Drama* 8 (1965) 3–40.

Bibliography

Exum, J. Cheryl. *Fragmented Women: Feminist (Sub)versions of Biblical Narratives.* Valley Forge, PA: Trinity Press International, 1993.

———. *Tragedy and Biblical Narrative: Arrows of the Almighty.* Cambridge: Cambridge University Press, 1992.

Falck, Robert, and Martin Picker."Contrafactum." In *The New Grove Dictionary of Music and Musicians,* edited by Staney Sadie, Vol. 6, 367–70. New York: Macmillan, 2001.

Fast, Susan. *In the Houses of the Holy: Led Zeppelin and the Power of Rock Music.* Oxford: Oxford University Press, 2001.

Fausto-Sterling, Anne. *Myths of Gender: Biological Theories about Men and Women.* New York: BasicBooks, 1992.

Feldman, Martha. "The Absent Mother in Opera Seria." In *Siren Songs: Representations of Gender and Sexuality in Opera,* edited by Mary Ann Smart, 29–46. Princeton, NJ: Princeton University Press, 2000.

———. *City Culture and the Madrigal at Venice.* Berkeley: University of California Press, 1995.

Fernbach, David. *The Spiral Path: A Gay Contribution to Human Survival.* Boston: Alyson Publications, 1981.

Ferrell, Lori Anne. *The Bible and the People.* New Haven: Yale University Press, 2008.

Fetterley, Judith. *The Resisting Reader: A Feminist Approach to American Fiction.* Bloomington: Indiana University Press, 1978.

Feuerbach, Ludwig. *The Essence of Christianity.* Translated by George Eliot. New York: Harper, 1957.

Fewell, Danna Nolan. "Deconstructive Criticism: Achsah and the (E)razed City of Writing." In *Judges and Method: New Approaches in Biblical Studies,* edited Gale A. Yee, 119–45. Minneapolis: Fortress, 1995.

Fewell, Danna Nolan, and David M. Gunn. *Gender, Power, and Promise: The Subject of the Bible's First Story.* Nashville: Abingdon, 1993.

Fish, Stanley. *Is There a Text in This Class? The Authority of Interpretive Communities.* Cambridge: Harvard University Press, 1980.

Flynn, Elizabeth A., and Patrocinio P. Schweickart, eds. *Gender and Reading: Essays on Readers, Texts, and Contexts.* Baltimore: Johns Hopkins University Press, 1986.

Fokkelman, J.P. *Narrative Art and Poetry in the Books of Samuel: A Full Interpretation Based on Stylistic and Structural Analyses, Volume 2: The Crossing Fates.* Dover, NH: Van Gorcum, 1986.

Fortunato, John. "The Last Committee on Sexuality (Ever)." *Christianity and Crisis* (February 18, 1991) 34–35.

Foucault, Michel. *The Archeology of Knowledge.* Translated by A. M. Sheridan Smith. New York: Harper & Row, 1972.

———. *The History of Sexuality, Volume 1: An Introduction.* Translated by Robert Hurley. New York: Vintage, 1980.

———. *The Order of Things: An Archeology of the Human Sciences.* New York: Vintage, 1973.

———. "What is an Author?" In *Language, Counter-Memory, Practice: Selected Essays and Interviews,* edited by Donald F. Bouchard, 113–38. Ithaca, NY: Cornell University Press, 1977.

Fradenburg, Louise, and Carla Freccero eds. *Premodern Sexualities.* New York: Routledge, 1996.

Freccero, Carla. *Queer/Early/Modern.* Durham: Duke University Press, 2006.

Frei, Hans. *The Eclipse of Biblical Narrative: A Study in Eighteenth- and Nineteenth-Century Hermeneutics.* New Haven, CT: Yale University Press, 1974.

Friedman, Richard Eliot. *Who Wrote the Bible?* San Francisco: HarperSanFrancisco, 1989.

Frontain, Raymond-Jean. "The Fortune in David's Eyes." *The Gay and Lesbian Review Worldwide* (July-August 2006). http://www.glreview.com/issues/13.4/13.4-frontain. php (accessed August 31, 2010).

Frontain, Raymond-Jean, and Jan Wojcik, eds. *The David Myth in Western Literature.* West Lafayette, IN: Purdue University Press, 1980.

Frow, John. *Marxism and Literary Theory.* Oxford: Blackwell, 1986.

Frymer-Kensky, Tikva. *In the Wake of the Goddesses: Women, Culture, and the Biblical Transformation of Pagan Myth.* New York: Free Press, 1992.

Fuchs, Esther. "'For I Have the Way of Women': Deception, Gender, and Ideology in Biblical Narrative." *Semeia* 42 (1988) 68–83.

———. "Who is Hiding the Truth? Deceptive Women and Biblical Androcentrism." In *Feminist Perspectives on Biblical Scholarship*, ed. Adela Yarbro Collins, 137–44. Atlanta: Scholars Press, 1985.

Fuller, Sophie, and Lloyd Whitsell, eds. *Queer Episodes in Music and Modern Identity.* Urbana: University of Illinois Press, 2002.

Fulton, Christopher. "The Boy Stripped by His Elders: Art and Adolescence in Renaissance Florence." *Art Journal* 56:2 How Men Look: On the Masculine Ideal and the Body Beautiful (1997) 31–40.

Fung, Richard. "Looking for my Penis: The Eroticized Asian in Gay Video Porn." In *How Do I Look? Queer Film and Video*, edited by Bad Object-Choices, 145–60. Seattle: Bay Press, 1991.

Gadamer, Hans-Georg. *Truth and Method*, 2nd rev. ed. Translated by Joel Weinsheimer and Donald G. Marshall. New York: Continuum, 1989.

Gagnon, Robert A. J. *The Bible and Homosexual Practice: Texts and Hermeneutics.* Nashville: Abingdon, 2001.

———. "Gays and the Bible: A Response to Walter Wink." *The Christian Century* (August 14–27, 2002) 40–43.

Galeano, Eduardo. *Open Veins of Latin America: Five Centuries of the Pillage of a Continent.* Translated by Cedric Belfrage. New York: Monthly Review, 1973.

Geertz, Clifford. *The Interpretation of Cultures: Selected Essays.* New York: Basic, 1973.

George, Mark. "Assuming the Body of the Heir Apparent: David's Lament." In *Reading Bibles, Writing Bodies*, edited by Timothy K. Beal and David M. Gunn, 164–74. London: Routledge, 1997.

Gilligan, Carol. *In a Different Voice: Psychological Theory and Women's Development.* Cambridge: Harvard University Press, 1982.

Gilman, Charlotte Perkins. *His Religion and Hers: A Study of the Faith of Our Fathers and the Work of Our Mothers.* Westport, CT: Hyperion, 1976.

Ginzberg, Louis. *The Legends of the Jews*, 7 vols. Baltimore: Johns Hopkins University Press, 1998.

Gluckman, Amy, and Betsy Reed, eds. *Homo Economics: Capitalism, Community, and Lesbian and Gay Life.* New York: Routledge, 1997.

Godt, Irving. "Prince Henry as Absalom in David's Lamentations." *Music and Letters* 61 (1981) 318–30.

Goehr, Lydia. *The Imaginary Museum of Musical Works: An Essay in the Philosophy of Music.* New York: Oxford University Press, 1992.

Bibliography

Goldberg, Jonathan. *Sodometries: Renaissance Texts, Modern Sexualities*. Stanford, CA: Stanford University Press, 1992.

Goldenberg, Naomi. "Archetypal Theory and the Separation of Mind and Body: Reason Enough to Turn to Freud?" In *Weaving the Visions: New Patterns in Feminist Spirituality*, edited by Judith Plaskow and Carol P. Christ, 244–55. San Francisco: Harper & Row, 1989.

Goss, Robert. *Jesus Acted Up: A Gay and Lesbian Manifesto*. San Francisco: HarperSanFrancisco, 1993.

Gössmann, Elisabeth. "History of Biblical Interpretation by European Women." In *Searching the Scriptures: Volume 1: A Feminist Introduction*, edited by Elisabeth Schüssler Fiorenza, 27–40. New York: Crossroad, 1993.

Grabbe, Lester L., ed. *Did Moses Speak Attic? Jewish Historiography and Scripture in the Hellenistic Period*. Sheffield: Sheffield University Press, 2001.

Gramit, David. "Constructing a Victorian Schubert: Music, Biography, and Cultural Values." *Nineteenth-Century Music* 17:1 (1993) 65–78.

Grant, Robert M. *A Short History of the Interpretation of the Bible*, 2nd ed. Philadelphia: Fortress, 1984.

Greenberg, David F. *The Construction of Homosexuality*. Chicago: University of Chicago Press, 1988.

Greenberg, Steven. *Wrestling with God and Men: Homosexuality in the Jewish Tradition*. Madison, WI: University of Wisconsin Press, 2004.

Greenblatt, Stephen. *Shakespearean Negotiations: The Circulation of Social Energy in Renaissance England*. Berkeley: University of California Press, 1988.

Grenz, Stanley J. *Welcoming, But Not Affirming: An Evangelical Response to Homosexuality*. Louisville, KY: Westminster John Knox, 1998.

Guck, Marion. "Music Loving, or, the Relationship with the Piece." *Journal of Musicology* 15:3 (1997) 343–52.

Guest, Deryn. *When Deborah Met Jael: Lesbian Biblical Hermeneutics*. London: SCM, 2005.

Guest, Deryn, et al., eds. *The Queer Bible Commentary*. London: SCM, 2006.

Guha, Ranjit. *History at the Limit of World-History*. New York: Columbia University Press, 2002.

Gunn, David. *The Fate of King Saul: An Interpretation of a Biblical Story*. Sheffield: University of Sheffield, 1980.

Habermas, Jürgen. "A Review of Gadamer's *Truth and Method*." In *Hermeneutics and Modern Philosophy*, edited by Brice R. Wachterhauser, 243–76. Albany: State University of New York Press, 1986.

Hackett, Jo Ann. "1 and 2 Samuel." In *The Women's Bible Commentary*, edited by Carol A. Newsom and Sharon H. Ringe, 85–95. Louisville, KY: Westminster John Knox, 1992.

Halperin, David M. *How to Do the History of Homosexuality*. Chicago: University of Chicago Press, 2002.

———. *One Hundred Years of Homosexuality: And Other Essays on Greek Love*. New York: Routledge, 1990.

Halpern, Baruch. *David's Secret Demons: Messiah, Murderer, Traitor, King*. Grand Rapids: Eerdmans, 2001.

Hamm, Charles. "Privileging the Moment of Reception: Music and Radio in South Africa." In *Music and Text: Critical Inquiries*, edited by Steven Paul Scher, 21–37. Cambridge: Cambridge University Press, 1992.

Hanning, Barbara Russano. "Monteverdi's Three Genera: A Study in Terminology." In *Musical Humanism and Its Legacy: Essays in Honor of Claude Palisca*, edited by Nancy Kovaleff Baker and Barbara Russano Hanning, 145–70. Stuyvesant, NY: Pendragon Press, 1992.

Harding, James E. *The Love of David and Jonathan: Ideology, Text, Reception.* Sheffield: Equinox, 2013.

Harley, John. *Orlando Gibbons and the Gibbons Family of Musicians.* Aldershot: Ashgate, 1999.

Harnack, Adolf von. *What is Christianity.* Translated by Thomas Baily Saunders. New York: Harper & Row, 1957.

Harris. Ellen T. *Handel as Orpheus: Voice and Desire in the Chamber Cantatas.* Cambridge, MA: Harvard University Press, 2001.

———. "Homosexual Context and Identity: Reflections on the Reception of *Handel as Orpheus.*" In *Queer People: Negotiations and Expressions of Homosexuality, 1700–1800*, edited by Chris Mounsey and Caroline Gonda, 41–66. Lewisburg: Bucknell University Press, 2007.

———. "Silence as Sound: Handel's Sublime Pauses." *Journal of Musicology* 22:4 (2005) 521–58.

Harrison, Beverly Wildung. *Making the Connections: Essays in Feminist Social Ethics*, edited by Carol S. Robb. Boston: Beacon, 1985.

———. *Our Right to Choose: Toward a New Ethic of Abortion.* Boston: Beacon, 1983.

Hart, Vaughan. *Art and Magic in the Court of the Stuarts.* London: Routledge, 1994.

Hartman, Keith. *Congregations in Conflict: The Battle over Homosexuality.* New Brunswick, NJ: Rutgers University Press, 1996.

Harvey, Van A. *The Historian and the Believer: The Morality of Historical Knowledge and Christian Belief.* Philadelphia: Westminster, 1966.

Haskell, Harry. *The Early Music Revival: A History.* London: Thames and Hudson, 1988.

Haynes, Bruce. *The End of Early Music: A Period Performer's History of Music for the Twenty-First Century.* Oxford: Oxford University Press, 2007.

Heacock, Anthony. *Jonathan Loved David: Manly Love in the Bible and the Hermeneutics of Sex.* Sheffield: Sheffield Phoenix Press, 2011.

———. "Wrongly Framed? The 'David and Jonathan Narrative' and the Writing of Biblical Homosexuality [sic]." *The Bible and Critical Theory* 3:2 (2007) 22.1–22.14.

Heisig, James W. "Non-I and Thou: Nishida, Buber, and the Moral Consequences of Self-Actualization." *Philosophy East and West* 50:2 (2000) 179–207.

Held, Virginia, ed. *Justice and Care: Essential Readings in Feminist Ethics.* Boulder: Westview, 1995.

Helfand, Duke. "Gay Issues May Splinter Churches." *Los Angeles Times* (May 26, 2009). http://www.latimes.com/news/local/la-me-marriage26-2009may26,0,4342616.story?page=1 (accessed May 26, 2009).

Helminiak, Daniel A. *What the Bible Really Says about Homosexuality*, Millennium ed. Tajique, NM: Alamo Square, 2000.

Hengel, Martin. *Judaism and Hellenism: Studies in Their Encounter during the Early Hellenistic Period.* Translated by John Bowden. Philadelphia: Fortress, 1974.

Hewitt, Marsha Aileen. *Critical Theory of Religion: A Feminist Analysis.* Minneapolis: Fortress Press. 1995.

Bibliography

Heyward, Carter. "Doing Theology in a Counterrevolutionary Situation." In *The Future of Liberation Theology: Essays in Honor of Gustavo Gutierrez*, edited by Marc H. Ellis and Otto Maduro, 397–409. Maryknoll, NY: Orbis, 1989.

———. *God in the Balance: Christian Spirituality in Times of Terror*. Cleveland: Pilgrim, 2002.

———. *Our Passion for Justice: Images of Power, Sexuality, and Liberation*. New York: Pilgrim, 1984.

———. *The Redemption of God: A Theology of Mutual Relation*. Lanham, MD: University Press of America, 1982.

———. *Staying Power: Reflections on Gender, Justice, and Compassion*. Cleveland: Pilgrim, 1995.

———. *Touching Our Strength: The Erotic as Power and the Love of God*. San Francisco: Harper & Row, 1989.

———. *When Boundaries Betray Us: Beyond Illusions of What Is Ethical in Therapy and Life*. San Francisco: HarperSanFrancisco, 1993.

Heyward, Carter, with the Amanecida Collective. *Revolutionary Forgiveness: Feminist Reflections on Nicaragua*. Maryknoll, NY: Orbis, 1987.

Hicks, Anthony. "Handel's *Saul*." In *Handel Studies: A Gedenkschrift for Howard Serwer*, edited by Richard G. King , 247–51. Hillsdale, NY: Pendragon Press, 2009.

Hill, Christopher. *The World Turned Upside Down: Radical Ideas During the English Revolution*. New York: Viking Press, 1972.

Himbaza, Innocent, Adrien Schenker, and Jean-Baptiste Edart. *Clarifications sur l'homosexualité dans la Bible*. Paris: Cerf, 2007.

Hite, Devan. "Pursuing the 'Root of Jesse': Investigating the Male Relationships of David and Jesus post-*Psychopathia Sexualis*." Paper given at the American Academy of Religion, San Diego, 2007.

Ho, Craig Y. S. "The Stories of the Family Troubles of Judah and David: A Study of Their Literary Links." *Vetus Testamentum* 49:4 (1999) 514–31.

Holsinger, Bruce. *Music, Body, and Desire in Medieval Culture: Hildegard of Bingen to Chaucer*. Stanford, CA: Stanford University Press, 2001.

———. "Sodomy and Resurrection: The Homoerotic Subject of the *Divine Comedy*." In *Premodern Sexualities*, edited by Louise Fradenburg and Carla Freccero, 243–74. New York, Routledge, 1996.

Holstun, James. *Ehud's Dagger: Class Struggle in the English Revolution*. London: Verso, 2000.

Hood, Mantle. "The Challenge of Bi-Musicality." *Ethnomusicology* 4:2 (1960) 55–59.

Hood, Robert E. *Must God Remain Greek? Afro Cultures and God-Talk*. Minneapolis: Fortress, 1990.

Hopcke, Robert H. *Jung, Jungians, and Homosexuality*. Boston: Shambhala, 1989.

Horner, Tom. *Jonathan Loved David: Homosexuality in Biblical Times*. Philadelphia: Westminster, 1978.

Horowitz, Joseph. *Classical Music in America: A History of Its Rise and Fall*. New York: Norton, 2005.

Howard, Thomas A. *Religion and the Rise of Historicism: W. M. L. De Wette, Jacob Burckhardt, and the Theological Origins of Nineteenth-Century Historical Consciousness*. Cambridge: Cambridge University Press, 2000.

Hughes, Richard T. *Myths America Lives By*. Urbana: University of Illinois Press, 2005.

Hunt, Mary. *Fierce Tenderness: A Feminist Theology of Friendship*. New York: Crossroad, 1991.

———. "Medals on Our Blouses? A Feminist Theological Look at Women in Combat." In *Feminist Theological Ethics: A Reader*, edited by Lois Daly, 315–25. Louisville, KY: Westminster John Knox, 1994.

Hutson, Lorna. *The Usurer's Daughter: Male Friendship and Fictions of Women in Sixteenth-Century England*. New York: Routledge, 1994.

Ingarden, Roman. *The Work of Music and the Problem of Its Identity*. Translated by Adam Czierniawski. Berkeley: University of California Press, 1986.

Ingram, David. "The Historical Genesis of the Gadamer/Habermas Controversy." *Auslegung* 10 (1983) 86–151.

———. "The Possibility of a Communication Ethic Reconsidered: Habermas, Gadamer, and Bourdieu on Discourse." *Man and World* 15 (1982) 149–61.

Isherwood, Lisa. "Interview by Lisa Isherwood with Carter Heyward." *Feminist Theology* 25 (2000) 105–11.

Jackson, Earl, Jr. *Strategies of Deviance: Studies in Gay Male Representation*. Bloomington: Indiana University Press, 1995.

Jaeger, C. Stephen. *The Envy of Angels: Cathedral Schools and Social Ideals in Medieval Europe, 950–1250*. Philadelphia: University of Pennsylvania Press, 1994.

Jakobsen, Janet R., and Ann Pellegrini, eds. *Secularisms*. Durham: Duke University Press, 2008.

Jantzen, Grace. *Becoming Divine: Towards a Feminist Philosophy of Religion*. Bloomington: Indiana University Press, 1999.

———. "Good Sex: Beyond Private Pleasure." in *Good Sex: Feminist Perspectives from the World's Religions*, edited by Patricia Beattie Jung, Mary E. Hunt, and Radhika Balakrishnan, 3–14. New Brunswick: Rutgers University Press, 2002.

Jennings, Theodore. *Jacob's Wound: Homoerotic Narrative in the Literature of Ancient Israel*. New York: Continuum, 2005.

———. *Plato or Paul?: The Origins of Western Homophobia*. Cleveland: Pilgrim, 2009.

Jobling, David. *1 Samuel*. Collegeville, MN: Liturgical, 1998.

Johnson, Barbara. *The Feminist Difference: Literature, Psychoanalysis, Race, and Gender*. Cambridge: Harvard University Press, 1998.

Johnston, Mark Albert. *Beard Fetish in Early Modern England: Sex, Gender, and Registers of Value*. Surrey: Ashgate, 2011.

Jones, Ann Rosalind. *The Currency of Eros: Women's Love Lyric in Europe, 1540–1620*. Bloomington: Indiana University Press, 1990.

Kaiser, Otto. "David und Jonathan: Tradition, Redaktion, und Geschichte in I Sam 16–20: Ein Versuch." *Ephemerides Theologicae Lovaniensis* 66 (1990) 281–96.

Katz, David S. *God's Last Word: Reading the English Bible from the Reformation to Fundamentalism*. New Haven: Yale University Press, 2004.

Katz, Jonathan Ned. *The Invention of Heterosexuality*. New York: Dutton, 1995.

———. *Love Stories: Sex Between Men before Homosexuality*. Chicago: University of Chicago Press, 2001.

Katz, Mark. *Capturing Sound: How Technology Has Changed Music*. Berkeley: University of California Press, 2004.

Kaufman, Gordon. *God the Problem*. Cambridge: Harvard University Press, 1972.

Keller, Catherine. *Face of the Deep: A Theology of Becoming*. London and New York: Routledge, 2003.

Bibliography

———. *From a Broken Web: Separation, Sexism, and the Self.* Boston: Beacon, 1986.

Kendall, Kathryn M. "Women in Lesotho and the (Western) Construction of Homophobia." In *Female Desires: Same-Sex Relations and Transgender Practices across Cultures*, edited by Evelyn Blackwood and Saskia E. Wieringa, 157–78. New York: Columbia University Press, 1999.

Kendall, R. T. *Calvin and English Calvinism to 1649.* New York: Oxford University Press, 1979.

Kerman, Joseph. *Contemplating Music: Challenges to Musicology.* Cambridge: Harvard University Press, 1985.

———. "A Few Canonic Variations." In *Write All These Down: Essays on Music*, 33–50. Berkeley: University of California Press, 1994.

Kerman, Joseph, et al. "The Early Music Debate: Ancients, Moderns, Postmoderns." *Journal of Musicology* 10:1 (1992) 113–30.

Kingsbury, Henry. *Music, Talent, and Performance: A Conservatory Cultural System.* Philadelphia: Temple University Press, 1988.

Kirkendale, Ursula. "The Source for Bach's *Musical Offering*: The *Institutio oratoria* of Quintilian." *Journal of the American Musicological Society* 33:1 (1980) 88–141.

Kirkendale, Warren. "Ciceronians versus Aristotelians on the Ricercar as Exordium, from Bembo to Bach." *Journal of the American Musicological Society* 32:1 (1979) 1–44.

Knauf, E. A. "Die Priesterschrift und die Geschichten der Deuteronomisten." In *The Future of the Deuteronomistic History* ed. Thoms Römer, 102–18. Leuven: Leuven University Press, 2000.

Knight, Gladys. *David the King.* New York: Dial Press, 1946.

Koch, Timothy R. "Cruising as Methodology: Homoeroticism and the Scriptures." In *Queer Commentary and the Hebrew Bible*, edited by Ken Stone, 169–80. Cleveland: Pilgrim, 2001.

Koestenbaum, Wayne. *Double Talk: The Erotics of Male Literary Collaboration.* New York: Routledge, 1989.

———. *The Queen's Throat: Opera, Homosexuality, and the Mystery of Desire.* New York: Vintage, 1993.

———. "Queering the Pitch: A Posy of Definitions and Impersonations." In *Queering the Pitch: The New Gay and Lesbian Musicology*, edited by Philip Brett, Elizabeth Wood, and Gary C. Thomas, 1–5. New York: Routledge, 1994.

Kopelson, Kevin. *Beethoven's Kiss: Pianism, Perversion, and the Mastery of Desire.* Stanford, CA: Stanford University Press, 1996.

Kramer, Lawrence. "Culture and Musical Hermeneutics: The Salome Complex." *Cambridge Opera Journal* 2:3 (1990) 269–94.

———. *Why Classical Music Still Matters.* Berkeley: University of California Press, 2007.

Kristeva, Julia. *Revolution in Poetic Language.* Translated by Margaret Waller. New York: Columbia University Press, 1984.

Kugel, James L. *In Potiphar's House: The Interpretive Life of Biblical Texts.* Cambridge: Harvard University Press, 1990.

Kuhn, Thomas S. *The Structure of Scientific Revolutions*, 2nd ed. Chicago: University of Chicago Press, 1970.

Kwok Pui-lan. *Discovering the Bible in the Non-Biblical World.* Maryknoll, NY: Orbis, 1995.

LaMay, Thomasin. "Madalena Casulana: My Body Knows Unheard of Songs." In *Gender, Sexuality, and Early Music*, edited by Todd M. Borgerding, 41–71. New York: Routledge, 2002.

Lammers, Heike Sigrid. "The *Planctus* Repertory in the *Carmina Burana*." In *The Echo of Music: Essays in Honor of Marie Louise Göllner*, edited by Blair Sullivan, 75–99. Warren, MI: Harmonie Park, 2004.

Langlamet, François. "'David-Jonathan-Saül' ou le 'Livre de Jonathan' 1 Sam 16:14—2 Sam 1:27." *Revue Biblique* 101:3 (1994) 326–54.

———. "De 'David, Fils de Jessé' au 'Livre de Jonathan': Deux Éditions divergents de L'Ascension de David' en 1 Sam 16—2 Sam 1?" *Revue Biblique* 100:3 (1993) 321–57.

Le Guin, Elizabeth. *Boccherini's Body: An Essay in Carnal Musicology*. Berkeley: University of California Press, 2006.

League, Kathleen RoseAnne. "Radical Formalism and the Working Class: A Critical Articulation of Adorno and Bourdieu." MA thesis, DePaul University, 1992.

Lebrecht, Norman. *Who Killed Classical Music? Maestros, Managers, and Corporate Politics*. Seacaucus, NJ: Carol, 1997.

Lerner, Gerda. *The Creation of Feminist Consciousness: From the Middle Ages to Eighteen-seventy*. New York: Oxford University Press, 1993.

Leuchter, Mark. *The Polemics of Exile in Jeremiah 26–45*. Cambridge: Cambridge University Press, 2008.

Levinas, Emmanuel. *Totality and Infinity: An Essay on Exteriority*. Translated by Alphonso Lingis. Pittsburgh: Duquesne University Press, 1969.

Levine, Lawrence. *Highbrow/Lowbrow: The Making of Cultural Hierarchy in America*. Cambridge: Harvard University Press, 1988.

Levy, Janet. "Covert and Casual Values in Recent Writing About Music." *Journal of Musicology* 5:1 (1987) 3–27.

Lewin, Tamar. "Are These Parties for Real?" *New York Times*, (June 30, 2005). http://www.nytimes.com/2005/06/30/fashion/thursdaystyles/30rainbow.html.

Linafelt, Tod. "Taking Women in Samuel: Readers/Responses/Responsibility." In *Reading Between Texts: Intertextuality and the Hebrew Bible*, edited by Danna Nolan Fewell, 99–113. Louisville, KY: Westminster John Knox, 1992.

Linscheid, John. "Our Story in God's Story: How I Began Reading the Bible through Gay Eyes." *The Other Side* 23:6 (1987) 32–36.

Lohfink, Norbert. *Theology of the Pentateuch: Themes of the Priestly Narrative and Deuteronomy*. Translated by Linda M. Maloney. Minneapolis: Fortress, 1994.

Lorde, Audre. *Sister Outsider*. Freedom, CA: Crossing, 1984.

Lüdemann, Gerd. *The Unholy in Holy Scripture: The Dark Side of the Bible*. Louisville, KY: Westminster John Knox, 1997.

McCarter, P. Kyle. *1 Samuel: A New Translation with Introduction and Commentary*. Anchor Bible. New York: Doubleday, 1980.

McClary, Susan. "The Blasphemy of Talking Politics During Bach Year." In *Music and Society: The Politics of Composition, Performance, and Reception*, edited by Richard Leppert and Susan McClary, 13–62. Cambridge: Cambridge University Press, 1987.

———. "Constructions of Subjectivity in Schubert's Music." In *Queering the Pitch: The New Gay and Lesbian Musicology*, edited by Philip Brett, Elizabeth Wood, and Gary C. Thomas, 205–33. New York: Routledge, 1994.

———. "Different Drummers: Theorizing Music by Women Composers." In *Musics and Feminisms*, edited by Sally McArthur and Cate Poynton, 79–86. Sydney: Australian Music Centre, 1999.

———. *Feminine Endings: Music: Gender, and Sexuality*. Minneapolis: University of Minnesota Press, 1991.

———. "Music and Sexuality: On the Steblin/Solomon Debate." *Nineteenth-Century Music* 17:1 (1993) 83–88.

———. *Reading Music: Selected Essays*. Aldershot: Ashgate, 2007.

———. "Terminal Prestige: The Case of Avant-Garde Music Composition." In *Keeping Score: Music, Disciplinarity, Culture*, edited by David Schwarz, Anahid Kassabian, and Lawrence Siegel, 54–74. Charlottesville: University of Virginia Press, 1997.

McCleary, Rollan. *A Special Illumination: Authority, Inspiration, and Heresy in Gay Spirituality*. London: Equinox, 2004.

MacCulloch, Diarmaid. *The Reformation: A History*. New York: Viking, 2003.

McDonald, Dennis Ronald. *The Legend and the Apostle: The Battle for Paul in Story and Canon*. Philadelphia: Westminster, 1983.

McGeary, Thomas. "Gendering Opera: Italian Opera as the Feminine Other in Britain, 1700–42." *Journal of Musicological Research* 14 (1994) 17–34.

———. "Review: A Gay-Studies Handel." *Early Music* 30:4 (2002) 608–12.

McGuire, Brian Patrick. *Friendship and Community: The Monastic Experience, 350–1250*. Kalamazoo, MI: Cistercian, 1988.

McKenzie, Steven. *King David: A Biography*. Oxford: Oxford University Press, 2000.

McKnight, Edgar V. *The Bible and the Reader: An Introduction to Literary Criticism*. Philadelphia: Fortress, 1985.

Manuel, Peter. *Cassette Culture: Popular Music and Technology in North India*. Chicago: Chicago University Press, 1993.

Marcuse. Herbert. *Eros and Civilization: A Philosophical Inquiry into Freud*. Boston: Beacon, 1966.

Margolis, Joseph. *Historied Thought, Constructed World: A Conceptual Primer for the Turn of the Millennium*. Berkeley: University of California Press, 1995.

Marissen. Michael. *Lutheranism, Anti-Judaism, and Bach's St. John Passion: With an Annotated Literal Translation of the Libretto*. New York: Oxford University Press, 1998.

Masten, Jeffrey. *Textual Intercourse: Collaboration, Authorship, and Sexualities in Renaissance Drama*. Cambridge: Cambridge University Press, 1997.

Mathews, Shailer. *The Growth of the Idea of God*. New York: Macmillan, 1931.

Maus, Fred. "Glamour and Evasion: The Fabulous Ambivalence of the Pet Shop Boys." *Popular Music* 20:3 (2001) 379–93.

———. "Learning from 'Occasional' Writing." *Repercussions* 6:2 (2001) 5–23.

———. "Love Stories." *Repercussions* 4:2 (1995) 86–96.

———. "Masculine Discourse in Music Theory." *Perspectives of New Music* 31:2 (1993) 264–93.

Mendenhall, George. *Law and Covenant in Israel and the Ancient Near East*. Pittsburgh: Biblical Colloquium, 1955

Miller, D. A. *Place for Us: Essay on the Broadway Musical*. Cambridge: Harvard University Press, 1998.

Miller, Felicia. "*Farinelli*'s Electronic Hermaphrodite and the Contralto Tradition." In *The Work of Opera: Genre, Nationhood, and Sexual Difference*, edited by Richard Dellamora and Daniel Fischlin, 73–92. New York: Columbia University Press, 1997.

Miller, Leta E., and Fredric Lieberman. *Lou Harrison: Composing a World*. New York: Oxford University Press, 1998.

Miscall, Peter. *1 Samuel: A Literary Reading*. Bloomington: Indiana University Press, 1986.

Monson, Craig. *Disembodied Voices: Music and Culture in an Early Modern Italian Convent*. Berkeley: University of California Press, 1995.

———. "Thomas Myriell's Manuscript Collections: One View of Musical Taste in Jacobean London." *Journal of the American Musicological Society* 30:3 (1977) 419–65.

Moon, Dawne. *God, Sex, and Politics: Homosexuality and Everyday Theologies*. Chicago: University of Chicago Press, 2004.

Moore, Allan. Review of *Progressive Rock Recosidered*, edited by Kevin Holm-Hudson (New York: Routledge, 2002). *Twentieth-Century Music* 1:2 (2004) 293–97.

Moore, Stephen. *God's Beauty Parlor: And Other Queer Spaces In and Around the Bible*. Stanford: Stanford University Press, 2001.

Moroney, Muffie. "A Conversation with Carter Heyward, Pioneer Episcopal Priest." http://www.brigidsplace.org/journal/A-Conversation-with-Carter-Heyward.asp (accessed January 30, 2008).

Morris, Mitchell. "On Gaily Reading Music." *Repercussions* 1:1 (1992) 48–64.

———. "Musical Virtues." In *Beyond Structural Listening?: Postmodern Modes of Hearing*, edited by Andrew Dell'Antonio, 44–69. Berkeley: University of California Press, 2004.

———. "Reading as an Opera Queen." In *Musicology and Difference: Gender and Sexuality in Music Scholarship*, edited by Ruth A. Solie, 184–200. Berkeley: University of California Press, 1993.

Mosala, Itemelung. *Biblical Hermeneutics and Black Theology in South Africa*. Grand Rapids: Eerdmans, 1989.

Mowitt, John. "The Sound of Music in the Era of Its Electronic Reproducibility." In *Music and Society: The Politics of Composition, Performance and Reception*, edited by Richard Leppert and Susan McClary, 173–97. Cambridge: Cambridge University Press, 1987.

Mud Flower Collective. *God's Fierce Whimsy: Christian Feminism in Christian Education*. New York: Pilgrim Press, 1985.

Mullen, Theodore E. *Narrative History and Ethnic Boundaries: The Deuteronomistic Historian and the Creation of Israelite National Identity*. Atlanta, GA: Scholars, 1993.

Muxfeldt, Kristina. "Political Crimes and Liberty, or Why Would Schubert Eat a Peacock?" *Nineteenth-Century Music* 17:1 (1993) 47–64.

Nakanose, Shigeyuki. *Josiah's Passover: Sociology and the Liberating Bible*. Maryknoll, NY: Orbis, 1993.

Naphy, William. "Sodomy in Early Modern Geneva: Various Definitions, Diverse Verdicts." In *Sodomy in Early Modern Europe*, edited by Tom Betteridge, 94–111. Manchester: Manchester University Press, 2002.

Nardelli, Jean-Fabrice. *Homosexuality and Liminality in the* Gilgameš *and* Samuel. Amsterdam: Hakkert, 2007.

Nelson, James B. *Embodiment: An Approach to Sexuality and Christian Theology*. Minneapolis: Augsburg, 1978.

Nessan, Craig. *Orthopraxis or Heresy: The North American Theological Response to Latin American Liberation Theology.* Atlanta: Scholars, 1989.

Neubauer, John. *The Emancipation of Music from Language: Departure from Mimesis in Eighteenth-Century Aesthetics.* New Haven: Yale University Press, 1986.

Neusner, Jacob. "The Doctrine of Torah." In *The Blackwell Companion to Judaism,* edited by Jacob Neusner and Alan J. Avery-Peck, 193–211. Oxford: Blackwell, 2000.

Niditch, Susan. *Oral World and Written Word: Ancient Israelite Literature.* Louisville, KY: Westminster John Knox, 1996.

Niebuhr, Reinhold. *Moral Man and Immoral Society.* New York: Charles Scribner's Sons, 1960.

Nietzsche, Friedrich. *Sämtliche Werke: Kritische Studienausgabe in 15 Einzelbänden,* edited by Giorgio Colli and Mazzino Montinari. Berlin: de Gruyter, 1988.

Nissinen, Martti. *Homoeroticism in the Biblical World: A Historical Perspective.* Translated by Kirsi Stjerna. Minneapolis: Fortress, 1998.

———. "Die Liebe von David und Jonathan als Frage der modernen Exegese." *Biblica* 80 (1994) 249–63.

Noll, Kurt L. *The Faces of David.* Sheffield: Sheffield Academic, 1997.

Norris, David. "Homosexual People and the Christian Churches in Ireland: A Minority and Its Oppressors." *The Crane Bag* 5:1 (1981) 31–37.

Norton, Rictor. *Mother Clap's Molly House: The Gay Subculture in England, 1700–1830.* Stroud, Gloucestershire: Chalford, 2006.

Noth, Martin. *The Deuteronomistic History.* Sheffield: JSOT Press, 1981.

Oestreich, James R. "Hallelujah Indeed: Debating Handel's Anti-Semitism." *New York Times* (April 23, 2007) B3.

Olyan, Saul. "'Surpassing the Love of Women': Another Look at 2 Samuel 1:26 and the Relationship of David and Jonathan." In *Authorizing Marriage? Canon, Tradition, and Critique in the Blessing of Same-Sex Unions,* edited by Mark D. Jordan, 7–16. Princeton, NJ: Princeton University Press, 2006.

———. "'And With a Male You Shall Not Lie the Lying down of a Woman': On the Meaning and Significance of Leviticus 18:22 and 20:13." *Journal of the History of Sexuality,* Vol. 5, No. 2 (October, 1994), 179–206.

Owens, Jessie Ann. "Introduction: Soundscapes of Early Modern England." In *"Noyses, sounds, and sweet aires": Music in Early Modern England,* edited by Jessie Ann Owens, 8–19. Washington, DC: Folger Shakespeare Library, 2006.

Paddison, Max. *Adorno's Aesthetics of Music.* Cambridge: Cambridge University Press, 1993.

Pagels, Elaine. *Adam, Eve, and the Serpent.* New York: Random House, 1988.

Pardes, Ilana. *Countertraditions in the Bible: A Feminist Approach.* Cambridge: Harvard University Press, 1992.

Parris, David Paul. *Reception Theory and Biblical Hermeneutics.* Eugene, OR: Pickwick, 2009.

Patai, Raphael. *Sex and Family in the Bible and Middle East.* Garden City, NY: Doubleday, 1959.

Patel, Aniruddh D. *Music, Language, and the Brain.* Oxford: Oxford University Press, 2008.

Pauck, Wilhelm, ed. *Melanchthon and Bucer.* Louisville, KY: Westminster John Knox, 1969.

Pequigney, Joseph. "Sodomy in Dante's *Inferno* and *Purgatorio.*" *Representations* 36 (1991) 22–42.

Peraino, Judith A. "I Am An Opera: Identifying with Henry Purcell's *Dido and Aeneas.*" In *En Travesti: Women, Gender Subversion, Opera,* edited by Corinne E. Blackmer and Patricia Juliana Smith, 99–131. New York: Columbia University Press, 1995.

———. *Listening to the Sirens: Musical Technologies of Queer Identity from Homer to Hedwig.* Berkeley: University of California Press, 2006.

———. Review of *Music, Body and Desire in Medieval Culture: Hildegard of Bingen to Chaucer,* by Bruce Holsinger, (Stanford, CA: Stanford University Press, 2001). *Journal of the American Musicological Society* 57:2 (2004) 374–34.

———. "'Rip Her to Shreds': Women's Music According to a Butch-Femme Aesthetic." *Repercussions* 1:1 (1992) 19–47.

Perlitt, Lothar. "Händels *Saul*: Text und Quelle." In *Musikalische Quellen—Quellen zur Musikgeschichte: Festschrift für Martin Staehlin zum 65. Geburtstag,* 287–97. Göttingen: Vandhoeck & Ruprecht, 2002.

Perry, Curtis. *Literature and Favoritism in Early Modern England.* Cambridge: Cambridge University Press, 2006.

Phillips, Peter. "Performance Practice in 16th-Century English Choral Music." *Early Music* 6 (1978) 191–98.

———. *What We Really Do: The Tallis Scholars.* London: Musical Times, 2003.

Pickering, Judith. "*Mulier in ecclesia taceat*: The Silencing of Women in the Authentic Performance Movement." In *Musics and Feminisms,* edited by Sally Macarthur and Cate Poynton, 99–108. Syndey: Australian Music Center, 1999.

Pike, Lionel. *Hexachords in Late Renaissance Music.* Aldershot: Ashgate, 1998.

Pixley, Jorge. *Biblical Israel: A People's History.* Minneapolis: Fortress, 1992.

Placher, William C. *The Domestication of Transcendence: How Modern Thinking about God Went Wrong.* Louisville, KY: Westminster John Knox, 1996.

Plaskow, Judith. *Sex, Sin, and Grace: Women's Experience and the Theologies of Reinhold Niebuhr and Paul Tillich.* Lanham, MD: University Press of America, 1980.

———. *Standing Again at Sinai: Judaism from a Feminist Perspective.* San Francisco: HarperSanFrancisco, 1991.

Plumb, J. H. *The Commercialisation of Leisure in Eighteenth-Century England.* Reading: University of Reading, 1973.

Pomykala, Kenneth E. "Images of David in Early Judaism." In *Of Scribes and Sages: Early Jewish Interpretation and Transmission of Scripture, Volume 1: Ancient Versions and Traditions,* edited by Craig A. Evans, 33–46. London: T. & T. Clark, 2004.

Popper, Karl. *The Poverty of Historicism.* New York: Harper and Row, 1964.

Proudfoot, Wayne. *Religious Experience.* Berkeley: University of California Press, 1985.

Proulx, Annie. *Close Range: Wyoming Stories.* New York: Simon and Schuster, 1999.

Prusak, Bernard P. "Woman: Seductive Siren and Source of Sin?" In *Religion and Sexism: Images of Women in the Jewish and Christian Traditions,* edited by Rosemary Radford Ruether, 89–116. New York: Simon and Schuster, 1974.

Puar, Jasbir K. *Terrorist Assemblages: Homonationalism in Queer Times.* Durham: Duke University Press, 2007.

Puckett, David L. *John Calvin's Exegesis of the Old Testament.* Louisville, KY: Westminster John Knox, 1995.

Questier, Michael C. *Conversion, Politics, and Religion in England, 1580–1625.* Cambridge: Cambridge University Press, 1996.

Bibliography

Rabinowitz, Peter J. "Chord and Discourse: Listening through the Written Word." In *Music and Text: Critical Inquiries*, edited by Steven Paul Scher, 38–56. Cambridge: Cambridge University Press, 1992.

Raffo, Susan, ed. *Queerly Classed: Gay Men and Lesbians Write about Class*. Boston: South End, 1997.

Rambuss, Richard. *Closet Devotions*. Durham and London: Duke University Press, 1998.

Rand, Calvin. "Two Meanings of Historicism in the Writings of Dilthey, Troeltsch, and Meinecke." *Journal of the History of Ideas* 25 (1964) 503–18.

Ratti, Rakesh, ed. *A Lotus of Another Color: An Unfolding of the South Asian Gay and Lesbian Experience*. Boston: Alyson, 1993.

Reynolds, Thomas. "Reconsidering Schleiermacher and the Problem of Religious Diversity: Toward a Dialectical Pluralism." *Journal of the American Academy of Religion* 73:1 (2005) 151–81.

Rich, Adrienne. *Blood, Bread and Poetry: Selected Prose, 1979–1985*. New York: Norton, 1986.

Ricoeur, Paul. "Hermeneutics and the Critique of Ideology." In *Hermeneutics and Modern Philosophy*, edited by Brice R. Wachterhauser, 300–42. Albany: State University of New York Press, 1986.

Riley, Denise. *"Am I That Name?" Feminism and the Category of "Women" in History*. Minneapolis: University of Minnesota Press, 1988.

Robertson, Carol E., ed. *Musical Repercussions of 1492: Encounters in Text and Performance*. Washington, DC: Smithsonian Institution Press, 1992.

Robison, Brian. "Somebody is Digging My Bones: King Crimson's 'Dinosaur' as (Post) Progressive Historiography." In *Progressive Rock Reconsidered*, edited by Kevin Holm-Hudson, 221–42. New York: Routledge, 2002.

Rogers, Eugene F., Jr. *Sexuality and the Christian Body: Their Way into the Triune God*. Oxford: Blackwell, 1999.

Rogers, Jack. "Biblical Interpretation regarding Homosexuality in the Recent History of the Presbyterian Church (U.S.A.)." *Review of Religious Research* 41:2 (1999) 223–38.

Rogers, Jack B., and Donald K. McKim, *The Authority and Interpretation of the Bible: An Historical Approach*. San Francisco: Harper and Row, 1979.

Rogerson, John. *Old Testament Criticism in the Nineteenth Century: England and Germany*. Philadelphia: Fortress, 1985.

Römer, Thomas. *The So-Called Deuteronomistic History: A Sociological, Historical, and Literary Introduction*. London: T. & T. Clark, 2005.

Römer, Thomas, and Loyse Bonjour. *Homosexualité dans le Proche-Orient et la Bible*. Geneva: Labor et Fides, 2005.

Rorem, Ned. *Knowing When to Stop: A Memoir*. New York: Simon & Schuster, 1994.

Roscoe, Will, ed. *Living the Spirit: A Gay American Indian Anthology*. New York: St. Martin's, 1988.

Rosenberg, Joel. *King and Kin: Political Allegory in the Hebrew Bible*. Bloomington: Indiana University Press, 1986.

Rosenwald, Lawrence. "On Prejudice and Early Music." *Historical Performance* 5 (1992) 69–71.

Rudy, Kathy. *Sex and the Church: Gender, Homosexuality, and the Transformation of Christian Ethics*. Boston: Beacon, 1997.

———. "Subjectivity and Belief." In *Queer Theology: Rethinking the Western Body*, edited by Gerard Loughlin, 37–49. Malden, MA: Blackwell, 2007.

Ruether, Rosemary Radford. "Asceticism and Feminism: Strange Bedmates?" In *Sex and God: Some Varieties of Women's Religious Experience*, edited by Linda Hurcombe, 229–50. New York: Routledge, 1987.

———. *Christianity and the Making of the Modern Family*. Boston: Beacon, 2000.

———. *Liberation Theology: Human Hope Confronts Christian History and American Power*. New York: Paulist, 1972.

———. *New Woman/New Earth: Sexist Ideologies and Human Liberation*. San Francisco: Harper & Row, 1975.

———. "Prophets and Humanists: Types of Religious Feminism in Stuart England." *Journal of Religion* 70:1 (1990) 1–18.

———. "Religion and Society: Sacred Canopy vs. Prophetic Critique." In *Expanding the View: Gustavo Gutierrez and the Future of Liberation Theology*, edited by Marc H. Ellis and Otto Maduro, 72–76. Maryknoll, NY: Orbis, 1988.

———. *Sexism and God-talk: Toward a Feminist Theology*. Boston: Beacon, 1983.

———. "Spirit and Matter, Public and Private: The Challenge of Feminism to Traditional Dualisms." In *Embodied Love: Sensuality and Relationship as Feminist Values*, edited by Paula M. Cooey, Sharon A. Farmer, and Mary Ellen Ross, 65–76. San Francisco: Harper & Row, 1987.

———. *Women and Redemption: A Theological History*. Minneapolis: Fortress, 1998.

———. *Women-Church: Theology and Practice of Feminist Liturgical Communities*. Boston: Beacon, 1985.

Ruys, Juanita Feros. "*Planctus magis quam cantici*: The generic significance of Abelard's *planctus*." *Plainsong and Medieval Music* 11:1 (2002) 37–44.

Rycenga, Jennifer. "Lesbian Compositional Process: One Lover-Composer's Perspective." In *Queering the Pitch: The New Gay and Lesbian Musicology*, edited by Philip Brett, Elizabeth Wood, and Gary C. Thomas, 275–296. New York: Routledge, 1994.

———. "Sisterhood: A Loving Lesbian Ear Listens to Progressive Heterosexual Women's Rock Music." In *Keeping Score: Music, Disciplinarity, Culture*, 204–28. Charlottesville: University of Virginia Press, 1997.

———. "Tales of Change within the Sound: Form, Lyrics, and Philosophy in the Music of Yes." In *Progressive Rock Reconsidered*, edited by Kevin Holm-Hudson, 143–66. New York: Routledge, 2002.

Said, Edward W. *Beginnings: Intention and Method*. New York: Columbia University Press, 1985.

Sands, Kathleen M. *Escape from Paradise: Evil and Tragedy in Feminist Theology*. Minneapolis: Fortress, 1994.

———. "Uses of the Thea(o)logian: Sex and Theodicy in Religious Feminism." *Journal of Feminist Studies in Religion* 8:1 (1992) 7–33.

Sanford, Sally, et al. "More Responses to 'On Prejudice and Early Music.'" *Historical Performance* 6:1 (1992) 39–41

Scanzoni, Letha, and Virginia Ramey Mollenkott. *Is the Homosexual My Neighbor? Another Christian View*. San Francisco: Harper & Row, 1980.

Schneider, Laurel C. *Re-Imagining the Divine: Confronting the Backlash against Feminist Theology*. Cleveland: Pilgrim, 1998

Schneider, Laurie. "Donatello's Bronze David." *Art Bulletin* 15 (1973) 213–16.

———. "Donatello and Caravaggio: The Iconography of Decapitation." *American Imago* 33 (1976) 76–91.

Bibliography

Schneider, Tammi. *Mothers of Promise: Women in the Book of Genesis.* Grand Rapids: Baker Academic, 2008.

Schniedewind, William. *How the Bible Became a Book: The Textualization of Ancient Israel.* New York: Cambridge University Press, 2004.

Scholes, Percy A. *The Puritans and Music in England and New England: A Contribution to the Cultural History of Two Nations.* London: Oxford University Press, 1934.

Schroer, Silvia, and Thomas Staubli. "Saul, David und Jonatan—eine Deriecksgeschichte?" *Bibel und Kirche* 51 (1996) 15–22. Translated as "Saul, David and Jonathan—The Story of a Triangle? A Contribution to the Issue of Homosexuality in the First Testament." In *Samuel and Kings*, edited by Athalya Brenner, 22–36. A Feminist Companion to the Bible (Second Series). Sheffield: Sheffield Academic, 2000.

Schüssler Fiorenza, Elisabeth. *But She Said: Feminist Practices of Biblical Interpretation.* Boston: Beacon, 1992.

———. *Discipleship of Equals: A Critical Feminist Ekklesia-logy of Liberation.* New York: Crossroad, 1993.

———. *In Memory of Her: A Feminist Theological Reconstruction of Christian Origins.* New York: Crossroad, 1983.

———. "The Will to Choose or Reject: Continuing Our Critical Work." In *Feminist Interpretation of the Bible*, edited by Letty M. Russell, 125–36. Philadelphia: Westminster, 1985

Schwichtenberg, Cathy, ed. *The Madonna Connection: Representational Politics, Subcultural Identities, and Cultural Theory.* Boulder: Westview, 1993.

Scott, Joan W. "'Experience.'" In *Feminists Theorize the Political*, edited by Judith Butler and Joan W. Scott, 22–40. New York: Routledge, 1992.

Sedgwick, Eve Kosofsky. *Epistemology of the Closet.* Berkeley: University of California Press, 1990.

Segundo, Juan Luis. *The Liberation of Theology.* Maryknoll, NY: Orbis, 1976.

Sharf, Robert H. "The Zen of Japanese Nationalism." In *Curators of the Buddha: The Study of Buddhism Under Colonialism*, edited by Donald S. Lopez, Jr., 107–60. Chicago, University of Chicago Press, 1995.

Shelemay, Kay Kaufman. "Toward an Ethnomusicology of the Early Music Movement: Thoughts on Bridging Disciplines and Musical Worlds." *Ethnomusicology* 45:1 (2001) 1–29.

Sherman, Bernard D. *Inside Early Music: Conversations with Performers.* New York: Oxford University Press, 1997.

Shuger, Debora Kuller. *The Renaissance Bible: Scholarship, Sacrifice, and Subjectivity.* Berkeley: University of California Press, 1994.

Siker, Jeffrey S., ed. *Homosexuality in the Church: Both Sides of the Debate.* Louisville, KY: Westminster John Knox, 1994.

Silverman, Kaja. *The Acoustic Mirror: The Female Voice in Psychoanalysis and Cinema.* Bloomington: Indiana University Press, 1988.

Skinner, Quentin. "Meaning and Understanding in the History of Ideas." *History and Theory* 8:1 (1969) 3–53.

Small, Christopher. *Musicking: The Meanings of Performing and Listening.* Middleton, CT: Wesleyan University Press, 1998.

Smalley, Beryl. *The Study of the Bible in the Middle Ages.* Notre Dame, IN: Notre Dame University Press, 1964.

Smith, Barbara, ed. *Home Girls: A Black Feminist Anthology.* New York: Kitchen Table, 1983.

Smith, Bruce. *The Acoustic World of Early Modern England: Attending to the O-Factor.* Chicago: University of Chicago Press, 1999.

———. *Homosexual Desire in Shakespeare's England: A Cultural Poetics.* Chicago: University of Chicago Press, 1991.

Smith, David L. "Catholic, Anglican, or Puritan? Edward Sackville, Fourth Earl of Dorset, and the Ambiguities of Religion in Early Stuart England." In *Religion, Literature, and Politics in Post-Reformation England, 1540-1688,* edited by Donna B. Hamilton and Richard Strier, 115-37.Cambridge: Cambridge University Press, 1996.

Smith, Hilda L. *Reason's Disciples: Seventeenth-Century English Feminists.* Urbana: University of Illinois Press, 1982.

Smith, Paul. *Discerning the Subject.* Minneapolis: University of Minnesota Press, 1988.

Smith, Ruth. *Handel's Oratorios and Eighteenth-Century Thought.* Cambridge: Cambridge University Press, 1995.

———. "Love between Men in Jennens' and Handel's *Saul.*" In *Queer People: Negotiations and Expressions of Homosexuality, 1700-1800,* edited by Chris Mounsey and Caroline Gonda, 226-45. Lewisburg: Bucknell University Press, 2007.

Soelle, Dorothee. *Suffering.* Translated by Everett R. Kalin. Philadelphia: Fortress, 1975.

———. *Thinking About God: An Introduction to Theology.* Translated by John Bowden. Philadelphia: Trinity Press International, 1990.

Solomon, Maynard. "Franz Schubert and the Peacocks of Benvenuto Cellini." *Nineteenth-Century Music* 12:3 (1989) 193-206.

———. "Schubert: Some Consequences of Nostalgia." *Nineteenth-Century Music* 17:1 (1993) 34-46.

Steblin, Rita. "The Peacock's Tale: Schubert's Sexuality Reconsidered." *Nineteenth-Century Music* 17:1 (1993) 5-33.

Stefani, Gino. "A Theory of Musical Competence." *Semiotica: Journal of the International Association of Semiotic Studies* 66:1/3 Special Issue: Semiotics of Music, edited by Eero Tarasti (1987) 7-22.

Steinberg, Leo. *The Sexuality of Christ in Renaissance Art and Modern Oblivion.* Chicago: University of Chicago Press, 1996.

Steiner, Ruth. "David's Lament for Saul and Jonathan." In *Commemoration, Ritual and Performance: Essays in Medieval and Early Modern Music,* edited by Jane Morlet Hardie with David Harvey, 5-15. Ottawa: Institute of Mediæval Music, 2006.

Steiner, Wendy, ed. *The Sign in Music and Literature.* Austin: University of Texas Press, 1981.

Sterne, Jonathan. "The MP3 as Cultural Artifact." *New Media and Society* 8:5 (2006) 825-42.

Stevens, John."Planctus." *The New Grove Dictionary of Music and Musicians,* edited by Staney Sadie, Vol. 19, 890-92. New York: Macmillan, 2001.

Stoebe, Hans Joachim. *Das zweite Buch Samuelis.* Gütersloh: Gütersloher, 1994.

Stone, Ken. "1 and 2 Samuel." In *The Queer Bible Commentary,* edited by Deryn Guest, Robert E. Goss, Mona West, and Thomas Bohache, 195-221. London: SCM, 2006.

———. *Practicing Safer Texts: Food, Sex, and Bible in Queer Perspective.* London: T. & T. Clark, 2005.

———. *Sex, Honor, and Power in the Deuteronomistic History.* Sheffield: Sheffield Academic, 1996.

Stone, Ken, ed. *Queer Commentary and the Hebrew Bible*. London: Sheffield Academic, 2001.

Straw, Will. "Sizing Up Record Collections: Gender and Connoisseurship in Rock Music Culture." In *Sexing the Groove: Popular Music and Gender*, 3–16. New York: Routledge, 1994.

Stuart, Elizabeth. *Just Good Friends: Towards a Lesbian and Gay Theology of Relationships*. London: Mowbray, 1995.

Subotnik, Rose Rosengard. *Deconstructive Variations: Music and Reason in Western Society*. Minneapolis: University of Minnesota Press, 1996.

———. *Developing Variations: Style and Ideology in Western Music*. Minneapolis: University of Minnesota Press, 1991.

Suleiman, Susan R., and Inge Crosman, eds. *The Reader in the Text: Essays on Audience and Interpretation*. Princeton, NJ: Princeton University Press, 1980.

Sweeney, Marvin A. *I & II Kings: A Commentary*. Old Testament Library. Louisville, KY: Westminster John Knox, 2007.

Sycamore, Matilda Bernstein, ed. *That's Revolting! Queer Strategies for Resisting Assimilation*. Brooklyn: Soft Skull, 2008.

Taruskin, Richard. *The Danger of Music and Other Anti-Utopian Essays*. Berkeley: University of California Press, 2009.

———. "Material Gains: Assessing Susan McClary." *Music and Letters* 90:3 (2009) 453–67.

———. "The Pastness of the Present and the Presence of the Past." In *Authenticity and Early Music*, edited by Nicholas Kenyon, 137–207 Oxford: Oxford University Press, 1988.

———. *Stravinsky and the Russian Traditions: A Biography of the Works through Mavra*. Berkeley: University of California Press, 1996.

———. *Text and Act: Essays on Music and Performance*. New York: Oxford University Press, 1995.

Taves, Ann. *Fits, Trances, and Visions: Experiencing Religion and Explaining Experience from Wesley to James*. Princeton, NJ: Princeton University Press, 1999.

Théberge, Paul. *Any Sound You Can Imagine: Making Music/Consuming Technology*. Hanover, NH: University Press of New England, 1997.

Thomas, Gary C. "'Was George Frederic Handel Gay?': On Closet Questions and Cultural Politics." In *Queering the Pitch: The New Gay and Lesbian Musicology*, edited by Philip Brett, Elizabeth Wood, and Gary C. Thomas, 155–203. New York: Routledge, 1994.

Thompson, J. A. "The Significance of the Verb *Love* in the David-Jonathan Narratives in 1 Samuel." *Vetus Testamentum* 24 (1974) 334–38.

Thompson, John L. *Writing the Wrongs: Women of the Old Testament among Biblical Commentators from Philo through the Reformation*. Oxford: Oxford University Press, 2001.

Thompson, Mark, ed. *Gay Spirit: Myth and Meaning*. New York: St. Martin's, 1987.

Thompson, Thomas L. *The Mythic Past: Biblical Archaeology and the Myth of Israel*. New York: Basic, 1999.

Tillich, Paul. *Biblical Religion and the Search for Ultimate Reality*. Chicago: University of Chicago Press, 1955.

Tomlinson, Gary. *Music in Renaissance Magic: Toward a Historiography of Others*. Chicago: University of Chicago Press, 1983.

Tompkins, Jane P., ed. *Reader-Response Criticism: From Formalism to Post-Structuralism.* Baltimore: Johns Hopkins University Press, 1980.

Torrance, Thomas F. *The Hermeneutics of John Calvin.* Edinburgh: Scottish Academic, 1988.

Tov, Emanuel. "The Composition of 1 Samuel 16–18 in the Light of the Septuagint Version." In *Empirical Models for Biblical Criticism*, edited by Jeffrey H. Tigay, 97–130. Philadelphia: University of Pennsylvania Press, 1985.

Traub, Valerie. *The Renaissance of Lesbianism in Early Modern England.* Cambridge: Cambridge University Press, 2002.

Trible, Phyllis. *God and the Rhetoric of Sexuality.* Philadelphia: Fortress, 1978.

Troeltsch, Ernst. *Writings on Theology and Religion.* Translated and edited by Robert Morgan and Michael Pye. Louisville, KY: Westminster John Knox, 1977.

Tsumura, David Toshio. *The First Book of Samuel.* The New International Commentary on the Old Testament. Grand Rapids: Eerdmans, 2007.

Udis-Kessler, Amanda. *Queer Inclusion in the United Methodist Church.* New York: Routledge, 2008.

van der Toorn, Karel. *Scribal Culture and the Making of the Hebrew Bible.* Cambridge: Harvard University Press, 2007.

van Wolde, Ellen. "Sentiments as Culturally Constructed Emotions: Anger and Love in the Hebrew Bible." *Biblical Interpretation* 16 (2008) 1–24.

Vaughan, Judith. *Sociality, Ethics, and Social Change: A Critical Appraisal of Reinhold Niebuhr's Ethics in the Light of Rosemary Ruether's Works.* Lanham, MD: University Press of America, 1983.

Veijola, Timo. *Die ewige Dynastie: David und die Entstehung seiner Dynastie nach deuteronomistischen Darstellung.* Helsinki : Suomalainen Tiedeakatemia, 1975.

von der Horst, Dirk. "*Gelone mio*: Reflections on the 1982 *Concerto Vocale* Recording of Cesti's *Orontea*." Paper written for directed study with Suzanne G. Cusick, University of Virginia, Spring 1998.

———. "'God Leaves His Throne': Sexual Politics and Theological Discourse in Ralph Vaughan Williams's *Job: A Masque for Dancing*." Paper written for Kurt Westerberg, DePaul University, 1992.

———. "Precarious Pleasures: Situating 'Close to the Edge' in Conflicting Male Desires." In *Progressive Rock Reconsidered*, edited Kevin Holm-Hudson, 167–82. New York: Routledge, 2002.

Walker, Alice. *Living by the Word: Selected Writings, 1973–1987.* San Diego: Harcourt Brace Jovanovich, 1988.

———. "A Name is Sometimes an Ancestor Saying Hi, I'm with You." In *Living by the Word: Selected Writings, 1973–1987.* San Diego: Harcourt Brace Jovanovich, 1988.

Walls, Peter. "London, 1603–1649." In *Music and Society: The Early Baroque Era*, edited by Curtis Price, 270–304. Englewood Cliffs, NJ: Prentice Hall, 1993.

Warner, Michael. *The Trouble with Normal: Sex, Politics, and the Ethics of Queer Life.* Cambridge: Harvard University Press, 1999.

Webster, James. "Music, Pathology, Sexuality, Beethoven, Schubert." *Nineteenth-Century Music* 17:1 (1993) 89–93.

Weinfeld, Moshe. "ברית." In *Theological Dictionary of the Old Testament*, edited by Johannes Botterwick and Helmer Ringgren. Translated by John T. Willis, volume 2, 253–79. Grand Rapids: Eerdmans, 1975.

Bibliography

Weiss Piero, and Richard Taruskin. *Music in the Western World: A History in Documents.* New York: Schirmer, 1984.

Welch, Sharon. *A Feminist Ethic of Risk*, rev. ed. Minneapolis: Fortress, 2000.

Weston, Kath. *Families We Choose: Lesbians, Gays, Kinship.* New York: Columbia University Press, 1997.

White, Hayden. *Figural Realism: Studies in the Mimesis Effect.* Baltimore, MD: Johns Hopkins University Press, 1999.

———. *Metahistory: The Historical Imagination in Nineteenth-Century Europe.* Baltimore, MD: Johns Hopkins University Press, 1973.

Wilks Timothy, ed. *Prince Henry Revived: Image and Exemplarity in Early Modern England.* London: Holberton, 2007.

Willetts, Pamela J. "The Identity of Thomas Myriell." *Music and Letters* 53:4 (October, 1972), 431–33.

Williams, Robert. *Just As I Am: A Practical Guide to Being Out, Proud, and Christian.* New York: Perennial, 1993.

Wilson, Nancy L. *Our Tribe: Queer Folks, God, Jesus, and the Bible.* San Francisco: HarperSanFrancisco, 1995.

Wink, Walter. "To Hell with Gays: Sex and the Bible." *The Christian Century* (June 5–12, 2002) 32–34.

Winter, Robert. "Whose Schubert?" *Nineteenth-Century Music* 17:1 (1993) 94–101.

Witte, John Jr., and Robert M. Kingdon. *Sex, Marriage, and Family in John Calvin's Geneva, Volume 1: Courtship, Engagement, and Marriage.* Grand Rapids: Eerdmans, 2005.

Wold, Donald J. *Out of Order: Homosexuality in the Bible and the Ancient Near East.* Grand Rapids: Baker, 1998.

Worton Michael, and Judith Still, eds. *Intertextuality: Theories and Practices.* Manchester: Manchester University Press, 1990.

Woźniak, Jerzy. "Drei verschiedene literarische Beschreibungen des Bundes zwischen Jonathan und David." *Biblische Zeitschrift* 27:2 (1983) 213–18.

Wyman, Walter E. Jr. "Revelation and the Doctrine of Faith: Historical Revelation within the Limits of Historical Consciousness." *Journal of Religion* 78:1 (1998) 38–63.

Young, Michael B. *King James and the History of Homosexuality.* New York: New York University Press, 2000.

Young, Norman J. *History and Existential Theology: The Role of History in the Thought of Rudolf Bultmann.* Philadelphia: Westminster Press, 1969.

Zehnder, Markus. "Exegetische Beobachtungen zu den David-Jonathan-Geschichten." *Biblica* 79 (1998) 153–79.

Zerubavel, Eviatar. *Time Maps: Collective Memory and the Social Shape of the Past.* Chicago: University of Chicago Press, 2003.

Zuidervaart, Lambert. *Adorno's Aesthetic Theory: The Redemption of Illusion.* Cambridge: MIT Press, 1991.

Zwelling, Jeremy. "The Fictions of Biblical History." *History and Theory* 39:1 (2000) 117–41.

DISCOGRAPHY

XVIII-21 Musique des Lumières, Jean-Christophe Frisch, dir. *Negro Spirituals au Brésil Baroque.* K617 FRANCE K617130 (2000).

Bach, Johann Sebastian. *Cantatas.* The Monteverdi Choir and the English Baroque Soloists, John Eliot Gardiner, director. Deutsche Grammophon D120541 (1992).

de Machaut, Guillaume. *L'art musical et poétique de Guillaume de Machaut.* Ensemble Guillaume de Machaut de Paris. Disques Ados 203712 (1977).

———. *Remede de Fortune.* Ensemble Project Ars Nova. New Albion Records D105812 (1994).

Dobkin, Alix. *Living with Lavender Jane.* Ladyslipper, Inc. WWWA001/2 (1997).

Ensemble Organum. *Polyphonie Aquitaine du XIIe Siecle: Saint Martial de Limoges.* Ensemble Organum. Marcel Pérès, dir. Harmonia Mundi HMC 901134 (1984).

Gibbons, Orlando. *Hymns and Songs of the Church.* Tonus Peregrinus, Antony Pitts, director. Naxos 8.557681, 2006.

Handel, George Frederick. *Saul.* Concentus Musicus, Nicholas Harnoncourt, cond. Teldec 2292–42651-2 (1986).

———. *Saul.* Gabrieli Consort and Players, Paul McCreesh, cond. Deutsche Grammophon 474 510–2 (2004).

———. *Saul.* RIAS Kammerchor.Concerto Köln. René Jacobs, cond. Harmonia Mundi 901877.78 (2005).

The Harp Consort, Andrew Lawrence-King, dir. *Missa Mexicana.* Harmonia Mundi 907293 (2002).

Parker, William. *The Listeners.* New World Records 80475–2 (1978).

Schein, Johann Hermann. *Israelisbrünnlein.* Rheinische Kantorei, Hermann Max, cond. Capriccio 10 290/91 (1992).

Simone, Nina. *The Best of Nina Simone.* PolyGram Records, Inc. 822846–2, (1969).

Tomkins, Thomas. *The Great Service.* The Tallis Scholars, Peter Phillips, director. Gimell Records CDGIM 024, 1991.

———. *Choral and Organ Music.* Oxford Camerata, Jeremy Summerly, director. Naxos 8.553794, 1999.

———. *Cathedral Music by Thomas Tomkins.* Choir of St. George's Chapel, Windsor. Christopher Robinson, conductor. Hyperion, CDH55066, 2001 (recorded 1989).

Weelkes, Thomas. *Cathedral Music.* Winchester Cathedral Choir, David Hill, dir. Hyperion Records CDA66477, 1992.

———. *Madrgigals and Anthems.* Anthony Rooley, dir. ASV CD GAU 195, 1999.

Index

Index

Made in the USA
Columbia, SC
09 February 2020

87720116R00111